**Louis I. Kahn
and the Yale Center for British Art**

Louis I. Kahn
and the Yale Center for British Art

A Conservation Plan
Peter Inskip and Stephen Gee
in association with Constance Clement

Yale Center for British Art
New Haven, Conneticut

Yale University Press
New Haven and London

Published by
Yale Center for British Art
P.O. Box 208280, New Haven, CT 06520-8280
britishart.yale.edu

Distributed by
Yale University Press
P.O. Box 209040, New Haven, CT 06520-9040
www.yalebooks.com/art

Designed by Pearce Marchbank RDI www.pearcemarchbank.com
Artwork and design assistance by Otis Marchbank
Production coordinated by Miko McGinty at Miko McGinty Inc.
Copyedited by Guilland Sutherland and Jason Best
Typeset in Yale Design and Gill Sans
Typesetting by Tina Henderson and Otis Marchbank
Printed on 135gsm Gardapat Kiara
Printed in Italy by Trifolio S.R.L., Verona, Italy

Facing previous page:
The Yale Center for British Art, looking north along High Street toward the central campus

Library of Congress Cataloging-in-Publication Data

Inskip, Peter.
Louis I. Kahn and the Yale Center for British Art : a conservation plan / Peter Inskip, Stephen Gee ; in association with Constance Clement.
p. cm.
ISBN 978-0-300-17164-8 (alk. paper)
1. Yale Center for British Art. 2. Kahn, Louis I., 1901–1974. 3. Art museum architecture — Conservation and restoration — Connecticut — New Haven — Planning. 4. Museum buildings — Conservation and restoration — Connecticut — New Haven — Planning. 5. New Haven (Conn.) — Buildings, structures, etc. I. Kahn, Louis I., 1901–1974. II. Gee, Stephen. III. Clement, Constance. IV. Title.
N590.I57 2011
7271.7092-dc22
2011017647

Contents

Director's foreword 7

Introduction 13

Acknowledgments 15

Understanding the place 19

The site and setting of the building 41

Assessment of cultural significance 49
As a building by Louis I. Kahn 51
Degree of survival and intactness 53
As a museum housing a specific collection 55
As urban fabric 56
Statement of cultural significance 59
Levels of cultural significance 60

Conservation policies 63
Method of approach 65
General policies 66
Exterior of the building 69
External spaces 79
Interior of the building 87
Structure and building systems 125
External materials 140
Internal materials 165

Floor plans 187

Selected further reading 197

Index 198

The Entrance Court with the interior shades raised, permitting views into the galleries at the time of the Paul Mellon centennial in 2007

An elegant harmony characterizes the relationship between the magnificent collection for which the Yale Center for British Art is renowned and the beautiful building in which it is housed. Both were gifts of Paul Mellon (Yale College, Class of 1929) to his alma mater, and the building, which was designed by Louis I. Kahn, was created with unusual sensitivity to the public display of the collection as well as to its use in teaching and research. Since the building opened to the public in the spring of 1977, it has been regarded as one of Kahn's greatest works, receiving the Twenty-five Year Award from the American Institute of Architects in 2005 as an architectural landmark that has proven its sustained cultural value and contributed significantly to the architectural heritage of the nation.

Deeply valued by each successive director and by the staff, the building has received the same thoughtful care and attention as the works of art that it contains. In addition to a strict regime of routine maintenance and minor renovations, two major restoration campaigns have been undertaken to replace windows with condensation problems (1996) and to renovate the roof (1998). The closure of the building for work on its roof also afforded the opportunity for the replacement of worn carpeting, as well as frayed Belgian linen that covered the walls and "pogo" partition walls in the galleries.

When I arrived as Director in 2002, the building appeared to be in fine health, and the interiors looked splendid. Nonetheless, a discussion over the replacement of two elevator control panels led us to realize how quickly even minor, well-meaning, but misconceived, design and maintenance decisions might cause an architecturally significant building to drift from its original form in unsatisfactory ways. To undertake an assessment of where such drift might already have occurred and to help guide similar decisions in the future, we formed a Building Conservation Committee, which included representatives from the staff along with architects and architectural historians from Yale's School of Architecture and the University's Facilities Office. The Center's Deputy Director, Constance Clement, agreed to serve as Chair, and the institution's first Director, Jules D. Prown, Paul Mellon Professor Emeritus of the History of Art, who oversaw the building's design and construction with Louis Kahn, also joined the committee.

Additionally, we asked the London-based firm of Peter Inskip + Peter Jenkins Architects to serve as consulting conservation architects, based on their experience not only with great historic sites but also with modern buildings of outstanding cultural significance. Peter Inskip and his co-director, Stephen Gee, are recognized widely for their work in preparing conservation plans that establish the policies by which architectural sites of aesthetic and historical importance should be treated in terms of maintenance, repair, growth, and modification. The object of such a plan is to identify the key features of a site that characterize its cultural significance and to ensure that those features are always protected from alteration. Other features that are not considered as central to a site's definition may be allowed to change. This kind of assessment requires the thorough analysis of a site's form and the materials of which it is composed as well as historical research into the design and construction phases and any modifications that have taken place over time. Such plans take full institutional commitment and are best undertaken when a site is not under the pressure of immediate alteration or expansion, when conditions allow for the investment of time necessary to engage in a meticulous and systematic physical and intellectual appraisal, involving many members of staff and the appropriate expert consultants. These were precisely the conditions in which we found ourselves when our Building Conservation Committee was formed and, after several meetings, we decided that the time was right for us to commence with the preparation of a conservation plan for the Center.

By creating this plan during a period of relative calm, we have wished to equip ourselves with a document that will help to protect a great building from the inevitable strains caused by a growing collection, a program that continues to be enriched by the creative energies of a major research university, increasing public visitation, and an expanding staff to support these activities. We have paired this endeavor with a study of our physical requirements projected twenty years into the future, led by Cooper, Robertson & Partners. Together, the Center's Conservation Plan and the physical requirements analysis will help us to preserve our building's most precious features as the institution develops in a healthy and carefully managed way. When the time comes, these complementary documents should prepare us to consider an expanded facility to accommodate the Center's growth without imperiling Louis Kahn's masterpiece. In the meantime, we tested some of the ideas posited here when we moved several staff offices to 270 Crown Street, a small building generously given to the Center by the University in 2008 in order to relieve the pressure of a growing staff on office space within the Kahn building.

Although physical requirements analyses for architectural sites of cultural significance are common in the United States, conservation plans are not, and from the start we have hoped that our plan might serve as an example for other important sites in this country. Indeed, we hope to encourage the development of these plans as part of the building process, at the time when information on the original design and construction is still readily accessible and those involved are available to offer their insights. From our own experience, we recognize how valuable the early development of a conservation plan is for the Center, and we are deeply grateful to Peter Inskip and Stephen Gee for engaging us in the process, especially while many who worked on the design and construction of the building have been able to participate and while the majority of the firms that manufactured or supplied materials remain in business.

We owe our consultants an enormous debt for bringing their masterful expertise to bear on our landmark building and for teaching us, with care and patience, how to analyze the very special structure in which the Center thrives. The pursuit has been most enjoyable, and I have no doubt that the resulting report will serve us well into the future. We will undertake a regular reassessment of the plan to confirm that it is still viable and to make corrections, additions, and refinements as our knowledge of the building grows and as new priorities come into play.

The in-depth understanding that we have gained of the condition of the structure and the materials of which it is composed has resulted in a list of projects that need to be addressed. We are beginning to draw up a hierarchy of these, along with an assessment of how much each will cost, so that a work schedule can be projected. Alongside implementing the standard protocols for maintaining the building that are now so clearly laid out in our Conservation Plan, correcting those features of the building that have drifted from their original design and repairing the materials that have begun to show signs of wear will be an enormously satisfying endeavor.

Amy Meyers, Director, New Haven, June 2011

Facing page:
J. M. W. Turner (1775–1851)
Staffa, Fingal's Cave (detail), 1831–32
Oil on canvas
Acquired by Paul Mellon in 1977

Following pages:
William Blake (1757–1827)
The Parable of the Wise and Foolish Virgins (detail), ca. 1825
Watercolor with pen and black ink on medium, moderately textured, cream wove paper
Acquired by Paul Mellon in 1941

George Stubbs (1724–1806)
A Lion Attacking a Horse (detail), 1762
Oil on canvas
Acquired by Paul Mellon in 1960

Introduction

This document sets out conservation policies for the building that houses the Yale Center for British Art, based on an assessment of its cultural significance.

The Center was designed to provide a permanent home for the collection of British art formed by Paul Mellon. His collection focuses primarily on the extended eighteenth century and is of outstanding quality. It is, without doubt, the best and most comprehensive collection of British art outside the United Kingdom. Mr. Mellon's gift was princely, but also discreet. It is the works of art, presented in a comfortable and generous setting, that take center stage, rather than the institution as a monument to the donor.

The building was designed by Louis I. Kahn, probably the most significant American architect of the second half of the twentieth century. The program stipulated that the paintings were to be viewed in daylight in room-like volumes. The building was to be state-of-the-art: the facilities provided for the storage and care of the collection were to be of the highest standards; daylighting studies were informed by the latest international research; and the museum experience and comfort of visitors and staff were all very carefully considered. The conclusion of this plan is that the Yale Center for British Art is a building of outstanding cultural significance. Not only are the primary spaces within the Center of exceptional importance, but virtually every space is of value because of the consistent approach that was taken in the design of each aspect. In addition, the Center was beautifully made and crafted.

Of paramount importance is the fact that the Center is not just a major building of the twentieth century but an institution providing a setting that complements Mr. Mellon's collection and facilitates the continuity of its mission as a center for the study of British art. It is a place concerned with the human experience of looking at and working with great works of art in a remarkable building.

Major alterations are acceptable if they maintain the Center as a leading museum and academic institution. The growth of the collection and the importance of hosting temporary exhibitions, including works from external sources, have both exerted pressure on the galleries, but the spaces appear to be inherently flexible and can accommodate change. Other areas are highly specific: the reading rooms and the lecture hall have been designed as finite spaces, but changes have been required in the former to introduce additional storage, and improvements to the acoustics in the latter are perceived to be necessary now that it serves a wider range of functions. All this is complicated by rapid changes in the field of museum lighting and acoustics.

The Yale Center for British Art is very tightly planned in terms of space, and minor alterations have been carried out in response to growth in the numbers of staff. This has resulted in the subdivision of some areas and the increased occupancy of others. However, it is a characteristic of the interior that it should be spacious in terms of its subdivision. Since the assessment of the exterior concludes that the building is finite in its form and cannot be directly extended, it is likely that growth can only be accommodated acceptably by the transfer of some functions off site and the reallocation of space that is released to appropriate uses.

Some policies might be seen as long-term aims; others are immediate. What is important is that policies are reviewed periodically, first within five years and then every ten years, and are subject to confirmation, modification, or deletion.

Facing page:
The fourth-floor galleries

View from first-floor galleries across the Entrance Court, 2007

Acknowledgments

Our first thanks have to be to Amy Meyers, Director of the Yale Center for British Art (YCBA). It was her foresight to commission a conservation plan for the Center. Usually, such plans are prepared as a reaction to deterioration or to the threat of development, but to commission a plan for a building that was less than thirty years old, still remarkably intact, and in good condition was perceptive. It recognized the importance of Kahn's building as a landmark building in its own right that justified being curated as diligently as the outstanding collection that it houses. Throughout the project, the Director has given us every assistance, and her reviews of this document as it developed have been invaluable.

The use of conservation plans was pioneered by Professor James Semple Kerr in Australia in the 1980s, and his book *The Conservation Plan* (National Trust New South Wales, 1990) provided the foundation for the development of conservation plans that occurred in the United Kingdom at the end of the twentieth century, and has since been championed internationally by bodies such as the Getty Grant Program. Kerr's study of the Sydney Opera House in 1993 was a breakthrough because it dealt with a building of the recent past. This plan is deeply indebted to his example.

Jorn Utzon: Sydney Opera House, completed 1973

We are also grateful to the members of the Center's Building Conservation Committee, chaired by Constance Clement, Deputy Director. The committee's members have reviewed aspects of this plan as it progressed; they include, at the Center, Amy Meyers (Director), David Mills (former Associate Director for Finance and Administration), Angus Trumble (Senior Curator of Paintings and Sculpture), Theresa Fairbanks-Harris (Chief Paper Conservator), Mark Aronson (Chief Paintings Conservator), Richard F. Johnson (Installation Manager), Martin Staffaroni (Operations Manager); and, at Yale, Jules Prown (Paul Mellon Professor Emeritus in the History of Art), Lawrence Regan and Kristina Chmelar (Yale Office of Facilities), Alexander Purves (Professor Emeritus, Yale School of Architecture), and Sandy Isenstadt (formerly Assistant Professor, History of Art Department, Yale University).

We are greatly indebted to Jules Prown, the Center's Founding Director. His book *The Architecture of the Yale Center for British Art* (Yale University Press, 1977) served as our introduction to the building and was the foundation for our entire study. He answered queries and commented on drafts of this document, but, most importantly, he was always on hand to examine the building and discuss ideas on site.

Patricia Cummings Loud, Curator of Architecture and Museum Archivist at the Kimbell Art Museum in Fort Worth, Texas, also assisted in every way. Over the years, she has carried out significant research at the Louis I. Kahn Archive at the University of Pennsylvania in Philadelphia. Through her study of Kahn's drawings, she has unraveled the complex design history of the Yale Center for British Art, and she recorded its development in her book *The Art Museums of Louis I. Kahn*, which accompanied the exhibition that originated at the Duke University Museum of Art in 1989–90, and traveled to the Yale University Art Gallery, the Kimbell Art Museum, and the San Francisco Museum of Modern Art. This, together with Jules Prown's book, was invaluable for the section entitled "Understanding of the Place" in this Conservation Plan. To assist with this project, Patricia Loud revisited Yale in 2003 and extended her research by studying the Louis Isadore Kahn Collection (MS 1345) held by Manuscripts and Archives, Yale University Library. When we visited Texas she was the perfect guide not only to the Kimbell, but to the other twentieth-century art museum buildings in Dallas and Fort Worth.

Facing page:
Sunlight on the travertine floor
of the Entrance Court

Our contribution to understanding the history of the building has been to analyze the extent to which the design changed after Kahn's death in 1974. Former Curator and Assistant Dean Julia Moore Converse, current Curator Bill Whitaker, and Nancy Thorne gave us every assistance when we visited the Louis I. Kahn Archive at the University of Pennsylvania. It was an inspiration to see Kahn's sketches and presentation drawings, which Loud had so thoughtfully interpreted, but it was the revision notes added to his construction drawings by Pellechia and Meyers, the successor firm to Kahn's, that filled the lacunae in our knowledge of the final development of the design. These notes demonstrated that the completed building changed very little from the original concept and that nearly all details remain Kahn's.

We regret the death of Marshall Meyers before we started this study, as his respect for Kahn's original design intentions is so admirable. While several hundred drawings were needed to complete construction, the majority were essentially concerned with the formal adoption by Pellechia and Meyers of working drawings already produced by Kahn's office. Any revisions to design generally proved to be the minimum required to bring details in line with such things as updated building codes. David Mills helped with enquiries concerning more recent repair campaigns.

Stephen Cannon-Brookes, George Sexton, and his associate David Tozer have all consulted with us on the lighting of the building. We are especially indebted to Steven Hefferan who contributed to the development of the lighting policies.

Further material relating to the history of the building has been discovered at the Center during the research process and supplemented by a full set of the construction drawings that has been supplied by the Louis I. Kahn Archive in Philadelphia. Within Yale, Scott Thomas provided copies of the as-built drawings held in the University's Plan Room. During the last five years, Karen Denavit, the Center's Information Analyst, has been systematically reviewing and documenting all files relating to the establishment and construction of the institution; she has worked closely with Jules Prown and been vigilant for material pertaining to our own research.

Throughout the preparation of the Conservation Plan, we have enjoyed the assistance of Yale undergraduates and graduate students in the School of Architecture. These have included Kimberley Skelton (PhD History of Art '07), 2003–04; Bernard Zirnheld (MPhil History of Art '08), 2004–05; Eleanor Sokolow (BA '05), 2004–05; Nate Puksta (BA '07), 2004–05; Orly Friedman (BA '07), 2005–06; Sam Roche (MArch '07), 2006–07; Lydia Shook (BA '07), 2006–07; Whitney Kraus (MArch '08), 2007–08; Harvey Chung (MArch '10), 2008–09; Nicholas Hanna (MArch '09), 2008–09; Bill Kamens (BA '09), 2008–09; Joseph Messick (MArch '10), 2009–10; Ashley Ozburn (MArch '12), 2009–11; Shayari DeSilva (BA '11), 2010–11. Together, they have contributed to a building chronology, an inventory of original furnishings, an analysis of fabric, a study of the urban context of the building, and an inventory of the architectural drawings found at the Center. Their contribution has been extremely helpful, and their own enjoyment has been rewarding to us.

The study of materials has its foundation in the original specifications for the building held at the Center. Steve Wolff and Roy Matway of Allegheny Ludlum assisted with our understanding of how the steel might have been manufactured. Michael Morris (The Metropolitan Museum of Art) and Trevor Proudfoot (Cliveden Conservation Workshop) assisted in carrying out trials and materials analyses. The first tranche of microscopic paint analysis carried out by Pascale Patris (The Metropolitan Museum of Art) established original colors and finishes in the building. Eric Breitung (General Electric) tested the results of the coatings being trialed for the external steel panels. Paul Gaudette (Wiss, Jenney, Elstner Associates, Inc.) advised on the concrete. All aspects of the conservation of the building were reviewed within the Center by YCBA Conservators Mark Aronson and Theresa Fairbanks-Harris.

With the building systems, we were guided at the YCBA by Gene Saulino (former Building Engineer) on the mechanical plant, Len Constanza (Chief of Security) on the security issues, and George Conte (former Operations Manager) and Martin Staffaroni (current Operations Manager) on the care and maintenance of the Center; all four contributed to the chronology of the building. "The Consultation Report and Conservation Environment Renovation Program," prepared in June 2002 by the firm of Garrison/Lull Inc., provided an overview of the efficacy of the systems. Richard Johnson also offered insights into the building chronology and particularly to the alterations to the "pogos" and millwork finishes. Further advice came from Greg Shea (YCBA Senior Museum Technician) and Joe Branco (former YCBA Cabinetmaker). Unfortunately, we were not in New Haven for the lecture in April 2005 given by Abba Tor, the engineer responsible for the structural design of the building, but his notes have been helpful in filling some gaps.

Illustrations have been supplied by the Center's Registrar's Office and Public Relations Department. Richard Caspole, YCBA Photographer, has taken additional images especially for this book. Those of Kahn's drawings were supplied by the Louis I. Kahn Archive at the University of Pennsylvania. Peter Aaron of Esto was commissioned by the Center to photograph the building during the Paul Mellon centennial celebrations in 2007, and further photographs were taken by Francis Dzikowski of the same firm in 2010.

Eleanor Hughes, Associate Curator and Head of Exhibitions and Publications at the Center, has worked tirelessly to oversee the production of this book and contributed greatly to the editorial process. Her organizational skills, patience, and good humor have served the project well. She has liaised with both Pearce Marchbank, Royal Designer for Industry, at Studio Twenty in London, who has designed the book, and with Miko McGinty in New York who has overseen its production. We are indebted to the Center's Publications Assistant Craig Canfield for obtaining many of the images and seeking permission to use them and to Assistant Curator Imogen Hart for her helpful editorial suggestions. We also wish to thank copyeditors Guilland Sutherland and Jason Best.

On every visit to New Haven we enjoyed the warm welcome and assistance we received from the staff, docents, and guards at the Center, and the evident pride that each member has not only in Paul Mellon's collection of works of art but also in the outstanding building that was commissioned to house it.

Finally, we have to thank Constance Clement for her untiring help and guidance in the project. With the greatest generosity and good cheer, she has answered questions, persevered with inquiries, sought out materials and details, and recruited and guided the Yale students. Her support throughout has been unwavering.

Peter Inskip and Stephen Gee, London, June 2011

Following page:
Dedication panel in
the Entrance Court

THIS CENTER, WITH HIS COLLECTIONS
OF BRITISH ART AND BOOKS, IS THE GIFT OF PAUL MELLON
YALE COLLEGE, CLASS OF 1929

Understanding the place

Facing page:
Paul Mellon with portrait bust
of Thomas, 1st Baron Dartrey,
by Joseph Wilton, photographed
in 1977

In December 1966 President Kingman Brewster of Yale University and Mayor Richard C. Lee of New Haven announced the proposed gift to Yale of Paul Mellon's collection of British art. The Paul Mellon Collection, however, was highly specialized, homogeneous, and difficult to blend with others. The gift, therefore, included funds to acquire a site, construct a building, and establish a new institution within Yale, together with an endowment.

Paul Mellon developed a passionate interest in British life and sport during his postgraduate years at Clare College, Cambridge, and, in 1931, he started collecting illustrated books with sporting plates. In 1936 he began acquiring paintings, especially of horses, and subsequently expanded his collection of rare books. After 1959 he began collecting British art more seriously, acquiring within two and a half years four hundred paintings by artists such as Hogarth, Wright of Derby, Turner, Constable, and Stubbs. His interest veered from the traditional formal portraits collected by early twentieth-century Americans under the tutelage of legendary art dealer Joseph Duveen to genre paintings, sporting art, landscapes, marine paintings, urban views, conversation pieces, and informal portraits. Generally, these were medium- to small-scale pictures, but the discovery of early eighteenth-century country-house views in the late 1960s also introduced some large-scale works and an interest in architecture and historic landscape. In addition, sculpture was represented by portrait busts. The collection focused primarily on the extended eighteenth century, but sporting art led him to Munnings and the twentieth century, including works by Ben Nicholson. Watercolors and other works on paper were a natural extension of the collection of rare books. A large exhibition of Mr. Mellon's British art was presented at the Virginia Museum of Fine Arts, Richmond in 1963. This was followed by shows at the Royal Academy, London, during the winter of 1964–65, and at the Yale University Art Gallery in 1965. The catalog to the Virginia exhibition of 1963 confirms that by that date it was the finest collection of British art outside England.

At first the institution was to be called the Paul Mellon Center for British Art and British Studies, but, by 1974, at the request of the donor, Mr. Mellon's name was omitted from the title. He modestly felt that others might be hesitant to support the institution if the title was too personalized. In 1979 the collection comprised more than 1,200 paintings, 10,000 drawings, 20,000 prints, 20,000 rare books and manuscripts, and a small representative group of sculptures.[1] The collection has since grown with Mr. Mellon's bequest, and acquisitions purchased by means of the endowment fund have extended the range of the collection from medieval to contemporary British art. Major gifts by others have also enhanced the collection as envisaged by its benefactor. In 2010 the collection comprised 1,900 paintings, 50,000 works on paper, 35,000 rare books and manuscripts, and 200 sculptures.

The reference to British Studies was also removed from the title in 1976. However, it is important that the institution is not perceived solely as a museum or art gallery, but that it is also a center for research and study. This aspect was the positive contribution of the University in its discussions with the donor, and an interdisciplinary committee, chaired by Professor Louis L. Martz (Department of English), developed plans for the institution that would make optimum use of the Mellon Collection to enhance the academic, intellectual, and cultural life of the University. The committee's report divided the institution into three parts: art gallery and rare books, research library, and academic program.

[1] *The British Art Center at Yale: An Introduction for Visitors and Students* (New Haven: Yale Center for British Art, 1979), 3.

Louis Kahn at the Yale University Art Gallery, photographed in 1953

The Yale Center for British Art was also recognized as an institution that would enrich the cultural life of the City of New Haven, with Mayor Lee stating that it would bring "a new dimension of elegance" to the city.[2]

The site on Chapel Street, purchased by Yale University with a gift from Mr. Mellon, was bounded by High and York streets, and extended to the south side of the present parking lot. It had the advantage of being located immediately opposite the Yale University Art Gallery and close to other art faculties. However, the choice of site represented the extension of the academic area into land that was clearly seen as inner-city commercial property. Despite being in an area in the process of deterioration, the loss of taxable property was recognized as a concern to the city, and others were antagonistic to the expansion of the University into the city. The inclusion of commercial premises within the project was, therefore, proposed.

Professor Jules Prown (Department of History of Art) was appointed the first Director of the Center in July 1968 with the charge, in part, of acting as client on behalf of Yale for the procurement of the building. With its emphasis on a humanistic approach, his "Preliminary Thoughts on Architecture," prepared for President Brewster, could well have had Louis Kahn in mind as architect when it was written in 1969.[3] Prown recalls that other architects under consideration included Philip Johnson, Robert Venturi, and I. M. Pei. The last was the architect of the East Wing at the National Gallery of Art, the gift of Paul Mellon and his sister Ailsa Mellon Bruce to the nation, and would have been an obvious choice, but Prown's preference for Kahn was expressed to Mr. Mellon and President Brewster.

Kahn had taught at Yale from 1947 and continued to act as a visiting critic until 1957 while maintaining his own practice in Philadelphia. His extension to the Yale University Art Gallery (1951–53) was acknowledged as a very significant building. Kahn's reputation had risen steadily since the Yale commission, and he was internationally recognized with the award of the Gold Medal of the American Institute of Architects in 1971 and that of the Royal Institute of British Architects in 1972. His scheme for the Kimbell Art Museum in Fort Worth (1966–72) was under construction and promised to be an outstanding museum building, both innovative and humanistic. Kahn's reputation for failing to meet budgets or deadlines was well known, but it was accepted that the architectural quality of his buildings was outstanding.

In April 1969 Prown, Paul Mellon, and his lawyer Stoddard Stevens flew to California and met Kahn at the architect's Salk Institute in La Jolla, which had been completed in 1966. It was a visit that Prown considered "fruitful and successful in every way."[4] He was impressed by the rapport between client and architect as well as by the building itself. Prown also took Kahn to see Mr. Mellon's collections at his houses in Washington and Virginia; the architect was clearly sympathetic to the paintings and other works of art. These visits were important in forming Kahn's sense of what the building should be. Although Paul Mellon's colonial-style Brick House in Upperville, Virginia, was far removed from Kahn's aesthetic, he appreciated the domestic setting of the collection and responded positively to Mr. Mellon's intimate library. Both architect and patron had a tremendous love of old books, and the integration of a library with an art gallery was both special and appealing. A remark by Mr. Mellon that one needed to get close

Louis I. Kahn: Salk Institute, La Jolla, California, 1959–66

[2] "The Paul Mellon Center for British Art: A Classic Accommodation between Town and Gown," *Yale Alumni Magazine*, vol. 35, no. 7 (April 1972), 30–31.

[3] Jules David Prown, Annual Report, The Paul Mellon Center for British Art and British Studies, 1968–69.

[4] Prown to Kahn, April 30, 1969. Kahn Collection, Correspondence with Yale Mellon Office, J. Prown and H. Berg, File Box LIK 109, quoted in Patricia C. Loud, *The Art Museums of Louis I. Kahn* (Durham, NC, and London: Duke University Press, 1989), 233 n. 9.

The Brick House, Upperville, Virginia

Looking towards the library in the Brick House

to a painting in order to see it on a dull morning because one was in a house and not a museum had particular significance for the architect.[5] Prown found Kahn "responsive to people just as he is to art objects."[6] The appointment was formally confirmed in October 1969.

Prown's "Preliminary Thoughts" was included as an appendix to the "Building Design Program, Preliminary, The Paul Mellon Center for British Art and British Art Studies,"[7] which the Yale Office of Buildings and Grounds Planning Department issued to Kahn in January 1970. The program was based on a schedule of accommodation that had been developed by the University since the proposal of the gift. As well as the galleries and study center, it included a physical connection to the Yale University Art Gallery and, of course, the need for commercial space to maintain city taxes. Zoning requirements for off-street service and loading areas and for parking were noted. Area requirements called for 88,000 square feet of accommodation, including 40,000 square feet of gallery space to allow 600 paintings and 200 drawings to be on public view, a gallery of 3,000 square feet for changing exhibitions, and a reserve gallery of 5,000 square feet to house approximately 700 paintings; the remaining space accommodated the print room, libraries, lecture hall, and academic and staff offices. With an allowance for elevators, stairs, restrooms, mechanical rooms, service areas, and public spaces, the requirement of 88,000 square feet resulted in a building of 147,000 square feet, the net area representing 60 percent of the gross.[8] The requirements remained very much as first envisaged in 1967, but in 1970 reference was made to the possibility of the University Art Library occupying the site of the adjacent Baptist church at some time in the future, and a link to this would also be required.

Mr. Mellon's gift for the project, which was made by a transfer of securities, mostly Gulf Oil Corporation and Alcoa stock, totalled $23,063,973 and had been accomplished by 1970.[9] Within this sum, $6 million had been allocated for the construction of the Center.

The development and chronology of the design is set out clearly in Patricia Cummings Loud's exhibition catalog *The Art Museums of Louis I. Kahn*, which illustrates Kahn's design drawings from the Louis I. Kahn Collection then held by the Pennsylvania Historical and Museums Commission and the University of Pennsylvania.

The scheme that was to be called the First Program was developed by Kahn throughout 1970 with a preliminary presentation to Mr. Mellon in June of that year, and it is clear that the passionate desire of both the architect and the Director to achieve a significant work of architecture had become an overriding factor. In the fall estimates were prepared for a building that had a net area 20 percent larger than that originally envisaged. Based on a construction schedule starting in June 1971 and continuing until June 1973, costs were estimated at $14.8 million. This was more than double that which had been allocated and reflected not only the increased size of the building but the considerable rise in construction costs, which had gone up 42 percent since the gift. Further development of the scheme during the autumn raised the estimate to $15.2 million.[10] Kahn's office illustrated the proposal with beautifully rendered elevations during January 1971, and the architect wrote to Mr. Mellon in March of that year saying that "the building has developed to a maturity that I believe in, and I hope can be realized."[11]

[5] Loud, *The Art Museums of Louis I. Kahn*, 174–75, 233 n. 13.

[6] Prown quoted by Robert Kilpatrick, "Louis Kahn May Design Arts Center," *New Haven Register*, June 4, 1969. Prown later spoke of the compatibility he felt with Kahn: "Interview with Alessandra Latour, New Haven, Connecticut, June 23, 1982," in Alessandra Latour, ed., *Louis I. Kahn: l'uomo, il maestro* (Rome: Edizioni Kappa, 1986), 133–43, quoted in Loud, *The Art Museums of Louis I. Kahn*, 233 n. 10.

[7] Kahn Collection, Mellon 1 Program Void, File Box LIK112.

[8] Area Requirements, January 1970. Loud, *The Art Museums of Louis I. Kahn*, 295–96.

[9] Loud, *The Art Museums of Louis I. Kahn*, 235 n. 41.

[10] Loud, *The Art Museums of Louis I. Kahn*, 185.

[11] Kahn to Mellon, March 31, 1971. Kahn Collection, Master Files, 1969–73, Box LIK 10, quoted in Loud, *The Art Museums of Louis I. Kahn*, 235 n. 49.

Following pages:
First Program, model of
Chapel Street facade, 1971.
Louis I. Kahn Collection,
University of Pennsylvania

It was hoped that further funds would be forthcoming, but the escalating estimate of construction costs determined that the initial design for the Center was followed by a second design based on a substantially reduced program in order to stay within the available resources.

In response to the situation, the building program was drastically reduced during April 1971 to 70 percent of that originally envisaged, in effect 60 percent of the size of that presented in January 1971, and in May a "Revised Building Program, Preliminary with appendix of net areas 4/29/71" was issued by the Yale Buildings and Grounds Planning Department. To achieve this, the planned research library was eliminated on the basis that a new unified Art Library had been approved by the University for the site of the Calvary Baptist Church. (Kahn had been asked to make tentative schematic drawings in the hope that Mr. Mellon might also be tempted to support its construction.) This meant that only 10,000 immediate reference volumes would be required for the curatorial staff within the Center and also helped to reduce its staffing levels. In addition, the generous exhibition space for displaying the permanent collection was reduced to about half, and the lecture hall was scaled back to seat 200 instead of 400. Parking (for 100 cars minimum) was to be outside the building rather than in a basement. In July 1971 a budget limitation was set at $6,560,000 for construction of the building and $700,000 for furniture and equipment.[12] To this was added the cost of the landscaping, parking lot, etc., bringing the total to $7.9 million.

With the continuing dramatic rise in construction costs, and following discussions with Kenneth Froeberg of the George B. H. Macomber Construction Company, Prown wrote to Kahn stating that a further reduction of 8,500 square feet would be necessary in order to maintain the quality of construction required for the building, now estimated at $80 per square foot at July 1971 prices, as opposed to $54 at the time of the original budget estimate two years earlier.[13] Prown suggested that Kahn should consider transferring more programmed facilities to the basement and reducing the space devoted to rare books and the photo archive. The satisfactory condition of the paintings and the proximity of the facilities in the Yale University Art Gallery justified the omission of the paintings conservation studio.

Mr. Mellon realized that the reduction required a completely different design and accepted that it should be treated as a new commission to the architect. With the benefit of his experience designing the First Program, Kahn developed his proposals for the Second Program rapidly. In contrast to the range of schemes using different structures that had characterized the development of the First Program, the basic form that was to be realized in the Second Program was essentially established by July 1971, within two months of the revised brief.

Kahn began the Second Program design even before the arrival of the July budget, reducing the building's size in both its length and depth but retaining its relationship to the corner at the junction of High and Chapel streets. This pulled the Center away from the church, leaving the space between the two buildings to be developed as a sunken court around which further commercial activities could be introduced, again providing revenue to the city. The space released to the south became available for the external parking lot. The basic organization of the Center, however, remained characterized by

Model of Second Program (facades on Chapel and High streets), November 1972. Louis I. Kahn Collection, University of Pennsylvania

[12] Basic Requirements for Mellon Center Project, stamped received, Louis I. Kahn, July 12, 1971. Kahn Collection, Mellon, Minutes of Meetings 1971–73, File Box LIK 110, quoted in Loud, *The Art Museums of Louis I. Kahn*, 236 n. 57.

[13] Prown to Kahn, June 16, 1971. Kahn Collection, Correspondence Yale Mellon Office, J. Prown and H. Berg, File Box LIK 109, quoted in Loud, *The Art Museums of Louis I. Kahn*, 235 n. 54.

four factors that had been constant in the First Program designs:

1. The use of the first floor primarily for commercial purposes, except for the entrance foyer and auditorium.
2. The placing of the Center on the second floor and above.
3. The division of the Center into gallery and study sides arranged around two courts.
4. The location of the paintings galleries on the top floor to exploit natural light.

The fundamental differences were the use of metal as the cladding, and the change in the approach to the structure. While metal cladding had been proposed for the mechanical service towers in the First Program, the building had been one of masonry and concrete with the weighty appearance found in several of Kahn's other works. It was a radical change to use metal for all the infill panels on the elevations of the Second Program, and its treatment as a part of the glazing (opaque and transparent windows) was something totally new in Kahn's work.

For the structural engineering of both the First and Second programs, Kahn had turned to Pfisterer-Tor Associates. Henry Pfisterer, an associate professor of architectural engineering on the Yale faculty, had been assigned as adviser to the Yale University Art Gallery project twenty years earlier. However, because of Pfisterer's health, his partner, Abba Tor, was responsible for the work on the Center. Instead of the Vierendeel beams that had provided the large-scale, open-plan galleries and parking lot beneath the building, Kahn adopted the use of a simple concrete frame supporting concrete slabs on a repetitive 20-foot square grid. On the fourth floor this resulted in a separate skylight above each grid, moving the galleries away from using split vaults that would have recalled those at the Kimbell Art Museum. Because of the integration of the mechanical and structural systems that Kahn and Tor developed, Tor observed that "this serene and modest looking building, with columns spaced on a 20-foot, or occasionally 40-foot grid, nothing to excite structurally, contains several well hidden structural innovations. Kahn had a unique talent to study, learn, and understand in depth the possibilities and constraints of the structural and mechanical systems, and integrate them in a most organic way with his architectural concepts. Like a great conductor, he could get the best results out of his orchestra."[14]

During the next three months the scheme was refined with the development of details such as the corner portico and the skylights to the fourth-floor galleries. The scheme was approved by Mr. Mellon in New York on November 3, 1971, and preliminary working drawings were instructed to be complete by January 1972. Prown drafted a statement on the museum, commenting that in the galleries "Kahn hoped the visitor would feel that he was in a comfortable house – one with small room-like spaces and pleasant little areas in which to view an object closely, or just sit and relax."[15]

Final working drawings were issued to the Macomber Construction Company a year later in February 1973 and construction started. However, by March the contractors were claiming delays in receiving information that would extend the construction period. Small changes in the building requirements also contributed to the delay, and the preparation of a revised budget indicated that, by August, costs were agreed to have increased by $481,342. The principal causes for the claims for delay centered on the development of the skylight and the need for fire shutters on the openings to the courts, but they

Following pages:
The Second Program, Chapel Street elevation, as realized, with the Center distanced from the Yale Repertory Theatre by the insertion of a space containing the Lower Court

[14] Abba A. Tor, "The Structure of the Yale-Mellon Center for British Arts and British Studies" (lecture, Yale Center for British Art, November 4, 2005).

[15] Draft with notations, Release, Preliminary Design, The Paul Mellon Center for British Art and British Studies, November 23, 1971. Kahn Collection, News Clippings, Mellon Art Gallery (Yale), File Box LIK 111, quoted in Loud, *The Art Museums of Louis I. Kahn*, 237 n. 85.

Kahn's Phillips Exeter Academy Library, 1965-72, with furnishings by Benjamin Baldwin

also related to Kahn's ceaseless efforts to improve the design. In the fall of 1973, with Kahn often abroad and the need to respond more quickly to the contractor, Marshall Meyers was brought in as Kahn's on-site representative three days a week. Meyers had previously worked for Kahn as his project architect on the Kimbell but had since set up his own practice with Anthony Pellecchia in Philadelphia. The release of information, however, remained critical, and Macomber advised that completion would not be before May 1975, fifteen months later than first envisaged by Yale.

On March 17, 1974, Louis Kahn died of a heart attack. With considerable rapidity, Prown ensured that the commission was assigned to Pellecchia and Meyers rather than remaining with Kahn's office, which was to be disbanded. By that time, drawings for nearly every detail had been completed by Kahn, and the amount of outstanding design work was, therefore, very limited. However, each drawing had to be adopted by the new firm of architects to ensure their formal responsibility for the design. Where design required finalizing, continuity could be ensured, as both partners had worked for Kahn and knew his approach. The furnishing of the building was carried out with Benjamin Baldwin, who had collaborated with Kahn on the Phillips Exeter Academy Library (1965–72).

The Yale Center for British Art was opened on April 19, 1977, eleven years after the announcement of Paul Mellon's gift to the University. Its gross area is 114,153 square feet, and total project cost was given as $12.5 million, a cost of $108 per square foot.[16]

With the completion of the building, Jules Prown relinquished the post of Director and returned to his academic work in the Department of the History of Art. The remaining final design decisions, therefore, fell to Edmund Pillsbury, the Center's Director from 1976 to 1981. These related to the handrails in the staircase, cloth sun shades for the windows, acoustical treatments in the Lecture Hall, the "pogo" partition walls, the photo studio, the carpentry shop, the matting and framing area, the sales desk, the lights in the reading rooms on the second floor and the festive lights in the Entrance Court, as well as building graphics.

Under the leadership of Duncan Robinson, the Director from 1981 to 1995, the Center renewed its efforts to address ongoing condensation problems and issues with its roof; the roof of a single bay at the northwest corner of the building was devoted to a trial over the course of a year. The exterior steel panels of the building were re-caulked, a backup system for the fire shutters was installed, and new louvered, white-oak shutters replaced the cloth sun shades on the inside of the windows. Due to problems with the original pogo panels, the spring-loaded poles that held the panels in position were replaced with new threaded devices that bolt into the concrete ceilings. The sales desk was moved from the undercroft near the entrance to what is now the Docent Room, and eventually an entirely new museum shop was constructed in one of the commercial spaces in the building facing High Street. In order to make the new shop accessible from the Center, the director sought the advice of Marshall Meyers about breaking through the concrete wall between it and the Entrance Court; this opening was then filled with new oak-and-glass doors that serve as the point of entry into the shop from the Center. The fourth-floor offices of the Paintings Department were also reconfigured. Additional projects included ongoing work on the air handling, mechanical, electrical, security, and other systems.

View of the construction of the first two stories of the Center from the Art and Architecture Building, March 6, 1974 (less than two weeks before Kahn's death)

[16] Jules David Prown, *The Architecture of the Yale Center for British Art*, 3rd ed. (1977; repr., New Haven: Yale University Press, 2009), 71.

Jules Prown, Paul Mellon, and
Kenneth Froeberg on site, April 11, 1974

One of the most time-consuming and challenging projects during Robinson's tenure related to the building's windows. With the help of a variety of consultants, the Center investigated the failure of the seals in the original windows and considered a variety of options, taking into account issues of reflection on the exterior and transparency on the interior. The vast majority of the Center's windows were replaced with new three-pane windows with adhesive UV filters, and window troughs were reengineered to include a weep system. The control room near the Center's loading dock was also renovated, and compact shelving was installed in several basement storage areas so that greater numbers of paintings could be accommodated.

During Patrick McCaughey's tenure as Director from 1996 to 2001, a comprehensive program of repair, renovation, and refurbishment of the building was undertaken. After years of planning, the Center's roof system was reengineered and renovated in 1998; all fifty-six skylight domes were dismantled and reassembled, and the flat roof was fitted with a new drainage system and mansards. Ancillary projects during the "Year of the Roof" included the replacement of worn wool carpet with synthetic carpet in the public galleries as well as in some non-public areas; the replacement of the soiled and discolored Belgian linen on the walls with new linen; the redesign of the original pogo panels and the repositioning of the pogos in the fourth-floor galleries; the transformation of the Study Gallery into the Long Gallery; and the relocation and design of a new information desk to serve visitors better and to improve security just off the Entrance Court in the undercroft. The conference room on the fourth floor became the Founder's Room, an alteration undertaken at the suggestion of Paul Mellon and with the advice of Bruce Budd, an interior designer recommended by Mrs. Mellon. Renovations were also made to the Paper Conservation Laboratory, the Registrar's Office and neighboring recording room, and the Reference Library. In addition, Ethernet wiring was installed, two basement areas were repurposed, a book storage area was converted to an art storage area (with new fire and security systems), and a restroom was demolished in order to create a new storage room for Center publications. New interior shades were purchased to prevent sunlight from falling on the paintings (due to the repositioning of the pogos), and fabric blinds were created for the second-floor galleries on the south side of the building. New white-oak cabinets were fabricated to accommodate the growing collection of prints and drawings in the Study Room. Subsequent to McCaughey's tenure, plans were carried out for the first phase of compact book storage in the Reference Library, Photo Archive, and Rare Books Department. Fluorescent lights were selected to replace the original incandescent lights above the stacks in the Reference Library, and efforts were made to retrofit the lights in the Entrance and Library courts. Shortly after the arrival of Amy Meyers as Director (2002–present), the second phase of compact book storage was completed, and the crate storage area in the basement was converted to two offices; these spaces are now shared by the Center's IT department and installation team.

Early in her tenure, Amy Meyers established a Building Conservation Committee comprised of relevant Center staff and representatives from the School of Architecture, the Department of the History of Art, and the University's Office of Facilities. She also appointed Peter Inskip of Peter Inskip + Peter Jenkins Architects to develop a

Visit of University officials to the construction site, 1974

Steps to Lower Court, restored

conservation plan for the building and engaged the services of Jared Edwards of Smith Edwards Architects to assist with design and oversight of various projects. These included the renovation of offices on the first, second, and third floors to accommodate additional staff; the upgrading of the cage area to better serve the needs of staff and caterers; and the creation of a new paintings conservation studio in the area formerly occupied by the Center's carpentry shop.

In late 2008 George Knight, of Knight Architecture LLC of New Haven; Paul Lanteri, of Wiss, Jenny, Elstner Associates, Inc.; and Turner Construction Company were appointed to work in collaboration with Yale's Office of Facilities on the conservation of the Lower Court, the area between the Center and the Yale Repertory Theatre. Repairs were necessary because of structural movement in the great flight of steps leading down to the Lower Court, making it hazardous. Trials were undertaken in 2009, and the renovations were executed in 2010.

Although a lot of work has been carried out since the Center opened in 1977, remarkably little has changed, and Kahn's design remains very much intact. Where interventions have occurred, such as the replacement of the windows in 1995–96 and the re-roofing in 1998, every effort was made to respect the architect's original design. Wherever possible, alterations have been reversible.

Following pages:
Sketches of the Second Program made by Louis Kahn in 1971, all from the Louis I. Kahn Collection, University of Pennsylvania unless otherwise stated

Facing page:
Portico looking towards the Entrance Court. Similar steel benches were also proposed by Kahn for the Lower Court. At the date of this sketch, the floor was to be stone paved and the walls clad with metal panels (805.466)

Page 34:
The Entrance Court, looking south. The court was first proposed as open to the sky with the entrance foyer on the west side protected by glazing. On each story, the walls were to be clad in metal panels. Glazed windows were to provide views out from the surrounding galleries (805.467)

Page 35:
The Library Court, looking east. This sketch shows the rotated square stair shaft and use of the space as originally intended as the Exhibition Court (805.471)

Page 36:
The Rare Books and Manuscripts Reading Room (805.474)

Page 37:
The Library Court, looking west, July 28, 1971, Louis Isadore Kahn Collection, Manuscripts and Archives, Yale University Library

Pages 38–39:
The High Street facade and view west on Chapel Street, October 15, 1971. The generous glazing to the galleries on the north elevation was reduced as the design developed (805.464)

Page 40:
The west facade and Lower Court, October 15, 1971 (805.465)

Inner Court entrance & Mellon

Four coffers 4'8"
deep. Top lined with
mosaic insulation
(specing)

Concrete
columns

Stone
floor

Concrete columns

Paul Mellon Center Yale U.
Looking into Entrance on
Chapel and High   Moore 71

The mental panel The quality of a painter
is turned into a mind of green fret like
base not so much a seat but can suggest
a place one can sit.

Paul Mellon Center, Yale University
Fountain Court

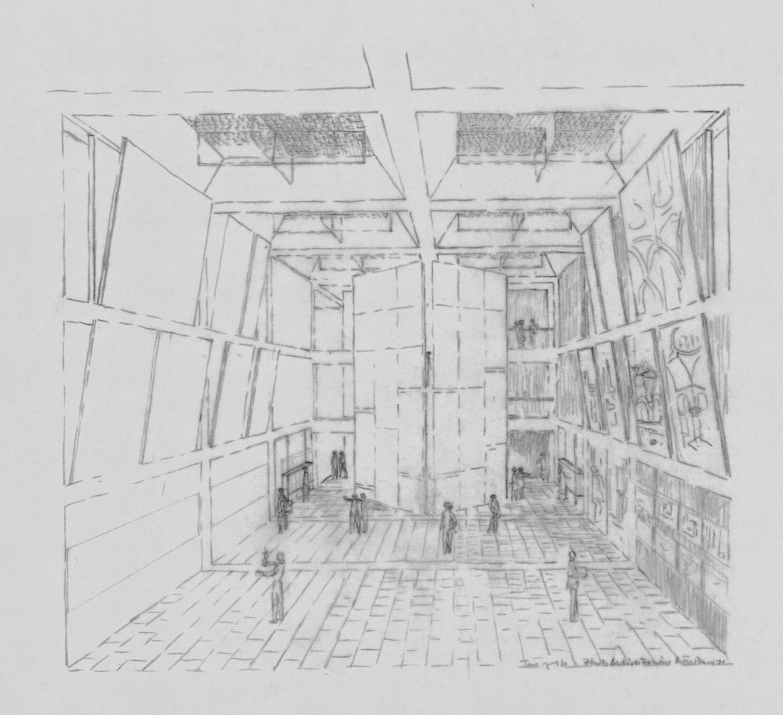

June 7/12   Photo Archive Exhibit & Gallery 72

The site and setting of the building

The original seventeenth-century plan of New Haven divided the city into nine perfect squares, the central of which formed an open Green that was bounded by what are now Elm, Church, College, and Chapel streets. This plan was maintained well into the eighteenth century. The Green was later subdivided with the introduction of Temple Street, and, by the end of the century, public buildings occupied the west half, while the east formed a public parade.[17]

Yale College had been constructed in 1717 in the southeast sector of the square immediately to the west of the Green, and the introduction of High Street, subdividing that square into east and west sections, followed the pattern seen in the rest of New Haven. It was natural for Yale's initial expansion to be contained within the area defined by Elm, College, Chapel, and High streets. By about 1840 the College occupied the whole of the area except for the corners on High Street, where a few residential properties recalled the earlier structure of the block.[18] By 1888 these had been cleared away, and the School of the Fine Arts had been constructed at the intersection of High and Chapel streets. The redevelopment of the south side of the block with the construction of Vanderbilt Hall and the replacement of Union Hall with Osborn Hall secured a strong University presence on the north side of Chapel Street by the end of the first decade of the twentieth century.

Apart from the central public square, the adjacent blocks originally were primarily residential. Yale gradually extended its campus westward across High Street. By the end of the nineteenth century, the entire west side of High between Elm and Chapel had been acquired by the University, and college buildings lined Library Street, in the center of the block. By the beginning of the twentieth century, Yale had extended through to York Street and beyond with the construction of Pierson College. Acquisition of properties on the south side of these blocks progressively extended frontage onto Chapel Street westward from High Street, where the east corner site had been acquired by 1888; additionally the University acquired three small adjacent properties by 1911. Further acquisitions to the west allowed the construction of the Yale Gallery of Fine Arts in 1927–28, bridging High Street to join with the School of the Fine Arts on the core block of the campus. The new gallery was to have extended from High Street to York Street, but only its east section was completed. The site of its proposed western wing is now occupied by Kahn's Yale University Art Gallery, which was finished in 1953 and first occupied as an art center.

Chapel Street, however, remained the southern boundary of Yale University, and the blocks beyond this were part of the City of New Haven, dominated by residential use but supplemented with the introduction of several public buildings. A commercial opera house had been constructed in 1860, behind what is now the Union League Café, and it was there that Charles Dickens performed his readings; the building was later adapted as the Hyperion Theater.

The city block bounded by Chapel and Crown, York and High, the north side of which is the site of the Yale Center for British Art, is shown as a low-density residential area in 1824, with detached houses arranged around its perimeter; a greater concentration of houses on the north side confirmed the importance of Chapel Street. By 1859 further houses had been introduced, increasing the density on the other three streets.

Louis I. Kahn's extension, 1951–53, to Egerton Swartwout's Yale Gallery of Fine Arts, 1927–28

[17] F. R. Honey, "Plan of New Haven in 1641," 1880, reproduced in Vincent Scully et.al., *Yale in New Haven: Architecture & Urbanism* (New Haven: Yale University, 2004) fig. 21; James Wadsworth, "Plan of the City of New Haven," 1748, reproduced in Vincent Scully et.al., *Yale in New Haven*, fig. 2; Amos Doolittle, "Plan of New Haven," 1812, reproduced in Scully et.al., *Yale in New Haven*, fig. 53.

[18] "Plan of the College," ca. 1841, reproduced in Scully et.al., *Yale in New Haven*, fig. 60.

Development plans

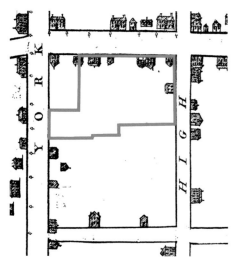

1824

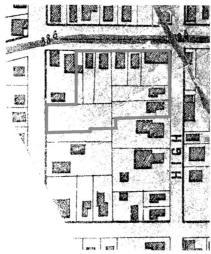

1859

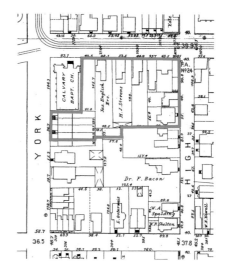

1911

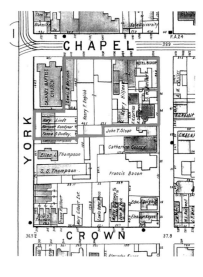

1924

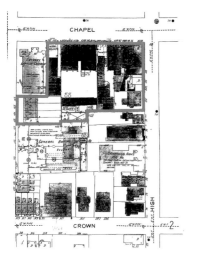

1971

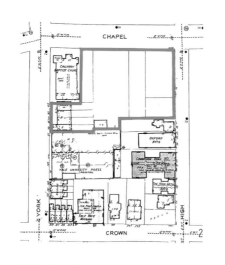

1973 site plan

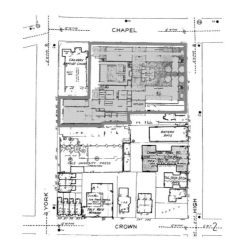

1973 First Program

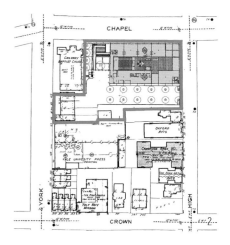

1974 Second Program

Paul Rudolph, Art and Architecture Building, 1959–63

The Calvary Baptist Church replaced three houses on the corner of York and Chapel in 1871. The redevelopment of the other freestanding houses on Chapel Street with commercial buildings that occupied the full width of their plots followed in the early twentieth century. By 1924, apart from the Calvary Baptist Church, the whole frontage was in redeveloped use with a funeral parlor next to the church, apartments and commercial units, and the Hotel Bishop on the corner of High. Although 1110 Chapel Street, the home of New Haven's WICC radio station, was refronted in the Art Deco style in 1938, none of the buildings could be considered architecturally distinguished. The other sides of the block remained residential, but development behind two properties on York Street belonging to the Thompson family resulted in the bakery of S. S. Thompson & Co. by 1924, further developed as the General Baking Co. On High Street one house was redeveloped as the Oxford Apartments, and the Highgate Apartments represent an infill within the garden of another property, which itself was replaced with the Cambridge Arms Apartment House by 1930. The Yale Hope Mission was built on Crown at about the same time.

A fire at the Hotel Bishop in 1945 resulted in loss of a life as well as damage to the building. It was not rebuilt. By 1973 the remaining residential properties on York had been adapted as rooming houses, and those on Crown had been turned into a laboratory and a clinic. The site of the bakery was rebuilt as a printing establishment for the Yale University Press. The block had, therefore, shifted from largely residential to commercial, with some connections to the University.

With the extension of the Yale University Art Gallery to the corner of York Street (Kahn, 1951–53) and the construction of the Art and Architecture building on the other side of York Street (Rudolph, 1959–63), a site for the Yale Center for British Art on the opposite side of Chapel Street was logical because of its proximity to other Yale arts facilities.

Site acquisition

At the time of acquisition, the site was chiefly occupied by stores and apartments, but it also included two restaurants, a garage, and the Calvary Baptist Church and its parish house. Many of the properties were in poor condition. The purchasing and gathering of lots for the construction of the Center was a relatively quick and easy process. The site was acquired through separate transactions with six individual land owners and involved eleven parcels of land.[19] The deeds were obtained between November 1966 and February 1968 by Yale University at an estimated cost of $1.5 million. Purchase of the Calvary Baptist Church came at a fortuitous time as the church was seeking to raise money to relocate to Orange, CT, in order to revive its dwindling congregation.

Facing page:
Development plans of the Chapel Street block. Although the whole of the frontage onto Chapel Street was acquired for the new Center, the Calvary Baptist Church was handed on to Yale University for the Yale Repertory Theatre and only the area outlined in blue was retained. The extent of Kahn's proposals for the First and Second programs is indicated in red. Extracts are taken from copies of plans in the Yale Center for British Art Archives.

The south side of Chapel Street, from the junction with High Street, looking west, photographed ca. 1963

[19] Information supplied by Wiggin & Dana, Counsellors at Law.

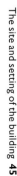

Rufus G. Russell, Yale Repertory Theatre
(formerly Calvary Baptist Church), 1871

Yale Repertory Theatre

Although not part of the Yale Center for British Art, the Yale Repertory Theatre building has to be considered as part of the Center's immediate setting. It was constructed as the Calvary Baptist Church and was designed by Rufus G. Russell (1823–1896), a New Haven architect. The church was built in 1871, just before the architect built the West Divinity Hall (1873–74) and about the same time that he designed the Winchester Observatory (constructed in a reduced form in 1882–83).[20] The church was acquired by Yale University when the site for the Center was assembled in 1966–68 by the University on behalf of Mr. Mellon. Its acquisition meant that the whole of the north side of the block between High Street and York Street was available for the Center.

It was found, however, that the space requirements for the new institution did not justify the full width of the block. Even with the very generous First Program, the building would have appeared stretched if it had occupied the full Chapel Street frontage, and Jules Prown felt that the visitor experience would not have been acceptable with such a low linear structure. Although it had been suggested that the church should be demolished and that the site might be landscaped to form part of the setting of the Center, the building was handed back to the University soon after it had been acquired.[21] All of Kahn's developed schemes illustrate the church retained in place, but the architect believed that it should be demolished. "He felt that it had outgrown its original function, and would eventually stand on the corner 'like a dumb animal.'"[22] Kahn returned to the idea of demolishing the church during the development of his schemes for the First Program with proposals for a new art library. However, Mr. Mellon did not offer funds for its construction, and nothing came of the proposal. With the Second Program, the Center drew further away from the church but retained its physical relationship to it through the construction of the Lower Court and terrace.

The church was in use by the Yale Repertory Theatre soon after its acquisition by the University. The Yale Rep had been founded in 1966 by Robert Brustein, Dean of the Yale School of Drama, with the goal of facilitating a meaningful collaboration between theater professionals and talented students. The building was refurbished by Patricia Tetrault in 1975 and, over the years, it has become one of the most distinguished regional theaters. Of the ninety world premieres that the Yale Rep has produced, four have won Pulitzer Prizes, and ten productions have received Tony Awards after being transferred to Broadway. The Rep was given a Tony for Outstanding Regional Theater in 1991. In 2002, the Yale School of Drama and Yale Repertory Theatre received the Governor's Arts Award from Governor John Rowland for artistic achievement and contribution to the arts in the state of Connecticut. Russell's building has been considerably altered in its conversion and the exterior has been modified extensively.

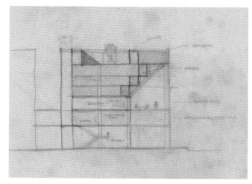

Kahn's preliminary study for an art library: section looking south with York Street on the right, 1970. Louis I. Kahn Collection, University of Pennsylvania (805.003)

Facing page:
The plan (top) and elevation (bottom) for Kahn's proposed art library on the site of the Calvary Baptist Church, with a bridge linking it to the Center's library (First Program), 1970. The proposal was not developed further. Louis I. Kahn Collection, University of Pennsylvania (805.007)

[20] Scully et al., *Yale in New Haven*, 139.

[21] Conversation between Peter Inskip and Jules Prown, ca. 2007–08.

[22] Prown, *The Architecture of the Yale Center for British Art*, 21.

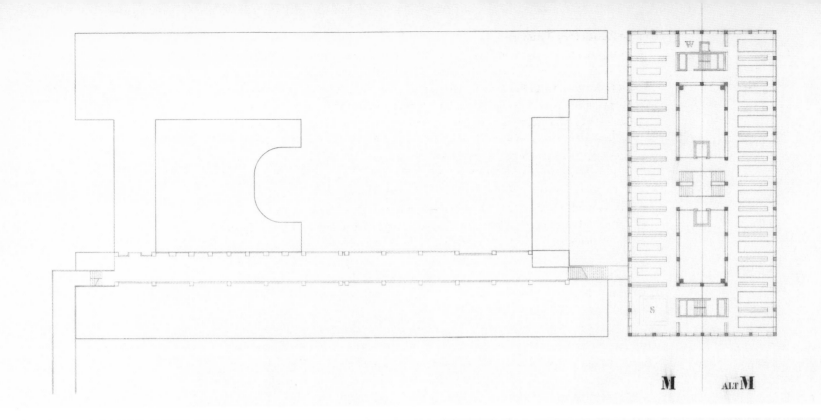

M · ᴀʟᴛ M

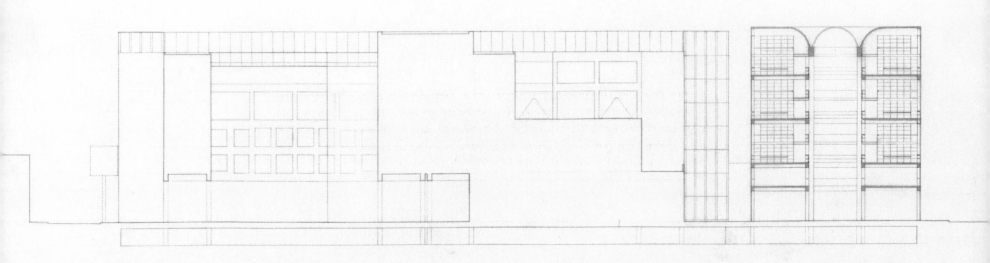

Sᴛ

Assessment of cultural significance

As a building by Louis I. Kahn

Although Louis Kahn was born in 1901, his fame and best work really belong to the next generation of architects who worked in the second half of the twentieth century. All the buildings that made him famous and gained him international recognition as one of the great innovative figures of world architecture were designed after he passed fifty. They are associated with two radical notions to which he attached great importance: the first was that any sound building must be rooted in its materiality and be proudly true to the way it is made; the second is a conviction that, however important the house, the factory, or the office might be, both as types and as elements in the configuration of the city, architecture must nonetheless concern itself primarily with the anatomy of society, and therefore with its institutions. The constant involvement with institutional buildings and the nature of public space is, therefore, a refrain that runs through his postwar work. Kahn's most important buildings were churches, synagogues, universities, and museums.

Kahn's earlier work, which had focused around the city of Philadelphia, had mainly been low-cost housing projects of the garden-city type, but little went beyond the drawing board. By 1939 his work as a partner of George Howe had gained him some recognition as an expert on low-cost housing. In addition, he had realized some projects for individual houses and a small synagogue.

After the Second World War, Kahn established his own Philadelphia office. The work was again mainly on individual private houses, but with his partner Oscar Storonov, he developed plans for an underdeveloped area of Philadelphia known as the "Triangle" for the City Planning Commission, and this confirmed his interest in public space. In the 1950s his projects for replanning Philadelphia were based on protecting the city from the excesses of automobile traffic by introducing a modern transport system. This was reinforced by his view that, within the city, the public building should be the positive marker of city grandeur and prosperity. All was a declaration about the essential nature of public and urban space.

Kahn's work in Philadelphia brought him international recognition, and at the same time he became recognized as an inspiring academic through his teaching at Harvard and, after 1945, at Yale, where he accepted a permanent appointment. It was through Kahn's introduction that Howe became Dean of the School of Architecture, and later it was Howe who urged the University to commission Kahn for a modest extension to the Yale University Art Gallery in 1951.

Kahn realized three distinctive museums in his life time, each of which satisfies its own program, functioning both as a work of art and, in practice, as a museum. Each is founded on Kahn's belief that museums can be places where individuals look at art objects in natural light. In them he gradually turned away from the universal space of the modernists that is so explicit in the Yale University Art Gallery. At the Kimbell Art Museum and the Yale Center for British Art, he developed ideas of looking at objects within defined, room-like spaces while still holding to the principle of flexibility. The Art Gallery was designed as an art center rather than just a gallery, and objects are only occasionally illuminated by natural light. At the Kimbell the director's idea was to create ambient light in which the viewer was aware of changes in natural light outdoors, but the objects could never really rely on natural light alone. At the Center, the need to rely

Facing page:
Fourth-floor galleries,
overlooking the Entrance Court

Cultural significance is a simple concept. Its purpose is to help in identifying and assessing the attributes which make a place of value to us and our society. An understanding of it is, therefore, a basic stage in any planning process. Once the significance of a place is understood, informed policy decisions can be made which will enable the significance to be retained, revealed, or, at least, impaired as little as possible. A clear understanding of the nature and degree of significance of a place will not only suggest constraints on future action, it will also introduce flexibility by identifying areas which can be adapted or developed with greater freedom.

James Semple Kerr, "The Conservation Plan,"
National Trust, New South Wales, 1990

Louis I. Kahn, Yale University Art Gallery, 1951–53

on natural light was expressed in the preliminary program, written before any architect was commissioned, and Kahn was engaged because of his sympathy and experience with that approach.

The Yale University Art Gallery (1951–53) is very tightly and simply organized, with crisp, insistent geometry in its volumes and in the manifest clarity of its structural detail. In addition, there is a clear, almost diagrammatic distinction between the served and the servant spaces that would become an important aspect of all Kahn's planning. Asserting the formal dignity of the service elements of a building while respecting the hierarchy of spaces in the plan is Kahn's deliberate challenge to the academic design method within which he had been taught. It is perhaps no accident that the change of direction in his work came directly after Kahn returned from visiting the monuments of ancient Greece. The Yale University Art Gallery was not only Kahn's first art gallery, but his first major building to be realized.

The Kimbell Art Museum (1966–72) was possibly Kahn's own favorite building among his works. The donor had died in 1964, leaving his collection to a trust together with funds to expand it and construct a new museum, which he wanted to be an outstanding piece of architecture. Patricia Loud notes that the program prepared by the museum's director, Richard Brown, was ideal for Kahn. Although it did detail requirements and costs, it did not rigidly prescribe the rooms so much as describe their qualities: "the experience of a visit to the museum should be one of warmth, mellowness and even elegance. . . . The spaces, forms and textures should maintain a harmonious simplicity and human proportion between the visitor and the building and the art objects observed."[23] Brown had also agreed that daylight was to be the main source of illumination, and the architect's response was for the strong Texas light that fell through a slit at the apex of the vaulted galleries to be diffused by a baffle so no direct light would fall on a work of art. The space was continuous but articulated by the vaults that extended over the galleries and by dividing screens that stopped short of the vault. After it was finished Kahn continued to describe it as "based on the room-like quality. And the natural light being the only acceptable light."[24] To a Fort Worth art editor, he described the museum by saying that it would not be "formidable, but like a friendly house" with "friendly-sized rooms [and a] beautiful environment of natural gardens."[25] He went on to say that "the paramount decision in making a space [for the Kimbell] was to honor natural light and not place art in a mausoleum atmosphere. . . . When the art was made, the mood of the day was obvious. In the galleries, you should always know if it's morning, afternoon or night." He continued to use the analogy of "a friendly home," adding "to emphasize important paintings, there will be houses within the house." As Loud observes, Brown considered the Kimbell to be "a contemporary version of the traditional palace of art: 'I like to think this is the palace of a great noble and that he has invited you into his home to enjoy his collection.'"[26]

After the Kimbell, the explicitness of the space in the Center might come as something of a surprise. However, the Center's program was complex, requiring Kahn to design for a highly specific existing collection based mainly on intimate works of art: domestic-scale pictures, works on paper, manuscripts, and rare books. There was also a need for spaces for scholars and university teaching.

Louis I. Kahn, Kimbell Art Museum, 1966–72

[23] Richard Brown, "Pre-Architectural Program" (1, C), in *In Pursuit of Quality: The Kimbell Art Museum* (Fort Worth: Kimbell Art Museum; New York: Distributed by H. N. Abrams, 1987), 319, quoted in Loud, *The Art Museums of Louis I. Kahn*, 264.

[24] Interview with William Marlin, Philadelphia, June 24, 1972, Kimbell Art Museum files, quoted in Loud, *The Art Museums of Louis I. Kahn*, 272 n. 41.

[25] Latryl Layton, "Kimbell Art Museum To Be 'Friendly House,'" *Fort Worth Press*, February 5, 1968, quoted in Loud, *The Art Museums of Louis I. Kahn*, 272 n. 44.

[26] Brown in Barbara Rose, "New Texas Boom, from Fort Worth to Corpus Christi, to Bring Together Great Art and Great Architecture," *Vogue* 160 (October 15, 1972), 130, quoted in Loud, *The Art Museums of Louis I. Kahn*, 264.

In the Center Kahn develops all the ideas about light and the importance of room-like volumes that he had expressed in the Kimbell, but the adoption of a 20-foot structural grid in place of the axial vault took this further. The 20-foot dimension, used by Alfred H. Barr, Jr. in the grid of the original Museum of Modern Art, was one Kahn considered the best for viewing art, and anything smaller he thought was not acceptable. (According to Kahn's widow, Esther, this applied even in his home, where he did not want paintings hanging in his living room, as the span was less than 20 feet and thus inappropriate for the display of art.)[27]

The Center is located within the Beaux Arts tradition of museums organized around courtyards. Its multiple-floor plan also implies the Roman palazzo and evokes museums of the past even more than the Kimbell with its porticoes and sacred-grove setting. The four-story plan also reflects that the building is on a restricted city-center site, and its urban quality is confirmed by its views back into its courts as much as those out to the surrounding city. The two internal courts that penetrate the block also relate the Center to other Kahn buildings (the Rochester Unitarian Church; the National Assembly at Dhaka; Eleanor Donnelly Erdman Hall, Bryn Mawr College; and the library at Phillips Exeter Academy), and the third court that lies to the west of the block provides the reference to monumental ruins so loved by the architect, as well as a fictive memory of a once larger scheme.

Each of Kahn's three art galleries is a highly significant work of architecture in its own right, but together they demonstrate the development of Kahn's approach to museum design. As Carter Wiseman has observed, "if the Yale Art Gallery had established the idea of served and servant spaces, and the Kimbell had redefined the role of natural light in an art museum, the Yale Center for British Art synthesized everything that had gone before. Here was a building laid out with a classical rigor, yet it embraced the realities of urban life and modern economics without apology. It provided a setting for its historical contents that was deeply respectful, yet also clearly modern. If the Center was less appealing to the camera than Salk, less monumental than Dhaka, less accessible as an ideal form than Exeter, and less overtly welcoming than the Kimbell, those apparent shortcomings constituted a remarkable advance. Here was a building the power of which did not reveal itself without repeated exposure and careful inquiry."[28]

View across the Library Court toward the cylindrical staircase and fourth-floor galleries

Degree of survival and intactness

Kahn's career resulted in comparatively few buildings being realized, and many proposals never went beyond the design stage. The 1960s saw a series of commissions for the public buildings that Kahn longed for: Mikveh Israel Synagogue in Philadelphia (1962); mother house for the Dominican nuns' congregation in Delaware County (1965); a new monastery for St. Andrew's in Valyermo, California (1966). But none of these was ever begun. The same problem faced two high-rise commissions: one in New York on the site of the Broadway Tabernacle, and an office tower in Kansas City. Neither came into being, the latter being transferred to Skidmore, Owings & Merrill after considerable design development, leaving Kahn bitter and disappointed. Lack of funds meant that the Holocaust Memorial in Battery Park, on which Kahn worked between 1966 and 1972, was never built. The plan for a memorial to Franklin D. Roosevelt was delayed for many years; and only now have funds for "Four Freedoms Park" been committed by New York City and the state thanks to the efforts of the Franklin and Eleanor Roosevelt Institute.

[27] Loud, *The Art Museums of Louis I. Kahn*, 265, 272 n. 49.

[28] Carter Wiseman, *Louis I. Kahn: Beyond Time and Style: A Life in Architecture* (New York: W. W. Norton, 2007), 261.

Louis I. Kahn, Bathhouse, Trenton Jewish Community Center, New Jersey, 1954–55

Kahn's masterpieces, such as the Salk Institute for Biological Sciences and the Kimbell Art Museum, have been well cared for, but other buildings have not. The Medical Services Center for the American Federation of Labor and Congress of Industrial Organizations (AFL-CIO) in Philadelphia was demolished for highway expansion in 1973, and the bathhouse at the Trenton Jewish Community Center became neglected and fell into disrepair but is now under restoration. Both the Yale University Art Gallery and the Alfred Newton Richards Medical Research Building, University of Pennsylvania, have undergone change.

However, at the time of Kahn's death, there were more prestigious commissions in his office than ever. An Israeli government center in Jerusalem had fallen victim to budget cuts in 1973, but the project for the Hurva Synagogue in Jerusalem was being developed, as were those for the Palazzo dei Congressi in Venice and the Menil Collection in Houston. Plans for revamping Independence Mall in Philadelphia were also underway. All were abandoned when Kahn's office was closed after his death.

The decision by Yale to entrust the completion of the Center to Pellechia and Meyers made sense, as Marshall Meyers had worked on behalf of the University to monitor and facilitate progress on construction while Kahn was still alive. His role as Kahn's project architect for the Kimbell also ensured the standards in execution that the architect would have required. Nearly every element in the Center's building had been detailed by Kahn's office before his death; the professional responsibility of Pellechia and Meyers after they took over was primarily one of site inspection rather than architectural design. Only a few details such as the stair handrails were amended, and those final furnishings that had to be selected were worked out by Meyers with Benjamin Baldwin, who had been involved with Kahn at the Kimbell and at Exeter. The Center can, therefore, be considered as designed by Kahn himself.

What is important is that the building also survives very much intact from when it was opened, with even its furnishings largely in place. Alterations have been very few: the adoption of one of the commercial units as a museum store, the frequent blocking of openings to reduce light in the second-floor galleries, alterations to the stacks and library to allow the introduction of compact storage, and changes resulting from the appropriation of the Lower Court by the restaurant. Minor changes have primarily been the result of "drift," such as the ad-hoc replacement of fittings, the introduction of additional services, and the modification of the pogos.

The Center can also be seen as important in the context of Yale. The commissioning of the Yale University Art Gallery in 1951 was recognized as the principal act through which the University embraced modern architecture after the war, and major developments followed with commissions to Eero Saarinen, Philip Johnson, Paul Rudolph, and Skidmore, Owings & Merrill. The appointment of Louis Kahn to design the Center, therefore, can be seen as evidence of the University's continuing patronage of the very best modern architecture in the second half of the twentieth century. The state in which the building has been maintained with so little alteration is confirmation of how well Kahn's design has served the community. This was acknowledged by the Twenty-five Year Award of the American Institute of Architects in 2005.

Louis I. Kahn, proposal for Hurva Synagogue, Jerusalem, 1965

As a museum housing a specific collection

The cultural significance of Kahn's building is enhanced by its association with Paul Mellon and his collection of British art. It is the most important collection of British art outside the United Kingdom: its size, its comprehensiveness, and its quality probably place it only just below the national collections of Great Britain. The Center is a very significant building housing a very significant collection.

Kahn's building must also be seen in the context of the other galleries donated to the nation by the Mellon family: the National Gallery of Art in Washington was given in 1936 by Paul Mellon's father, Andrew, together with his outstanding collection, and designed by John Russell Pope. The gallery's East Wing by I. M. Pei of 1978 was donated by Paul Mellon himself and his sister, Ailsa Mellon Bruce. Such gifts are twentieth-century examples of the tradition of great private American collections becoming public by will or by grant, which have their mid-nineteenth-century roots in the construction of the original Corcoran Gallery of Art in Washington.

The Center also rests firmly in the tradition of university museums dating back to the Ashmoleum Museum, Oxford, in the seventeenth century and continuing with the Fitzwilliam at Cambridge. The Trumbull Gallery at Yale became, in 1832, the first art gallery to be associated with a college in the United States. The construction of Swartwout's original Yale Gallery of Fine Arts building on Chapel Street to house the Jarves Collection, which had been acquired by Yale in 1871, eventually followed in 1928. At Harvard the Fogg Museum of Art was established by Elizabeth Perkins Fogg in 1895, and its present building is of 1927, by Coolidge, Shepley, Bulfinch & Abbott. These university museums combined teaching and public display, and the integration within the galleries, not only of curators' offices but also classrooms, meant that students and faculty as well as staff passed through the galleries and saw works of art on their way to destinations. This seriously influenced Prown's brief for the Center, reinforcing its role as an academic institution.

By the time Paul Mellon gave his collection of British art to Yale, the ideal of the museum as a monument in its own right had been replaced by the ideal of the museum as the perfect place to show, enjoy, and study works of art. Each aspect was particularly important to the donor: his paintings were to be shown appropriately, made accessible to the public free of charge, and to be the core of a study center within the University.

Although Mr. Mellon took a great interest in the project, once the gift to Yale had been formalized, the donor on the whole stood aside. After a visit to see the Salk, he accepted Yale's recommendation of the architect and did not interfere in the design or construction of the building, although, on occasion, he sometimes questioned the wisdom of proposals such as the placing of a car-park beneath a building housing his collection. When costs rose, he was firm that he did not wish to increase the available funds.

Where Mr. Mellon did contribute actively was in support of the idea that his collection should continue to be displayed in a domestic setting. On the whole, most of the pictures are small scale and were originally intended for that purpose, and Mr. Mellon had used them as such when he had started to collect, principally hanging them in the main rooms of the Brick House, the colonial-style building that he had constructed with his first wife, Mary Conover Brown, in Virginia following their marriage in 1935. After her death in 1946, Paul Mellon married Rachel (Bunny) Lambert Lloyd in 1948; they

John Russell Pope, National Gallery of Art, Washington, DC, 1937–41

I. M. Pei, East Wing of the National Gallery of Art, Washington, DC, 1978

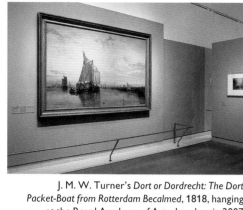

J. M. W. Turner's *Dort or Dordrecht: The Dort Packet-Boat from Rotterdam Becalmed*, 1818, hanging at the Royal Academy of Arts, London, in 2007

moved to Oak Spring, and the Brick House was largely given over to his pictures and books with additional space to house the growing collection made available in bedrooms on the second floor. In addition, other works were kept in Paul Mellon's residences in Washington and New York. The humanistic brief prepared by Jules Prown that focused on the paintings being viewed in daylight and in room-like volumes, therefore, continues Mr. Mellon's housing of his collection in a domestic setting. Kahn responded to this with great success through the subdivision of space, the handling of daylight, and the placing of windows. The variation in the levels of electric lighting also supports this quasi-domestic presentation. There is no evidence of spaces being designed for the installation of a specific work, but the building did provide appropriate opportunities for a display that revealed the quality of Mr. Mellon's collection.

The Turner Bay provides an example. Here Turner's painting *Dort or Dordrecht: The Dort Packet-Boat from Rotterdam Becalmed* ("The Dort") is displayed in a setting similar to that for which it was conceived at Farnley Hall in Yorkshire, with light falling across it from a window to the left. The association of the painting and its setting within Kahn's building is acknowledged as a highlight of a visit to the Center. The same picture was used as the centerpiece of the exhibition at the Royal Academy of Arts, London, in 2007 to celebrate the centennial of Paul Mellon's birth. Though still outstanding, when the work was displayed in a conventional, electrically lit gallery, it was no longer as powerful as when installed at Yale. The marriage of Mr. Mellon's collection with the Kahn building is borne out by the way that Constable's *Stratford Mill* was elevated when placed temporarily in the Turner Bay while the space was vacated by "The Dort."

As urban fabric

The purchase of the site for the Yale Center for British Art by the University meant that it would no longer be on the list of taxable property for the City of New Haven, since educational institutions are exempt. However, Yale decided to use the project as a medium to improve its status in the New Haven community. It achieved this by maintaining retail activities at street level, thus allowing the property to be taxed by the city. Kahn was enthusiastic about the proposal and handled it to great advantage. His four-story block maintains the urban form of the commercial south side of Chapel Street in contrast to the monumental University buildings on the north side. However, while the building was integrated into the street, he removed the museum from the bustle of the commercial sidewalk by setting it on the upper floors and placing its entrance at the heart of the first floor, approached through a deep portico. In addition, the division between museum and commercial activities is supported by the treatment of the elevation itself. By recessing the commercial facade to the rear face of the columns and setting it below a great transverse beam, Kahn discreetly differentiated the two elements, extending the sidewalk back into the commercial units, while the museum was set behind a flush facade through which visitors look out onto the life of the city.

The elevations of the Center are treated in a completely novel way for Kahn. Instead of masonry punctuated with voids, typical of his earlier work, the elevations celebrate the use of glazing through their reflections of the street, the buildings opposite, and the sky and light, and that glazing is set flush with its adjacent steel panels, which Kahn referred to as opaque windows. The whole adds iridescence to the street. The portico at

Top: The Turner Bay
Bottom: The same bay was adopted as the Constable Bay while "The Dort" was on exhibition in London in 2007.

Commercial shops opening onto the sidewalk on Chapel Street

In terms of its effort to relate a straightforward downtown street usage to the more inward-turning needs of an art museum, the Mellon Center may well be the first symbol of a new Yale-New Haven co-operation and interdependence.

"Retail Shops and a Yale Museum,"
New Haven Register, February 23, 1972

Commercial unit in the Lower Court,
extending beneath the terrace

the corner of Chapel and High, as well as marking the entrance to the Center, is symbolic of the relationship between the city and the University. The Lower Court is an important element in relationship to Chapel Street. It allowed the church room to breathe but, through its treatment as a monumental ruin, it also recalls Kahn's larger schemes that occupied the complete street frontage and so retains the integrity of the urban block. In addition, the planting of the parking lot to the south of the building maintains the sides of the block onto High and York streets.

From within the building, views out of its large windows place the Center within the context of the city. In its citation for the Twenty-five Year Award in 2005, the AIA stated that the building is "a gentle urbane masterpiece. It offers a quiet foil to its more demonstrative neighbors, and from the interior, it frames and augments them."[29]

Top: The Chapel Street facade
Bottom: Commercial storefronts on High Street

[29] "British Art Center Wins Design Award," *New Haven Register*, April 7, 1978.

Statement of cultural significance

The Yale Center for British Art building is culturally significant as:

1. An outstanding piece of architecture by one of the most significant architects of the second half of the twentieth century.

Both the client and architect were determined that the building should be a significant piece of architecture. The integrity of the building and the consistency in the handling of space and materials by Kahn demonstrate that this was achieved.

Within Kahn's oeuvre the Center combines ideas from the Yale University Art Gallery extension, Phillips Exeter Academy Library, and the Kimbell Art Museum, but they are brought together in a highly original way that has no precedent in his previous work.

2. An outstanding example of a building type.

The building is exemplary as a public art gallery without compromising its use as an academic institution.

Its success in meeting the requirements that the collection should be shown in natural daylight and in room-like volumes enhances the works of art and contributes significantly to visitor enjoyment.

3. It maintains the urban fabric of New Haven.

The building has a sense of responsibility to the city as a whole and, despite the introduction of a monumental art gallery, does not disrupt the definition of the commercial street.

The significance is enhanced through its association with Paul Mellon and his outstanding collection of British art.

The visitor experience of seeing such a significant collection within such a significant building is one of exceptional importance.

The cultural significance of the building is vulnerable from:

1. The need to accommodate:

a) the growth of the collection.

b) the increased levels of staffing needed to preserve and add to the collection, and to run its academic and public programs.

2. A drift away from the original architectural intentions and detail through:

a) changing patterns of use (e.g., the appropriation of the actual space of the courtyard by the commercial unit that lines two of its sides).

b) accretive change through replacement of small details including worn fixtures, carpets, etc.

c) response to environmental issues, security, etc.

Facing page:
The north side of the fourth-floor galleries, looking west

Levels of cultural significance

The assessment of levels of significance helps to justify a flexible approach to the treatment of the place: the greater the significance, the greater the need for careful decision making. The corollary is also valid: the lesser the significance, the freer may be its treatment, always provided that aspects of greater significance remain undamaged.

As these assessments are made without regard to conservation and management issues, there is no formal link between the level of significance and the subsequent policies. Significance is, however, the most important of the factors to be considered when developing policies.

The hierarchy of levels chosen for the Center is best explained as a four-rung ladder. The top rung is for items of exceptional significance in a broad context. The next rung contains items of considerable significance that would warrant inclusion on any national or state register of places of significance. The second rung from the bottom contains the threshold for entry onto such registers. Items on the bottom rung, as the designation implies, are of little significance.

★★★★ Exceptional significance

★★★ Considerable significance

★★ Some significance

★ Little significance

▨ Intrusive

[ ] Removed

Assessment of levels of significance in the schedule has been made on the basis of the independent value of the element in question, tempered by consideration of the degree to which the element tends to reinforce or reduce the significance of the whole. For example, some items are visually intrusive and damage the character and quality of the space. These are identified in the schedule as intrusive (▨).

Exterior and setting

Roof	★★★
Views from adjacent roofs	★★★
Roof lights	★★★
Flat roof	★★
Mansard slope	★★★

Elevations	★★★★
North Elevation	★★★★
East Elevation	★★★★
South Elevation	★★★★
West Elevation	★★★★
Equality of standing of elevations	★★★★
Building as freestanding block	★★★★
Concrete frame	★★★★
Deep beam above first-floor level	★★★★
Fenestration	★★★★
Steel panels	★★★★
Hard landscape surfaces	★★

Portico	★★★★
Views into the Entrance Court	★★★★
Ceiling	★★★★
Steel walls	★★★★
Vitrines	★★★★
Paving	★★★★
Signage	★★
Fire hydrants	★
Sandwich boards	▨

Shops on High and Chapel	★★
Storefronts	★★★★
Steelwork	★★★★
Glazing	★★★★
Replacement handles	▨
Commercial shop interiors	★
Museum shop interior	★
Concrete elements and air shafts within shops	★★

Lower Court ★★★★

Staircase to Lower Court	★★★★
Bollards at street level	■
Handrails	★★
Tree in Lower Court	★★★
Paving	★★★★
Elevations to Lower Court	★★★★
Interior of commercial premises (restaurant)	★
[Restaurant canopy]	■
[Shed]	■
Umbrellas for summer dining	■
[Lattice screens to Lecture Hall lobby]	■

Terrace ★★★

Trees	★★★
Screen wall	★★
Elevator tower	★★
Brick walkway at street level	★★★
Stepped terrace	★★★★

Loading Bay ★★

Screen wall	★★
Bollards	★★
Rolling shutters	★★
Storage container	■

Car park ★★

Endwalls and signage	★★
Totem pole sign	■
Parking attendant's booth	★★
Sidewalk	★★
Truck bay	★★
Bollards	★
Lighting	★
Fencing	★★
Tree planting	★★★
Yellow painting of curbs	■
Chiller and cage enclosure	■

Interior

Spaces for public circulation and assembly ★★★★

Entrance Court	★★★★
Foyer	★★★
Elevator lobby	★★★
Circular stair and shaft	★★★★
Lobby to Lecture Hall	★★★
Elevators	★★
Docent Room	★★

Lecture Hall ★★★

Seating	★★
Acoustic panels	★★
Projection booth	★★
Concrete walls	★★★
Introduction of additional audio equipment and cabling	■

Public display ★★★★

Galleries ★★★★

Fourth-floor galleries	★★★★
Long Gallery	★★★
Third-floor galleries	★★★
Second-floor galleries	★★★
Views between galleries	★★★
Views across the Library and Entrance courts	★★★★
Skylights	★★★★
Structural frame	★★★★
Air shafts	★★★
Floor grid	★★★★
Pogos	★★★
Wall treatment	★★★
Windows	★★★★
Light fixtures	★★★

Library Court ★★★★

Openings into galleries	★★★★
Views into Reference Library and Study Room	★★★
Concrete stair shaft	★★★★
Clarity of concrete frame	★★★★
Oak paneling	★★★★
Rug	★★

Libraries ★★★★

Reference Library ★★★★

Reading Room	★★★★
Built-in joinery (carrels, bookcases)	★★★★
Compact bookshelving	■
Mezzanine	★★★★
Staircase	★★★★
Offices	★★
Air shaft	★★★

Rare Books and Manuscripts ★★★★

Reading room	★★★★
Built-in joinery (carrels, bookcases)	★★★★
Curatorial offices	★★
Research office	★★
Stacks	★

Prints and Drawings ★★★★

Study Room	★★★★
Built-in joinery (carrels, bookcases)	★★★★
Outer office, storage, and staircase	★★★
Curatorial offices	★★
Air shaft	★★★
Stacks	★

Office and ancillary spaces ★★

Fourth floor ★★

Offices off the Long Gallery	★★
Art storage	★
Paintings Department offices	★
Kitchenette	★
Founder's Room	★★★
Director's office	★★★

Third floor ★★

Offices	★★
Design and graphics	★★
Paper Conservation Laboratory	★★★
Paper Conservation offices	★★
Paper Conservation teaching room/ library	★★

Second floor ★★

Staff Lounge	★★
Seminar Room	★★

Back of house ★★

First floor ★★

Back hall	★★
Corridor	★★
Paintings Conservation Studio	★★
Security offices	★★
Control Room	
Cage	★
Loading dock	★

Basement ★★

Mechanical room	★★
Corridor	★★
Art storage	★★
Photo Studio	★
IT Department	★★

Other ★★

Restrooms	★★
Fire escape stairs	★

Following page:
Steel panels above the walkway on the south side of the building

Conservation policies

Method of approach

The policies laid out below have been devised to safeguard the cultural significance of the place while promoting good public access, sustainable use, and adaptation.

The policies are arranged thematically, not necessarily by priority, and are generally set within a context on which the policy is based. Where helpful, a policy is followed by issues that are examples of related work.

Explanation, terms, and structure

The purpose of the conservation policies set out below is to provide a guide to the development and care of the Center in a way that retains its significance. Such policies are framed to:
1. Retain the character and quality of the building and its immediate setting
2. Permit alterations and renovations that are compatible with the above and will make the place more effective in its intended uses
3. Identify elements that adversely affect the place and that are in need of modification or removal
4. Provide an approach to the replacement of deteriorated fabric
5. Draw attention to a need for the coordination and continuity of conservation decisions

In order to clarify terms used in this document, the following definitions have been adopted from the Burra Charter[30]:

Cultural significance means aesthetic, historic, scientific, or social value for past, present, or future generations.

Conservation means all the processes of looking after a place so as to retain its cultural significance. It includes maintenance and may, according to circumstance, include preservation, restoration, reconstruction, and adaptation and will usually be a combination of two or more of these.

Maintenance means the continuous protective care of the fabric, contents, and setting of a place, and is to be distinguished from repair. Repair involves restoration or reconstruction, and it should be treated accordingly.

Preservation means maintaining the fabric of a place in its existing state and retarding deterioration.

Restoration means returning the existing fabric of a place to a known earlier state by removing accretions or by reassembling existing components without the introduction of new material.

Reconstruction means returning a place as nearly as possible to a known earlier state and is distinguished by the introduction of material (new or old) into the fabric. This is not to be confused with conjectural reconstruction or re-creation.

Consolidation is the physical addition or application of adhesive or supportive materials to the actual fabric to ensure its continued durability or structural integrity.

Adaptation means modifying a place to suit proposed compatible uses.

Compatible means a use that involves no change to the culturally significant fabric, changes that are substantially reversible, or changes that require minimal impact.

Facing page:
Fourth-floor galleries showing carpet, travertine, and millwork, looking west across the Entrance Court

[30] The Burra Charter, a reworking of the Venice Charter, defines the basic principles and procedures to be followed in the conservation of Australian sites of cultural significance. It takes its title from the historic mining town of Burra, South Australia, where the charter was adopted at a meeting of the International Council on Monuments and Sites in 1979.

General policies **Acceptance of statement, assessments, and policies**

The Yale Center for British Art is committed to the conservation of its building designed by Louis I. Kahn and will realize this to the appropriate standards set out in this document and according to the following policies:

Policy 1

To accept as one of the bases of future planning the statement of cultural significance and the assessments of significance contained in this document.

Policy 2

To endorse the policies recommended and the options discussed throughout this document as a guide to future work by all stakeholders.

Policy 3

To review the policies in five years, followed by review every ten years.

Objectives

Policy 4

To realize wherever possible, when renovations are executed at the Center, the recovery of the cultural significance of the building and, in carrying them out, to respect generally accepted national and international conservation principles.

Conservation issues

Policy 5

To consider carefully temporary alterations of the space, whether in the form of works or use, so as not to diminish its cultural value.

Policy 6

To discourage diminishing the cultural significance of the place on the basis of "reversibility" as temporary alterations, including signage, often become long-term. Even alterations that are short-lived can negatively impact a visitor's perception of a place's cultural significance.

Management principles

Policy 7

To establish an ongoing program of actions to protect, maintain, and improve the cultural asset in order to achieve its conservation as a whole and in its constituent parts.

Policy 8

To ensure that the quality of the conservation work at the Center is of the same intellectual rigor that is characteristic of the best conservation practices.

Policy 9

To coordinate planning and decision-making affecting the entity of the cultural asset.

The place

The Assessment of Cultural Significance found that the Center's building is culturally significant as an outstanding work of architecture, and this significance is enhanced through its association with the collection of British art formed by Paul Mellon.

Policy 10

To maintain the experience of seeing Paul Mellon's collection within the building designed for it by Louis I. Kahn. It is a highly significant collection within a highly significant building, and each contributes to the other.

[The First Program] consisted of two great arched structures facing Chapel Street and divided by an expansion joint running up the middle of a central column. The material was to be brick and concrete like the ruins of Rome, and the long arches of the upper floors shaped the wide gallery spaces with their strange trajectories, lighted by thin ribbons of glass that as it were outlined the arches. It seemed excessive at the time; in retrospect it begins to seem marvelous and would have made a spectacular streetscape along Chapel. . . . Kahn then wholly rethought the building [for the Second Program] and came up with something that for the first time in many years had nothing to do with Roman ruins and was in fact brand new in his design. . . . Outside, too, the aspect of the building is determined by the bony concrete skeleton, between which panels of metal and of glass are set in ways that recall the very beginning of modern city architecture in the work of Karl Friedrich Schinkel and Henri Labrouste in the 1830s and 1840s. Mies van der Rohe's buildings at the Illinois Institute of Technology of the 1950s, which were to create a kind of modern classicism out of that system, are also recalled. In general the final design by Kahn seems to leave the rather Piranesian Romantic-Classicism of his Roman work to rejoin the more canonical development of modernism as it had begun to take shape in the realist-materialist period of the mid-nineteenth century. Such academic musings give way, however, before the miracle of incandescence that Kahn works in his panes of glass. Here was an architect who for years had done his best to eliminate glass from his work or at the very least to subordinate its visual effects. Now all of a sudden he turns to it and so fixes it on his facades that it is not only wholly unshaded by reveals but also spectacularly contrasted with absolutely dead, matte, unreflective panels of stainless steel, looking like deep gray slate, so that when the sun hits the glass it explodes with reflected light and reflects all the fine row of buildings across the street, Kahn's own Art Gallery among them.[31]

The British Art Center . . . seemed to mark important developments in [Kahn's] design. I have referred to the articulated wall system, but even more fundamental might have been a renewed sense of responsibility to the street and the city as a whole. The building acts even more than the Art Gallery does to define Chapel Street in a traditional way.[32]

External form

The Center can be seen as a freestanding building located at the intersection of High and Chapel streets. However, as well as addressing the two public streets, it also fronts the parking lot on the south and the Lower Court on the west. The fact that it was built hard up against the sidewalk ensured that no other structure abutted it on its east and north sides. The strength of the walkway adjacent to the south elevation, acting very much as an urban sidewalk rather than just a way through a car park, and the excavation of the Lower Court also ensure that the same condition applies to the south and west. Although the Center is not a freestanding pavilion set within a plaza as at the Beinecke Rare Book and Manuscript Library, its mass is just as finite and the possibility of direct extension is denied by its relationship to its surroundings.

   This freestanding quality was also characteristic of the earlier schemes. The location of the building tight against the intersection of Chapel and High streets was a constant in each. It was first mooted by Kahn that the building should extend on the west side

Facing page:
The Center from the intersection of High and Chapel streets, photographed in 1977

[31] Scully et al., *Yale in New Haven*, 332.
[32] Scully et al., *Yale in New Haven*, 335.

from High Street to York, "from river to river" as he described it,[33] but no drawing of this is known. As soon as it was realized that the scale of the program meant that the Center would not extend along the whole frontage on Chapel Street, the Calvary Baptist Church site on the corner of York Street was returned to the University. The plans for the First Program all show a four-story building set just back from the church to allow the west elevation to be unencumbered. Even when Kahn prepared tentative proposals for an associated art library on the site of the church, this was treated as a separate block with the two buildings connected only by a bridge at the third-floor level. The reductions of the Second Program freed up the west elevation even more by pulling it further away from the church. The space left between the two buildings was treated as a sunken court, which served both as a memory of the earlier scheme as well as a physical constraint on any development adjacent to the freestanding building.

The same is true of the south side of the building. Even when the built form in the First Program extended the full depth of the site, Kahn made the Center appear to be freestanding. This he achieved by setting the main body back from the southern boundary and by only building up to it with a single-story block that accommodated the entrance to the below-ground car park and service space. Above first-floor level, the building was inherently symmetrical about its east-west axis with the south elevation similar to that of the north. The reductions in space requirements brought about in the Second Program not only reduced the depth of the main block by about a third, but the elimination of the below-ground parking lot also removed the need for the single-story access wing. This released space for the present ground-level parking lot that runs along the south side of the Center and totally freed the building on its south side.

As built, all elevations are treated equally with an articulated concrete frame infilled with glass and steel panels. None is relegated to being the "back" of the building. Of course, predominance is given to the corner of Chapel and High Streets by cutting the 40-foot-square portico into the mass, but above the first floor the equality of the elevation is undisturbed. However, variations arise as the elevations respond to the specific use immediately behind the facade.

Roof

The roofscape was clearly intended as a fifth elevation and integral to the building below. In each of the designs for the Center, the roof is generated by the design of the skylights to the top-floor galleries. However, with the rigorous adoption of the 20-foot structural grid in the Second Program, the roof becomes related to the whole building rather than primarily to the fourth floor. In the earliest of these schemes, each bay is expressed on the elevation, first as a convex enclosure, then one with sloping sides. As the design developed, the separate enclosures were replaced with a continuous sloping mansard, above which the individual bays were articulated by their skylight.

An essential part of Kahn's brief was to provide consistent natural light throughout the top-floor galleries at the same time as maintaining the experience of the changes in the daylight. In addition, the amount of ultraviolet light entering the building had to be reduced. The plan for the lighting was developed with Richard Kelly, who

[33] Prown, *The Architecture of the Yale Center for British Art*, 20.

Roof, looking north toward the Yale University Art Gallery. The domed skylights over the Entrance Court are unshielded; those over the galleries are protected by louvers that were described by Kahn as "angry crabs."

had collaborated with Kahn on both the natural and electric lighting of the Kimbell. Proposals were determined between September 1972 and April 1973 through extensive trials, including mock-ups on the roof of a building at 20 Ashmun Street, and later in two bays of the fourth floor once it had been constructed. This achieved the intended light levels through the use of fixed metal louvers above the Plexiglas-domed skylights, below which a cassette diffused the light within the building. The louvers were set to reduce the amount of light entering when the sun is high in the sky in summer and let in more light when it is low in winter. As Richard Kelly believed that most of the damaging ultraviolet light comes from the north, there were no open louvers on that side. Prown reports that Kahn never liked the louvers and referred to them as "angry crabs," although he understood the need for them.[34] Except for the bays containing fire escape stairs, elevators, and air shafts, the skylights occur over every bay of the fourth floor. Louvers and diffusers, however, were intentionally omitted from the skylights over the Entrance Court, acknowledging that it is a quasi-external space rather than one where artworks might be displayed, considered, or stored. Thus, the roof expresses both the arrangement of the accommodation on the floors below and is parallel to the response of the elevations to the interior of the building. Furthermore, the interruption of the row of skylights above the fire stairs is clearly reflected above the mansard on three of the elevations.

Any services on the roof were considered within this context, with ventilation ducts carefully grouped within the discipline of the grid and the skylights.

Taller buildings nearby afford views of the roof of the Center, and Kahn's building stands as an exemplar of calm and considered design.

Frame

In the early projects a Vierendeel truss system was used to maximize open space on the upper floor of the building and for parking below. However, the reduction in the size of the building program and the siting of the parking lot adjacent to the south allowed Kahn to employ a simple post-and-slab structural system for the Second Program. This he applied consistently throughout the building.

The principle of truth to materials was expressed in the treatment of the concrete. It was very carefully crafted, and great care was taken with the formwork in order to get an extremely smooth surface; holes from the tie rods that held the forms in place are left open, and beads of concrete ooze out to mark the joining of the forms. If the bead is broken or chipped, that was accepted because it is part of the history of the building process. Abba Tor recalls that "[o]ne of the most important design features was the treatment of construction and formwork joints in the cast-in-place concrete. The formwork for this building was very carefully chosen and detailed so as to achieve the unique smooth texture, joint pattern and special 'raised-V' joint. The contractor, George B. H. Macomber Company Inc., from Boston, approached this challenge with 'Tender Loving Care,' and the workmen took home some of the struck forms, not as souvenirs but as furniture quality wood! The Finn-form plywood used for the forms could be reused for furniture, both in color and texture."[35]

[34] Jules David Prown, "Light and Truth: Louis Kahn's Yale Center for British Art" (lecture, Yale Center for British Art, May 2, 2007).
[35] Tor, "The Structure of the Yale-Mellon Center for British Arts and British Studies."

As load decreases on the upper stories, the columns reduce in width

Kahn's characteristic expression of the structure results in the columns becoming more slender as the building rises and loads are decreased. In addition, the beams spanning the two bays over the portico, the commercial units, the bays facing the parking lot, and the entrance to the foyer are heavier than those over a single 20-foot bay.

Vincent Scully has noted "how perfectly the heavy beam above the ground floor of the British Art Center defines the street . . . [and provides the] traditional urban base that [Kahn's] Art Gallery, in comparison with Swartwout's, tended to lack."[36] It is under this beam that one moves from the city into the portico. Similarly, the frame reflects the organization of the upper floors, and the insertion of double-height spaces is clearly legible. Thus the two-story reading room of the Reference Library is announced on the south elevation by the omission over three adjacent bays of the horizontal beam between the second and third floors where there was only a balcony rather than a floor to support, and the same is true where similar situations occur in the Rare Books and Manuscripts and Prints and Drawings departments.

Cladding

Prown recalls that, when Kahn first indicated that he intended to use stainless steel on the exterior, "[I] asked him if he had ever seen a metal-clad building that pleased him. 'No,' he said. 'But you like stainless steel for this building?' 'Yes!'"[37] He never referred to the metal as steel, even though that is what it is. He metaphorically called it lead or pewter, wanting a dark, matte, non-reflective surface. When asked by Prown to describe the building's appearance, he replied that "on a cloudy day it would look like a moth, on a sunny day like a butterfly."[38]

The building is clad with glass and steel panels stacked within the frame. Each material is used by Kahn to express its essential characteristics: of glass, transparency; of metal, malleability. In the facade the steel therefore bends to enfold the glass, and as it is sheet steel, the two materials are held almost on the same plane.

In parallel with this, Kahn also carefully considered the placing of the cladding in relation to the frame, and this gives a demarcation between commercial space and the Center. With the former, the cladding is set on the rear face of the concrete frame; with the latter, it is flush with the external face of the frame. In consequence, on the first floor this means that the storefronts on Chapel and High are recessive, but the cladding of the elements belonging to the Center is flush with the face of the columns.

Kahn's reference to the steel panels as "opaque windows"[39] suggests that he considered the whole elevation to be glazed and recalls the presentation perspectives of the Second Program in October 1971, which show the galleries facing onto Chapel Street totally glazed very much as some elevations of his earlier Yale University Art Gallery. As the scheme developed in response to the brief, the disposition of the transparent and opaque elements was determined by the internal function of the space. Just as the concrete frame announces the presence of the double-height spaces within the building, both the cladding and the fenestration respond to the internal arrangement. While each story is clad vertically with three horizontal panels, double-height spaces introduce "joker" panels to make up for the omission of the cross beam at mezzanine level, as well as the accom-

[36] Scully et al., *Yale in New Haven*, 334.

[37] Prown, *The Architecture of the Yale Center for British Art*, 48.

[38] Prown, "Lux et Veritas: Louis Kahn's last creation," *Apollo* 165, no. 542 (April 2007), 49.

[39] Prown, *The Architecture of the Yale Center for British Art*, 48.

modation of windows that extend down to the level of reading desks. The additional height of the fourth floor is reported on the facade by the presence of an extra half panel extending around the whole building. With the fenestration, story-height windows, arising from the need of the visitors in the galleries to pause and look out onto the city for relaxation, make the galleries legible on the facade. Similarly, the need for well-lit reading desks near windows and the placing of storage cabinets result in windows of different heights that declare the varying requirements of the libraries and offices. However, Prown recalls that sometimes Kahn went beyond the literal program: "There are slit windows in the book stacks, even when Kahn was told that light was not needed or wanted there. He persisted in including some windows, saying in one of his not infrequent parables that one day Picasso would come to the Center and go to the stacks, and the books would say, 'Picasso is here. Let's open the windows and have a party!'"[40] The full-height, slit windows in the stacks, therefore, can be seen as logical.

Fenestration responding to the needs of the mezzanine gallery and the carrels of the Reference Library

Policy 11
To maintain Kahn's building as a freestanding building.

Policy 12
To respect the roof as a designed element of the building.

This is especially important in relation to mechanical services, and any alteration to these must not be approached in an ad-hoc manner.

Policy 13
To retain the legibility of the internal organization of the building in its cladding while maintaining carefully considered elevations.

For example, if an office is modified as an extension to a display gallery, the nature of its windows, both clear and opaque, should be appropriate to the new use, and the feasibility of such a modification has to be considered within its impact on an elevation.

[40] Prown, "Light and Truth."

Portico

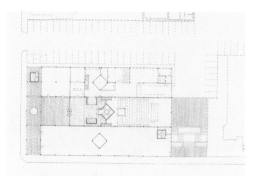

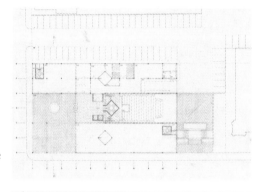

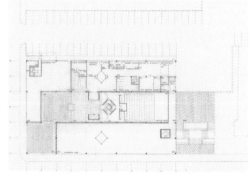

In contrast to the idea of entering the Center through a shopping mall that characterizes the First Program, the Second Program has the Center approached through a dedicated portico. At first, this was planned to run the full width of the High Street elevation,[41] but Kahn experimented with a corner entrance at the junction of Chapel and High during the summer of 1971, and by the fall he had definitely decided upon it. Prown believes that it was "probably in response to a wish expressed by President Brewster that the Center have an orientation both towards the University and the City."[42]

The clear omission of commercial activity across two bays on each facade at the corner of the two urban streets is particularly significant. The portico is a calm, open space with views through into the Entrance Court. Although it is the same structural double bay that forms the adjacent shops, the space clearly belongs to the Center. The square-plan form of two-by-two bays is the same as that of the Entrance Court beyond. The grid of the paving, reflecting the expressed beams, together with its array of downlighters, also relates the space through to the institution beyond. In an early design Kahn had made proposals for the flanking shops to open onto the portico, but this had been rejected, primarily because the donor did not like the idea of the commercial units being so close to the museum entrance, and it would have intruded on the use of the space as a transition between the street and the Center. The steel cladding to the walls is indicative of the exclusion of the commercial world on either side. The puncturing of these flank walls with vitrines, designed after Kahn's death by Pellecchia and Meyers and used to promote the exhibitions, confuses this, however, as it suggests a relationship to the commercial space behind them.

The use of the brick paving confirms that the space is external, and the 40-foot span openings on each of the two adjacent external facades open up the corner of the building at street level and make the space readily available to the city, a shortcut between sidewalks, a place to linger and talk, and a venue for occasional street music. At the same time, it is a portico welcoming people to the Center. To this end, the daylight beyond the portico within the Entrance Court is of considerable importance.

Policy 14

The contrast with the commercial activities is very significant and needs to be maintained to ensure that the portico cuts through the zone to the calm of the museum beyond.

Policy 15

The treatment of the flanking steel and glass walls is important, and the use and content of the vitrines has to be handled with care to ensure their clear association with the Center rather than appearing as part of the commercial units.

The portico as completed in 1977

The portico, first planned to extend six bays across the full width of the High Street elevation, was progressively reduced to the present corner solution. In each the Entrance Court is external and the stair is contained within a rotated square, rather than circular, tower. Kahn office drawings, July/August/October 1971, Louis I. Kahn Collection, University of Pennsylvania (805.006)

[41] Kahn, schematic first-floor plan, Louis I. Kahn Collection, 805.006, University of Pennsylvania and Pennsylvania Historical and Museum Commission.

[42] Prown, *The Architecture of the Yale Center for British Art*, 35 (Perspective sketch, October 15, 1971, fig. 22).

Policy 16

The treatment of the space as an open portico that welcomes visitors to the Center and is also part of the urban scene should be maintained. Attempts to gate it or enclose it would be unacceptable.

Policy 17

The view of the daylight in the Entrance Court beyond the portico is of great importance in welcoming visitors to the Center.

Commercial premises on High and Chapel streets

Commercial activity at street level was a requirement of the University and the New Haven Planning Department. In many ways, the Center is one of Kahn's most significant buildings because of its resulting physical relationship with New Haven. One of the great successes of the building is that his approach maintains the south side of Chapel Street clearly within the urban fabric of the city without compromising the presence of the Center, and it emphasizes how much the experience of walking along that sidewalk contrasts with using the one on the north where one is just passing University buildings.

The donor was not necessarily keen on the inclusion of commercial space, but it was part of the strategy for securing goodwill for the project and realizing the building to maintain the urban fabric. Commercial units were, therefore, entered directly from Chapel and High streets as a pragmatic and civilized gesture to the City of New Haven and to maintain the tax income to the city. Kahn realized this as an opportunity to give his design that traditional urban base, with the heavy beam above the first floor defining the realm of the street. The inclusion of the shops activates the street in the same manner as those found at the base of Roman palazzos; indeed, one charcoal sketch of the Center is labeled by Kahn as "Palazzo Melloni."[43]

Prown states that Kahn thought of the shop windows in his First Program design as "crystalline, sparkling beneath the museum,"[44] and he appears to have carried this idea through to the Second. As well as having this characteristic, the storefronts also maintain the materials of the upper elevations, giving uniformity to the design of the building. As the cladding is recessed, it not only protects a welcoming threshold outside the shops, but it distances the shops from the Center, which occupies the upper floors.

The uniform treatment of the storefronts, each containing a central door set between large glazed shop windows, meets Kahn's description that they would be "crystalline." This has been supported by the windows not being encumbered with signage, which has been successfully restricted to positions within the building and free of the glass. However, over the years ad-hoc repairs to door hardware and the like have resulted in modifications that need to be reversed to maintain the uniformity of the shop elevations.

Within, the shops each have their own identity, and it is the very ordinariness of the interiors that confirms the shops are part of the city rather than the museum building. Their fit-out was not by Kahn, and the interiors were left as shells for completion by the tenants. However, the continuity of the primary structural and services shafts that pass through the shops is important to the understanding of the building as a whole. Some

[43] Kahn, Schematic North Elevation, June 1970, Louis I. Kahn Collection, 805.200, University of Pennsylvania and Pennsylvania Historical and Museum Commission.

[44] Prown's recollection to Inskip, ca. 2005, describing the windows of the commercial units in the First Program, which were canted in and not flush with the street.

of these have been painted or covered over, making their legibility and their relationship with the upper floors hard to read. In addition, the introduction of drop ceilings compromises the interiors and reduces their relationship to the building in which they are placed.

Most of the shops have been outfitted with window display ledges immediately within the storefronts, but recent refurbishment at Atticus Bookstore has opened up the space adjacent to the window; this has resulted in a sense of continuity that extends the external space into the shop and allows the café seating inside the building to feel almost al fresco and part of the sidewalk.

The Center's Museum Shop was originally a small sales desk in the reception foyer off the Entrance Court, but later relocated to the Docent Room. It moved to its present location when the southernmost commercial shop on High Street became available in 1986. In 1992 its interior was designed by the Architecture Studio (later renamed Gray Organschi). Care has been taken to maintain the shop as a unit belonging to the street, but the use of similar woodwork to that in the Center, and the doorway into it from the Entrance Court, contradict the steel-clad wall that denotes the separation of museum and commercial space.

Atticus Bookstore, after the refurbishment in 2008 that resulted in freeing up the interior adjacent to the sidewalk on Chapel Street

Policy 18

To maintain the legibility of the primary elements, such as the structural frame and the diagonal air shafts, where they pass through the commercial units. Painting the primary concrete structure is not acceptable, and dropped ceilings should not be introduced.

Policy 19

To maintain the commercial units so that they are of the street and belong to the city, not the museum.

Where a commercial unit has been adopted by the museum as its shop, it should maintain its position in the street, and any secondary entrance from the museum should be as discreet as possible.

Policy 20

To maintain storefronts carefully in order to retain their overall uniformity and high standard of appearance. Signage needs to continue to be strictly controlled: sited within the building and small-scale, but legible.

Facing page:
The commercial shop, far left, nestled under the Center at street level, with the steps to the Lower Court

The Lower Court is an integral part of Kahn's building, rather than a piece of hard landscape adjacent to it. The architect's love of ruins is well documented and has influenced the design of many of his works. With the Lower Court, he can be seen constructing an actual "ruin," since it can be read as the foundations and remains of a basement story of a building that was never completed or has long since been demolished. Its colonization by nature is also suggested by the asymmetric, off-grid planting of the honey locust tree. The tree is not shown in the 1971 perspective but is illustrated in Kahn's plans of 1973. The court, of course, records the reduction of the design from the First Program, symbolizing the section of the Center that was never constructed.

The square court at the foot of the great steps responds to the Entrance Court, which it balances. It is clearly the third court of the building, occupying the sixth of the double 20-foot grids that extend along the street from the corner of High and placed on the central axis common to the two courts within the building. The paving with bands of New York bluestone crossing the brick, however, relates the area to the portico, both marking entrances into the Center. Using the model of the Roman palazzo, the Lower Court can be associated with the Center that might have surrounded it had the building not been cut back to structural Grid 11 in the reduction of the program. The space around the Court can also be interpreted as the basement of an unrealized part of the Center that has been colonized by an extension of the commercial world. Such a reading is supported by the monumentality of its great flight of steps that clearly belongs to a public building. Placing the steps opposite the entrance to the University Art Gallery reinforces the relationship between the two cultural institutions.

Kahn's last drawings show the Lower Court virtually as built, serving as an entrance to the Center together with a subordinate range of commercial activities. The entrance into the building was intended by Kahn to provide an alternative access to the Lecture Hall via the lobby off the Lower Court. The predominance of this is clarified by its fully glazed wall contrasting with the lower openings to the commercial units inhabiting the side walls, which are set below deep beams. As at street level, the facades of the commercial units are set back, aligned with the rear face of the concrete frame; that of the Lecture Hall lobby, however, is of the language of the Center and set flush. In recent years, the Lecture Hall lobby was significantly degraded, not only by the introduction of a lattice screen to conceal its windows, but also by its relegation to storage use.

Originally, it was intended that there would be two separate commercial units in the Lower Court: one to the south of the court (the present restaurant); the other on the north side extending back below the landing of a divided staircase. However, by April 1972 Kahn's drawings show the second relocated to the west of the court, joined up to the restaurant and serving as a bar. The independent elevator access from street level was introduced at the same time as the replanning of the restaurant. Presumably the change reflects the involvement of a possible tenant; there are no comparable fitting-out studies for the other commercial units at street level. The interior design of the restaurant and bar is by David Spiker and dates to 1979. However, in essence, the plan remains as drawn at the time of Kahn's death.

Model of the First Program, with the Center extending from High Street to the site of the Calvary Baptist Church, 1971, Louis I. Kahn Collection, University of Pennsylvania

The Lower Court and terrace from the roof of the Yale University Art Gallery

Facing page:
Louis I. Kahn, Study for entrance to the Center from the Lower Court, 1971, Louis I. Kahn Collection, University of Pennsylvania (805.403)

Top: Lattice and trellis introduced in 1987, photographed in 2005

Bottom: The entrance to the Lecture Hall lobby, screened over except for the fire exit doors, photographed in 2005

Illustration from a 1987 proposal for the commercial use of the Lower Court

In parallel with the rearrangement of the commercial space, there was a tightening of the design of the Lower Court. In the first proposals this had extended to the western boundary of the site. However, the court was now reduced in width to bring it onto grid, providing a 40-foot-square space, identical in plan to both the Entrance Court and the portico. As a consequence of this, the monumental staircase was redesigned as a straight run, and the stepped terrace was formed on the west side, above the bar. In addition, the promontory overlooking the steps, next to the shop at street level, was introduced to allow escape from the northwest fire stair to the sidewalk, since the quarter landing of the divided original stair was no longer available for this purpose. Kahn intended that the handrails should be freestanding, set adjacent to the containing walls, and that the lowest flight, which extended the full width of the Lower Court, was to be divided by a central rail aligning with the bluestone division of the court.

In the development of the final drawings by Pellecchia and Meyers in 1975, changes were made to meet safety codes: an additional landing was introduced, and the steps were arranged as four flights of seven steps (this elongated the fire stair promontory). In addition, the two intermediate handrails were introduced. Details were also modified: brick parapets were changed to concrete, taking them off grid, and a more complicated termination to the handrails, similar to their modification on the principal stair within the building, was designed by Pellecchia and Meyers.[45] The use of bright stainless steel is a move away from Kahn's selection of non-reflective steel.

The Lower Court is probably the area that has experienced the most change since the building was opened. It was intended as an essential entrance to the public auditorium as well as a location for additional commercial units, and it serves as an emergency egress from both the public and staff areas of the Center. For several years, the Lecture Hall Lobby was covered with lattice and reduced only to an emergency exit. With its relationship to the Center concealed, the monumentality of the court and its stair was rendered meaningless. As a result, the connection between the Center and the Yale University Art Gallery that is suggested by the stair has never been fully exploited.

Accretive development brought about the visual domination of the court by the restaurant since its use of the court is now the only activity there except in emergencies. This has been secured through the introduction of restaurant seating, planting, heaters, and canopies. The introduction of an aluminium canopy, designed by Spiker to emphasize one of the restaurant entrances, was an alteration denied to all the other commercial units in the building and conflicted with the entrance to the Center.[46] Lattice screens and trellis structures, together with a storage shed at the east end of the bottom landing, were designed by Eric Epstein in 1987. The removal of these added elements in 2008–09 has done much to recover the relationship of the court to the Center.

Except for the tree, which was intended by Kahn, the planting schemes in the Lower Court have been a problem. The introduction of pots and planters on the steps and in tubs within the court was very intrusive. Not only did it crowd the court, it blocked one third of the width of the steps, completely occupying the central section. The form of the planters, trellis, and lattice was also unsympathetic to Kahn's architecture and contradicted the intended monumentality of the space. A revised planting scheme introduced in 2008 as a temporary measure to address these problems has improved the situation.

The importance of the Lecture Hall lobby is confirmed by the hierarchic treatment of the glazing: flush with the framing and tall in contrast to the recessed, low glazing that is characteristic of the commercial space seen on the facing page, photographed in 2008.

Facing page: The Lower Court, from within the Lecture Hall lobby, during the restoration trials, photographed in 2008. The storage shed dating from 1987 has not yet been removed from the stair landing.

[45] Pellechia and Meyers, February 25, 1975, Louis I. Kahn Collection, University of Pennsylvania and Pennsylvania Historical and Museum Commission.

[46] Research by Constance Clement and Bill Kamens, November 2008, unraveled the design history of the Lower Court with the works by Spiker and Epstein.

A raking canopy and imitation columns were introduced in 1979 to emphasize one of the entrances to the commercial units in the Lower Court. They were removed in 2009.

The planters, storage shed, and trelliswork that were introduced in 1987 obscured the monumentality of the steps to the Lower Court.

Facing page:
The Lower Court and terrace relate the Center to the entrance of the Yale University Art Gallery across Chapel Street

The stainless-steel bollards between the top of the steps and the sidewalk on Chapel Street are modifications of the original design by Pellechia and Meyers, and the two western bollards date from 1987 (by Epstein). Chains between them were introduced subsequently, and signs relating to the restaurant have been added to the tops of the bollards in recent years. All have to be considered intrusive.

Policy 21
The Lower Court is an essential component of the Center, and its original meaning should be recovered.

Policy 22
Use of the commercial space in the Lower Court should respond to the fact that it lies within the orbit of the Center, in contrast to those which open directly to the street.

Policy 23
To respect the original landscape scheme of the Lower Court by restricting planting to a single tree.

Honey locust trees are relatively short-lived. In some respects the tree is now over-scale and replacement should be anticipated before it starts to deteriorate.

Terrace

While the Lower Court represents the eleventh and twelfth bays of the grid, the terrace occupies the thirteenth and fourteenth. The fourteenth, however, is curtailed by the transept of the church.

The terrace is an integral extension of the Lower Court. The upper landing of the steps to the court extends to the west and returns along its side as a balcony overlooking the court and its approach stair. To the west of this, the upper flight of steps also returns, running from the sidewalk south to the screen wall. The effect is that of an amphitheater and has some similarities to Kahn's first proposals for the area where a double stair provided a landing on the north side of the court that gave a vantage point to view the activities below. The concrete parapets surrounding the court are "softened" with the bluestone inserts in areas where spectators might lean. The effect of the ampitheater, however, was largely lost in recent years through the trellis and plant canopy that visually provided a roof over the court, denying the experience of views down into the Lower Court until they were removed in the spring of 2008.

While the west elevation of the court is carried up above the bar to form a balcony parapet, the south elevation above the restaurant extends to a higher level to serve as a screen to the loading bay. This is disengaged from the west elevation of the main building but extends to the west where the elevator access to the commercial unit below is contained within a concrete shaft. The tower containing the elevator is therefore integral to the design of the Center and is the termination of the overall composition extending from High Street to the Yale Repertory Theatre.

The steps to the Lower Court after the planters and storage shed were removed in 2008–09

The terrace located over the commercial space

The construction of the interior of the elevator tower continues that of the exterior, with poured-concrete ceiling and walls; it is parallel to the Lecture Hall lobby. The elevator itself is set behind a screen wall and treated as an insertion within the lobby. As with the other commercial areas, the concrete was intended to be undecorated, and the present red paint is intrusive and should be stripped.

The terrace extends back to the east side of the Yale Repertory Theatre, with the brick-and-bluestone paving continuing the materials indicative of the Center's external space. The trees on the terrace occupy the fourteenth bay, are planted within the grid, and complete the geometry of the site that extends from High Street to the Yale Rep.

Loading dock

The loading dock on the south of the screen wall that separates the parking lot from the Lower Court extends between the restaurant's elevator shaft and the west elevation of the Center. The area's simplicity, with its large-scale concrete wall protected by red painted bollards, is as designed by Kahn. The loading dock, originally planned adjacent to the wall, was moved one bay to the south early in the design to afford greater maneuverability.[47] The replanning, however, resulted in an inconvenient chicane inside the building.

Screen wall and loading dock as viewed from the parking lot

Top: The fencing to the parking lot was designed by Kahn, developed by Pellechia and Meyers in 1976, and reconstructed in 2008. Bottom: Screen wall at the High Street entrance to the parking lot, with return fencing

Parking lot

The below-ground garage, entered from a ramp off High Street, was replaced with an above-ground parking lot beside the building in the Second Program.

The cast-concrete, freestanding walls with their elegant signage at the High Street and York Street entrances date from the completion of the building.

The underlying grid of the building extends to the parking lot with the honey locust trees adjacent to the elevation planted at 40-foot centers, aligning with the column grid. The east row, however, is slightly displaced by the concrete screen wall that occupies Grid 1. Because of the restricted width of the parking lot, the further row of trees is set out at one-and-a-half bays south of the other. While the trees extend the depth of the building, they do not extend beyond the west elevation (Grid 12), and the pair on either side of the York Street entrance are intentionally isolated and not part of the grid.

Each tree was set by Kahn within a planting station formed by a radius-ended concrete curb that protects it from vehicles. The painting of the curbs yellow is intrusive, and the neat gravel infill has become overlaid with soil and weeds.

The walkway alongside the Center is of cast concrete set within a curb and is important in defining a route around the complete building, confirming that it is a freestanding structure. Two lamp posts light the sidewalk and correspond to the second pier from each end of the building and are original.

The south boundary fencing of two layers of painted Western red cedar slats set above a dwarf concrete wall was designed by Kahn. As the fencing was dilapidated and the rear section had been removed, it was renewed to Kahn's design in the fall of 2008.[48]

While the east half of the parking lot is well structured and remains much as intended, deterioration in the quality of the space is clearly noticeable at the west. This arises

Walkway along south facade

[47] Kahn, First floor plan, August 16, 1971, Louis I. Kahn Collection, University of Pennsylvania and Pennsylvania Historical and Museum Commission.

[48] Pellechia and Meyers, Drawing of parking lot, March 1976, Louis I. Kahn Collection, SKA-322, University of Pennsylvania and Pennsylvania Historical and Museum Commission.

Top: Chiller on south side of parking lot
Bottom: Planting within the parking lot.
The curbs are part of Kahn's design, but
were modified in 1974.

from the lot not being so clearly related to the building as it steps around the end of the church, and it is compounded by the introduction of a dedicated chiller that was sited in place of some parking bays on the south side, a problem in terms of noise as well as appearance. The parking attendant's booth is a neat structure designed by Pellecchia and Meyers in 1976.[49] However, the entrance has also been compromised by the introduction of various sandwich boards and other signs relating to the commercial use of the parking lot. This is further disfigured by the inappropriate graphics of gold lettering on a green ground, which is particularly noticeable because of the contrast with the high standard of graphics used on the rest of the site. The attendant's booth was originally painted green.

Policy 24
To recover the overall unity of the parking lot and its relationship with the building.

Policy 25
To maintain trees.

Policy 26
To maintain hard landscape.

Policy 27
To maintain boundary walls, fencing, etc.

Policy 28
To recover a high standard of graphics with specified range of colors and typefaces as originally designed.

Top: The entrance to the parking lot from High Street.
Bottom: The attendant's booth and totem-pole sign, at the York Street entrance, designed by Pellechia and Meyers in 1976. Later graphics and signage have become intrusive.

[49] Pellechia and Meyers, Yale Center for British Art plan, Louis I. Kahn Collection, University of Pennsylvania and Pennsylvania Historical and Museum Commission.

THIS CENTER WITH HIS COLLECTIONS
OF BRITISH ART AND BOOKS, IS THE GIFT OF PAUL MELLON
YALE COLLEGE, CLASS OF 1929

The constant in all of Kahn's designs for the Center is the organization of the building. In each, the Center is set on the upper stories above commercial space at street level. Each design places the Center's entrance at the core of the building within a commercial perimeter. Its model is the Roman palazzo where the accommodation on the upper floors is approached from a court screened from the street by shops.

On the second and third floors there is a constant east-west division demarcating public display and the libraries, while on the fourth floor the extension of the principal picture galleries over the whole of the plan unites these two parts of the Center.

In addition, the Entrance and Library courts that rise vertically through the building relate the individual sections to one another, unifying the disparate elements. The clarity of the organization meant that the first floor is always treated as a base to the Center.

Policy 29

Major alterations are acceptable where technical advance, expert advice, design quality, adequate resources, and meticulous construction can be combined to create facilities that will improve function and reinforce the significance of the Center provided that the work is planned in the context of an overall scheme and not taken piecemeal on an ad-hoc basis.

Policy 30

Reallocation of space to serve current use is acceptable as long as it remains within the organizational structure of the Center.

However, a wary approach to the subdivision of the existing offices and other spaces should be taken to ensure that the spacious character of the interior is maintained.

Use of space should respect the mechanical systems available.

The organization of the building is of fundamental significance to Kahn's design and should be respected when projects are being considered at any level, whether they be major alterations or the location of an exhibit.

Policy 31

To maintain commercial space at street level. Its use for non-commercial purposes would be an unacceptable contradiction of the organization of the building.

Policy 32

To maintain the pattern set by Kahn whereby the basement story serves the Center that occupies the second, third, and fourth floors of the building. Existing below-ground accommodation needs to remain discrete.

Facing page:
The Entrance Court as
seen from the foyer

Fourth floor
The top-lit fourth-floor galleries, where the Center's permanent collections of paintings and sculpture are displayed

Third floor
The electrically lit third-floor exhibition space, which was originally dedicated to works on paper

Second floor
The side-lit second-floor galleries, overlooking the Entrance Court

First floor
The entrance spaces are embedded within the commercial perimeter on the first floor, which forms a base for the galleries above

North window
closed with
wood shutters

openings
in wall for
daylight
created by
shutters
on the interior

High and chapel inner court entrance to the Mellon Center Yale U.
Scheme 1. to cover court with skylight construction.

Shutters let into
interior for display

High and Chapel inner court
Scheme 2. To expose court to the

Kahn filled the basement with what he termed "servant" spaces: restrooms, mechanical rooms, preparation areas, and storage for both the Center and the commercial units – specifically not galleries, libraries, or offices. If gallery space were ever constructed at this level, it would need to be articulated as being clearly apart from the institution, both architecturally and in terms of its mission. It is likely that it would provide very different gallery space from that designed by Kahn in terms of museum experience and daylighting.

Entrance spaces

Entrance Court

The concept of the four-story Entrance Court originated in the First Program. In the earlier designs the court provided common circulation space, giving access to both commercial space and the entrance lobby to the Center set at the heart of the plan.

In the Second Program the concept of the Entrance Court was retained, but it was reduced considerably in size, with the plan only being about two-thirds of that in the First Program. Commercial functions no longer opened off the court but were only approached from the street. The brightness and height of the court were intended to draw visitors through the low, dark portico from the surrounding streets. Once inside, visitors' awareness of the surrounding galleries on the upper floors was provided by openings in the upper stories, through which the galleries could be seen. The possibility of covering the court with skylights, rather than leaving it open to the sky, was firmed up following the development of the corner entrance in the fall of 1971.[50] If open to the sky, it was intended that the court should be brick paved (as found in the portico and the Lower Court), indicative of an external space, but the change to travertine, the material for interior paving, followed the decision to use skylights. In parallel, the elevations, which had been envisaged as being metal and glass when open to the elements, changed to oak panelling on the upper floors with openings giving views into the galleries. At street level, the metal cladding was retained, clearly demarcating the separation of the court from the surrounding commercial units. To meet the then-current codes, the openings onto the galleries had to be fitted with rolling fire shutters, and these appear very much as an afterthought.

In response to the need to control daylight to the galleries intended for works on paper, Kahn did not incorporate openings on the third floor. The current use of part of the second floor for loan exhibitions has resulted in the blocking up of some of the openings on that floor. Even if made to appear as if they are only closed by shades that have been lowered, the effect is intrusive, as the implication is false and antithetical to Kahn's philosophy.

The Entrance Court is illustrated by Kahn primarily as a place for entry, circulation, or for resting on benches. His drawings do not indicate any display within the court. This is corroborated by the unfiltered daylight falling through the four skylights: a space that was first intended as external remains quasi-external. The limited display of sculpture, however, has been successful from the time of the Center's opening. Neither the sculpture of William III, in place in the 1970s, nor Hepworth's *Biolith*, located there from

Facing page:
Louis I. Kahn, Schematic interior perspectives of the Entrance Court: "Scheme 1: To cover court with skylight construction"; "Scheme 2: To expose court court to the sky," 1971, Louis I. Kahn Collection, University of Pennsylvania (805.469 and 805.468)

[50] See Kahn's drawings on the facing page.

The entrance foyer is defined by the deep beam spanning the whole of the west side of the Entrance Court. The reception area, shown in 1977 located on the north side of the entrance foyer (top), was moved to the south (bottom) in 1998.

2005, have disrupted the sense of the space as an entrance court outside the collection, because both sculptures are monumental, outdoor pieces and only one piece was used at a time. The very occasional display of exceptionally large objects such as the William Morris glass (2005) or the John Virtue canvases (2006) also worked well, as they were clearly temporary installations, and the court returned to its former state as soon as each exhibition closed. Its use as a conventional gallery showing sculpture (equestrian bronzes, 2002–03) was much less successful because this extended public display of the permanent collection outside the galleries.

Policy 33

To maintain the Entrance Court as a space that is conceptually external, a place for entrance and contemplation. Kahn illustrates seating in the form of benches in his proposals for both the external and enclosed courts.

Policy 34

Colonization of the Entrance Court for use as a gallery or ancillary accommodation, such as a museum store, is inappropriate. The exception is the limited display of sculpture in the Entrance Court, which could be compatible with the quasi-external character of the space and the inherited memory of the original proposals for a court open to the sky. Even in such a case the use of sculpture must be compatible with that of an external court and not that of a sculpture gallery.

Policy 35

The openings to the galleries are of exceptional significance to the court and should be recovered. If a change in code permits, the removal of the fire shutters should be considered.

Policy 36

To respect the enclosure at first-floor level by stainless-steel cladding, which underlines the separation of the Center from the adjoining commercial areas.

Entrance foyer

A deep beam allows the whole of the west side of the lowest story of the Entrance Court to act as the entrance to the Center's single-story foyer. In this location Kahn had planned entrance doors set within a glazed screen to enclose the lobby, if the court had been open to the sky. The recognition of it as the entry point to the Center is, therefore, significant, and the cluster of downlighters marking it underscores its importance as visitors progress into the building. The foyer divides into three areas: reception and orientation, elevator and stair lobby, and the Lecture Hall lobby.

Reception

When first constructed, the reception desk was located at the north side of the reception area, but to improve the surveillance of the entrance and to provide a warmer welcome for visitors, it was relocated to the south side of the foyer in 1998. This has displaced coat racks that are now located in the Lecture Hall lobby. Occasional use of the original desk area as an exhibition space has not been successful, as it has meant that the collection has strayed below its second-floor boundary. However, it has proved useful for orientation, not only because the low space contains the noise of school visitors from rising through the building, but also because it remains the notional lobby to the building even after the decision to roof over the Entrance Court and omit the glazing that contained the foyer.

Guides and postcards had been sold at the reception desk originally before sales were moved to the Docent Room. However, the southeast commercial unit was acquired for use as the Museum Shop in 1986; a direct entrance into the shop was subsequently made from the museum foyer. The connection to the Center was sensitively achieved in that it joined into the foyer rather than the Entrance Court, but it weakened the clarity of the separation of the commercial units and the institution and has to be considered intrusive.

Lecture Hall lobby

Kahn's initial plans show doors in glazed screens on either side of the stair shaft in order to dedicate the west section of the entrance foyer to the Lecture Hall, but with the change from a rotated square to a circular stair shaft, the proposed doors were omitted and the area remained continuous with the rest of the single-story-space foyer.

This area is vulnerable to ad-hoc storage, largely arising from the fact that coat-check facilities are no longer available in the basement lobby or outside the Docent Room. In addition to millwork coat racks, storage units have been moved there. The space is also used to store wheelchairs and racks of stools, with the idea that this is acceptable since these items are out of sight and screened by the stair shaft. This, however, relegates the area to being left-over space. The storage is particularly intrusive when placed immediately against the stair enclosure, one of Kahn's primary architectural elements, particularly as this is the very point where visitors are introduced to the staircase.

Docent Room

The Docent Room is an adjunct of the entrance foyer. At different stages in the design, it was shown as a gallery sales area (October 1971) or an education space, and it has served both of these functions at various times. However, in one of the earliest proposals for the Second Program, it was intended as a truck dock. Although the room remains largely intact, it cannot be considered successful either as a meeting room or an extension of the foyer, since both daylighting and electric lighting are poor. Modification, or the introduction of alternative uses that supplement the foyer, could be considered.

Basement lobby

The basement lobby was associated through use with the first-floor foyer because it gives access to the visitors' restrooms and was originally planned by Kahn to provide a coat-check area with millwork racks in the space to the east of the elevators. However, this was not implemented, and concerns about security resulted in the use of coat racks in the Lecture Hall lobby. This has left a space at basement level that should be clearly within the public realm but is currently used for storage of display cases, barriers, and

Attempts to use the original reception desk area as an exhibition space for small objects have not been successful (top, photographed in 2003). However, it has served as a good orientation space for school groups, and the presence of Hepworth's *Sphere with Inner Form* (bottom, photographed in 2008), has proved compatible with this use as the sculpture's monumentality is suited to a quasi-external space.

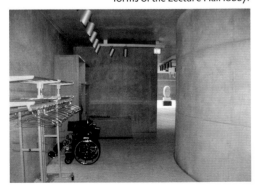

The ad-hoc storage of racks, cabinets, and other items disturbs the celebration of pure forms of the Lecture Hall lobby.

screens. Presently the lobby only serves the restrooms, but its size and scale requires more, and it should not feel abandoned. If security precludes the reinstatement of the coat racks, the area could be used for appropriate interpretation or seating for those waiting for their companions.

Originally intended as a coat check with millwork counters, the basement elevator lobby has been relegated to storage.

Restrooms

The restrooms contain original fixtures. The arrangement of the basins with their mirrors and lighting, similar to that in a theater dressing room, the use of the cinder-block walls, and the restriction of the white, ceramic-mosaic-tile cladding to those areas of the wall that might come in contact with users are part of the Kahn aesthetic and appear also at the Kimbell. The consistency of this application to all restrooms in the building also reflects the egalitarian approach that underlies its design. The location of staff restrooms on the upper levels off the galleries illustrates the architect's directness of approach, but the absence of labeling clearly indicates that they were not intended for public use by the time the building opened. Each restroom should be considered significant.

The basement restrooms are considered as much a piece of design as any of the other spaces in the Center. Kahn used the same lighting in his own living room in Philadelphia.

Policy 37

To ensure that the internal connection from the Center to the commercial unit that accommodates the Museum Shop is as discreet as possible. Introducing a lobby could assist in reinforcing the separation of the two elements.

Policy 38

To recognize the Lecture Hall lobby as a significant area and of comparable standing to the Lecture Hall that it serves. All lobby spaces need to be maintained free of ad-hoc storage.

Policy 39

The Docent Room is not a significant space, and alteration would be acceptable.

Policy 40

The basement lobby should be recovered as part of the entrance foyer.

Policy 41

The restrooms are spaces of significance and should be respected.

Lecture Hall

The Lecture Hall was a primary element of the brief from the outset, and its importance, as well as its location, is constant in each version of Kahn's design. The locus for lectures related to the collection and exhibitions, it remains at the heart of the Center; its use in recent years as a cinema and concert hall was not part of the original intent. The design is similar to, but more generous than, that used at the Kimbell. The treatment of the space as a rectangular concrete box is of considerable significance, and the discipline of the grid arising from the panels of the concrete formwork controls the space. Kahn had intended to design "tapestries" to provide acoustic absorption, and Prown believes that they would have been strong visual elements; the gray quilted panels were devised after Kahn's death by Marshall Meyers.

... under a majestic beam, is the auditorium, tough and simple, all concrete seats in a stern concrete box of space, totally different from the Cinema-1-2-3 effect of the carpeted auditorium that was excavated under the Art Gallery at about the same time, though that is not a bad room either.

Vincent Scully et al., *Yale in New Haven*

The concrete box is something to celebrate, as it is beautiful, but it is also the major constraint, as its shape limits its use in acoustic terms (rooms for music avoid parallel walls); what is more, the concrete cannot be chased or altered to accommodate sound systems without damage. To date, use has been primarily related to speech and film rather than music, but minor alterations and upgrading of services have resulted in cabling installed through surface-mounted plastic conduits — executed as carefully as possible but still to be regretted. Concerts have generally been held in the Library Court, but, with larger numbers attending such events, the court is proving to be too small and the improvement of the acoustics in the Lecture Hall has been under reconsideration.

As was found at the Sydney Opera House, acoustics is a very fast-moving science and care has to be taken as "attempts at improvement have the potential to cause needless damage to the very real character of a space," particularly if there is uncertainty about the appropriate solution.[51] The introduction of new uses such as concerts, therefore, might be inappropriate if the improvement to acoustics involved physical alteration to significant fabric.

The projection booth is part of Kahn's original scheme, but access is restricted by two steps and the environmental conditions are poor. Audio-visual requirements have changed considerably since the 1970s, and the projection equipment was brought up to date in 2010. In time, the booth itself might become redundant, and alternative use of the space might be considered.

The steps down the aisles are both steep and of different widths because they are interrupted by the platforms on which the seats are arranged. The step lights in the risers were intended to address this, but it is likely that health-and-safety requirements will result in the need to introduce some form of handrail. Care needs to be taken that a solution does not visually interrupt the space of the Lecture Hall.

Access for people with disabilities is also a problem. Space at the top of the auditorium is extremely limited, as the raking seats start immediately as one enters from the lobbies on either side of the projection booth. With no landing at the back of the hall, people in wheelchairs have to remain in the small lobbies on either side of the projection booth. The alternative arrangements allow those with disabilities to be escorted through the basement service areas that give back-of-house access to the floor of the

The Lecture Hall, seen from below, with its raked seating and projection booth

[51] James Semple Kerr, *A Revised Plan for the Conservation of the Sydney Opera House and its Site*, 3rd ed. (Sydney: Sydney Opera House Trust, 2004), 74.

Lecture Hall. Both arrangements are very unsatisfactory and need to be resolved, but it is the only instance within the Center where access to a major space is a problem.

The survival of its fittings is significant, but some seats are broken, treads are wearing, and the flip desks are becoming chipped.

The recesses in the ceiling and the dense hang of downlighters from the suspended track facilitate the unobtrusive positioning of suspended loudspeakers introduced to support the changes in use of the Lecture Hall.

Policy 42
To maintain the Lecture Hall and the projection booth to the best functional standards in the light of current knowledge.

Policy 43
To ensure that acoustic improvements respect Kahn's design and are based on an agreed priority use of the space as well as acoustic objectives.

Policy 44
To ensure that alterations do not leave the fabric of the Lecture Hall with a progressively increasing collection of drilled holes and minor alterations that affect its visual appearance and that new installations are contained in the least bulky housings so as to mitigate any visual intrusion into the Lecture Hall.

Policy 45
To ensure that the Lecture Hall does not become cluttered. Musical instruments should not remain in the space after a concert. If a permanent location is required for a piano, it is likely that it would be more suitable in the Library Court, which was seen by Kahn as a space that could be furnished with freestanding display cabinets and furniture.

Policy 46
To retain the original fabric of seating and acoustic quilts within the constraints of reason and depending on the circumstances. With the seating, retention would be first choice; partial replacement (e.g., reupholstery), second; total replacement in the character of Kahn's work, third.

Policy 47
To ensure the safety of visitors and to provide access for people with disabilities in a manner that causes the least visual intervention. If it was acceptable, a series of posts related to each row of the seating would be less intrusive than a continuous handrail.

Facing page:
The Lecture Hall

Vertical circulation

Elevator lobbies

The lobbies bring together the elevators and staircase. The public generally ascends to the galleries via the elevators and often returns via the staircase. Shared use of the lobby by the public and service elevators reflects the egalitarian approach to the design of the building. The elevator cars are original. The control panels are replacements.

The disengagement of the stair tower from the adjacent structure occurs on each floor save for the basement. On the upper floors this affords views back over the Library Court, while on the second and first floors it provides access to the Library Court and the Lecture Hall foyer respectively. The views on the upper floors allow orientation as visitors progress further into the building. At basement level, the attachment of the stair tower to the adjacent walls confirms that access is restricted, limited only to the restrooms and cloakroom space.

In earlier designs the freight elevator and the pair of passenger elevators were contained in shafts that were expressed as freestanding. Their size was determined by the cars, the difference being taken up in a surrounding travertine apron that adjusted them to the grid. The scheme later was developed to become two identically sized concrete shafts that also housed various air shafts. The freestanding quality, however, was not maintained, and the shafts appear more as lobby walls rather than independent objects. The travertine paving remained but is contained within the defined lobby.

The fourth-floor elevator lobby and the top of the staircase

Staircases

A major element of the Entrance Court in the First Program, the staircase rises to pass through the Library Court in the Second Program, thus transferring the vertical movement of the visitor into the heart of the building. Although no longer treated as an almost baroque feature, the stair remained expressed as an enclosed element; its transparent glazed walls were replaced with a concrete shaft with its own lens-lit roof, which stopped independently below the skylights that extend over the court. At first intended as a rotated square and then as a cylinder, the final design of the stairwell has obvious parallels with the stairs at the Yale University Art Gallery. The design of the stair is almost entirely Kahn, except the handrail, which was altered from an elliptical section by Pellechia and Meyers. The steps were detailed to be totally in travertine, but cost cutting before Kahn's death resulted in the present arrangement of travertine inserts to a concrete structure.

The display of both Hepworth's *Sphere with Inner Form* and the sculpture of William III at different periods within the stairwell has been unsatisfactory. The basement area at the foot of the stair is not only restricted, with inadequate space for viewing, but it is two stories below the spaces that are designated for gallery use, and consequently objects feel both stray and relegated to basement storage. The fact that the space at the foot of the stairwell is also decidedly internal meant that these two external sculptures were even more uncomfortable in this location.

Top of staircase with its laylight set well below the rooflights of the Library Court

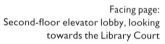

Facing page:
Second-floor elevator lobby, looking towards the Library Court

William III, by John Nost the Elder or John Cheere, displayed in the stairwell in 2006

Policy 48

The staircase is of exceptional significance and should be maintained without alteration.

Policy 49

The staircase should not be used as a place for display.

Fire escape staircases

Staircases are treated as utilitarian spaces, and the directness of their detailing remains consistent with the hierarchies of the rest of the building. Although servant spaces, they are a positive element to value.

Policy 50

To respect utilitarian spaces such as the fire escape stairs.

Public display galleries

Vulnerabilities

The public display galleries are under pressure from:

1. The growth of the collection;
2. The requirement that Paul Mellon's collection may not leave the building, except for short-term loan to other museums or ceremonial spaces at Yale;
3. The need to accommodate temporary loan exhibitions;
4. Changing requirements for conservation and the control of daylight stipulated in loan agreements;
5. Changing attitudes toward energy issues.

Gallery space

Two characteristics underlie the design of the galleries in Kahn's schemes for the Center: the importance placed on viewing pictures both in daylight and within room-like volumes.

Daylight

The use of daylight was critical to both the client and the architect. It is identified as such in Prown's "Preliminary Thoughts on Architecture" (January 1969), and Kahn's appointment at Yale followed his proposals to use skylights in the Kimbell Art Museum at Fort Worth (commissioned 1966). There the director had accepted that the strong Texas daylight would be unacceptable for lighting works of art, but he wanted museum visitors to be aware of the outside world as light levels changed. The arrangement of baffles below skylights thus allowed the variation of natural light to affect the mood of the gallery space, but the illumination of the works of art was, in reality, primarily electric. "The first aim in exhibit spaces," stated Kahn when describing the Kimbell, "was that paintings and drawings be seen in natural light in the true color seen by the artist. The mood and color of the sky, the time of day, season of the year will be seen."[52]

Prown recalled that "I wanted to go a step further – or perhaps more precisely a step backward – to traditional skylit galleries, to be able to rely on daylight alone to illumi-

The British Art Center is somehow the most stable, the most wholly serene, the quietest building one has ever experienced. It is built; it feels right, complete, permanent. This is also true of the gallery floors, especially, of course, of the top level where the light is filtered down through the skylights that Kahn loved so well and had studied previously in his design for the Kimbell. . . . The most moving space of all on the British Art Center's top floor is the corner bay in front of the great Turner, where one of the big square panes of glass opens onto Chapel Street. From there, somehow magnified and clarified as in an optical lens, the whole range of buildings along the street . . . is clearly visible.

Vincent Scully et al., *Yale in New Haven*

. . . [at the Center], as under the Art Gallery's dark canopy, the objects on display may take on a special sacral aura.

Vincent Scully et al., *Yale in New Haven*

[52] Loud, *The Art Museums of Louis I. Kahn*, 215.

Model of the proposed fourth-floor galleries from the First Program for the Center

Diffused top lighting and indirect side light from the garden court at the Kimbell Art Museum

nate pictures on sunny or bright overcast days."[53] This determined the basic arrangement of the Center: the placing of the main exhibition galleries on the top floor in order to exploit natural light. This arrangement served not only to enhance the display of objects but also possibly to suggest locations for individual works within the galleries as occurs in the Turner Bay.

As at the Kimbell, Kahn worked with Richard Kelly on both the control of daylight as well as electric lighting. Their approach was informed by contemporary research in the effects of light not only on works on paper but also on all types of painted surfaces that was being carried out elsewhere, particularly at the National Gallery in London and The Metropolitan Museum of Art in New York. "A Report on Deteriorating Effects of Modern Light Sources" by Laurence S. Harrison at The Metropolitan Museum of Art, which Kelly sent to Prown, made the point that all light, natural or electric, causes deterioration.

The objectives regarding daylight were set out in a memorandum from the client in October 1971:

The following represents our basic objectives:

1. *On a brilliant sunny day we would like to rely solely on natural light to illuminate the pictures; however, we do not want bright spots or hot spots on the floors and walls.*
2. *On bright but overcast days we would like to rely mostly on natural light for illumination, using little or no electric light to supplement it.*
3. *For less bright days we would use electric light, preferably incandescent, to bring the natural illumination up to an acceptable level.*
4. *We desire the option of eliminating all natural light from any gallery skylight.*
5. *We do not want any beam of light to fall directly on the floor or walls.*
6. *The light admitted to the skylight should come through clear glass or plastic, treated only to remove ultraviolet rays.*
7. *We want to be able to sense the change in the level of brightness of the sunlight available and do not object to sensing changes in the sun's position.*[54]

The use of skylights was fundamental in the design of the building. The unbaffled skylights in the Entrance Court declared the importance of light in the architectural concept but also emphasized that the space was not a gallery; light in the galleries was controlled to protect the works of art. For Prown, daylight would be admitted freely, while the "harmful elements of natural light, including the direct fall of sunlight, [would be prevented] from entering and damaging works of art."[55] Prown saw the eventual solution as a return to the traditional method of lighting gallery space, but with far greater control than previously available, thus eliminating damage. It was an escape from the enclosed free spaces and monotonous electric lighting of museums of the International School.

Loud noted that the lighting became one of the most difficult and prolonged phases of the design of the building. Kelly wanted to minimize northern light because of its stronger ultraviolet content and designed complex screening devices. In addition, electric lighting had to be accommodated. Kahn had not made designs final for the skylights at the time of his death, although Kelly's basic concept of a diffuser had met with his approval, and the structure for the skylight frame was decided.

[53] Prown, "Light and Truth."

[54] Memorandum on plans of August 26, October 7, October 11, 1971, Berg to Office of Louis I. Kahn, Louis I. Kahn Collection, Correspondence Yale Mellon Office, J. Prown and H. Berg, File Box LIK 109, quoted in Loud, *The Art Museums of Louis I. Kahn*, 237 n. 75.

[55] Prown to Kahn, November 20, 1972, Louis I. Kahn Collection, Mellon Correspondence, J. Prown and H. Berg II, File Box LIK 109, quoted in Loud, *The Art Museums of Louis I. Kahn*, 237 n. 87.

In 1972 and 1973, while the building was under construction, there was extensive experimentation with various ways of admitting light in a mock-up of a gallery bay constructed on the roof of the Physical Plant building on Ashmun Street. However, the skylight was still not completely resolved at the time of Kahn's death in 1974. Most details had been decided on: the external fixed louvers and the division of the roof of each bay into quadrants beneath Plexiglas domes with ultraviolet filters. Below each dome, inside the building, cassettes were to scramble the light and scatter it evenly on the interior wall surfaces.

The cassettes that Kelly had been working on with Kahn were described by Prown as an assemblage of Plexiglas dentils. The cassette was six inches deep, but Kahn was hoping that he could eventually develop a cassette that was shallower.[56] Two months after Kahn's death, Froeberg of Macomber was preparing drawings of an alternative version based on ready-made Parawedge elements in order to reduce costs. Both versions were mocked up in the building and tested in adjacent bays in November. Both worked equally well, diffusing the light and illuminating all the walls evenly, and neither drew attention to itself by being too bright or creating high spots on the floor. The Kahn/Kelly solution, however, was reported by Prown as more beautiful as an object in itself, but it cost $100,000 more than the contractor's proposal. To the regret of the designer and the first director, the cheaper version was chosen to maintain budgets.

Windows were also integral to Kahn's scheme for displaying the collection in varying daylight. The fully developed version of the First Program (January 1971) incorporated windows to provide views onto the street that would allow visual relief at the ends and center of the long elevations of the top-lit galleries on the fourth floor. The more conventional room-like galleries on the third floor, however, provided a wall of windows with screens at right angles to them on which pictures could be displayed with side light. Sliding wooden louvered shutters, concealed behind the wall linings when not in use, were planned to control the daylight coming in the windows.

This use of side light for displaying pictures was also adopted for the Second Program. In the October 1971 design (final presentation) the perspectives and drawings illustrate screens across the gallery windows looking onto Chapel Street that can be hinged open at right angles to the glazing to allow pictures to be displayed with side lighting or closed to form an external wall. The daylight on the south side of the building had to be more controlled. The Study Gallery was, therefore, seen as a purely top-lit space, with a continuous blank wall along the south elevation save for two windows on either side of the central column. A further window was planned in the center of the west wall to terminate the view down the gallery.

The acceptance that works on paper could not be shown in such conditions resulted in the third floor being treated as dark space, with no windows or openings onto the Entrance Court. However, a window was placed looking onto High Street to give relief.

Policy 51
To ensure that the display of works of art continues to respond to the varying nature of daylight.

The fourth-floor galleries

Facing page:
Lighting study for the First Program with Richard Kelly, from the Louis I. Kahn Collection, University of Pennsylvania (805.005)

Paul Mellon and Louis Kahn inspecting the lighting trials in the mock-up of a fourth-floor bay, June 14, 1973

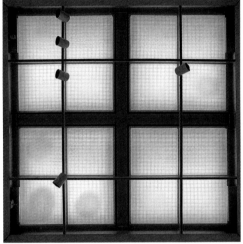

Top: The Kahn/Kelly proposal for the cassettes fixed under the skylights to diffuse the daylight, 1973
Bottom: The Macomber alternative that was accepted on the grounds of cost

[56] There was also the possibility that motorized louvers would be used, particularly over office areas. Macomber Coordination Meeting Notes, March 6, 1974, Yale Center for British Art Archives.

Room-like volumes

Kahn had visited Paul Mellon's house with Prown and understood the domestic setting of the pictures that the benefactor liked. It is clear that the architect was also inspired by his visits to England, where he saw British art in the setting of the English country house. His galleries from the First Program onwards reflect this with the use of double-height spaces and quasi-domestic settings achieved by the division of the space into small-scale volumes. In the final building this was realized by variations in the arrangement of pogos, and the judicious use of side light reinforced the chosen layout. The display of Turner's "Dort," with side lighting that recalls that of its original setting in the dining room at Farnley Hall, characterizes this effect at its most memorable. In the same vein, the oak-paneled, top-lit Library Court with its deep hang recalls the English great hall.

The majority of the pictures in the collection are small in scale and suitable for domestic use. Generally, Mr. Mellon did not collect large-scale English portraits, and the only substantially sized pictures are the country-house views and some paintings of animals. Stubbs's *A Lion Attacking a Horse* is shown in several of Kahn's preliminary sketches, but Prown believes that this was purely indicative of gallery space, and there was no specific direction as to the placement of the collection. The installation, therefore, is inherently flexible and under curatorial direction. The dense hang in the Study Gallery arose from the client as a response to the need for accessible storage. Such facilities had been developed at the National Gallery in London and the Brooklyn Museum. It is likely that the dense hang also reflected the trans-Atlantic admiration that had developed in the 1960s for the picture gallery at the Soane Museum in London with its dense hang and skylights.

Policy 52

To respect the quasi-domestic setting, with comparatively small, room-like volumes, in any alteration of the building or rearrangement of the pogos.

The galleries are also determined by a series of other considerations:

Display

Although Kahn's sketches of the Library Court indicated his intention that paintings might be hung on the millwork paneling, generally works of art in the galleries were to be displayed on linen panels treated either as freestanding pogos or as inserts to the concrete-framed bays that formed the external walls. Kahn's approach meant that no pictures, labels, or signage were hung on the concrete walls or steel panels.

The pogos were further variants of those used at the Yale University Art Gallery (1951–53) and the Kimbell Art Museum (1966–72), where Kahn had designed light-weight panels as independent display screens. In the former the panels were disengaged from both ceiling and floor by polecats, and in the latter they rested on the floor above gray baseboards and were anchored back to ceiling beams by offset metal plates. For the Yale Center Kahn's proposals again used polecats; the recessed baseboards were an introduction by Pellechia and Meyers after Kahn's death.

Facing page:
Second-floor galleries

Yale University Art Gallery, photographed in 1953

Fourth-floor galleries with original installation of pogos, photographed in 1977

In 1998 some of the natural linen on the Center's fourth floor was temporarily replaced with blue damask to provide a setting for portraits by Reynolds.

Kimbell Art Museum

Yale University Art Gallery

While the walls were filled with display panels of linen surrounded by an oak trim, the separation of the pogos from the structure was emphasized by the absence of the edge detail, and their linen-faced panels floated visually in the space. In his return to polecats Kahn also disengaged the base of the pogos from the travertine bands in the floor. Another proposal followed showing the bottom of the linen panel recessed into an oak beam that extended the full width of the screen, but the beam itself remained raised off the floor by polecats. After Kahn's death a baseboard was introduced and the pogos were made to appear closer to those at the Kimbell; they sat directly on the travertine and interrupted the continuity of the floor plane. In 1998 a protective trim, designed by Glenn Gregg, was introduced on the edges of the pogos to mitigate the soiling caused by visitors brushing the sides of the panels; this further altered the character of the pogos, reducing their contrast with the adjacent wall panels.

The panels were covered with natural Belgian linen, and, to achieve a uniform approach, this was applied in all galleries. At one point in the 1990s, the simplicity was disrupted by the replacement of the Belgian linen with blue damask in a "room" in the Long Gallery in an attempt to provide a "period" setting for a group of Reynolds portraits. The change of material proved intrusive to Kahn's chosen neutral aesthetic using natural materials and has since been reversed.

Analysis of Kahn's and Meyers's plans and photographs of the first installation allow deduction of Kahn's guidelines for positioning pogos, but they should not necessarily be restrictive. While the pogos allow for the creation of a variety of spaces, they should be:

1. positioned centrally along the 20-foot grid on which the columns are set out (i.e., on the travertine grid);
2. disengaged from the columns with a minimum offset of one foot from the column grid (i.e., to align with the return edge of the travertine floor grid);
3. limited to a range of widths of 3-foot increments. However, Kahn's first drawing shows uniform 12-foot-wide pogos applied throughout the fourth floor;
4. laid out to maintain the calm of the building and give a sense of graciousness and generosity;
5. arranged to maintain continuity of space and not used to provide solid partition walls.

Only by working within such constraints can an order and control of the space be possible rather than degenerating into unorganized space lacking structure.

It appears that Kahn's intention was that the display within the building should have a degree of flexibility. However, the architect's experience at the Yale University Art Gallery had shown that his tetrahedral ceiling had provided so much flexibility that subsequent installations had eroded the architectural coherence of the space. Opportunities to rearrange pogos at the Kimbell were constrained by the need for fixtures to relate to the exposed beams that edged the vault, and at the Center, this was further controlled by the discipline of the 20-foot grid.

Kahn illustrated the galleries divided by 12-foot-wide pogos, but they were assembled from 3-foot- and 6-foot-wide panels so that they should be manageable. The use of actual 9-foot- and 6-foot-wide pogos appear in the early installations. The small 3-foot-wide pogos were introduced only in the late 1990s, but the scale of the panel is not adequate to control the space architecturally.

Pogos covered in a colored fabric, arranged off-grid and on the diagonal in the exhibition *James Tissot: Victorian Life, Modern Love*, in 1999

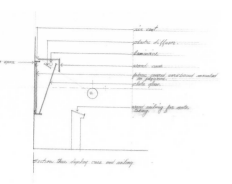

Estimator's drawing showing Kahn's design for display screens for works on paper, February 18, 1972, Louis I. Kahn Collection, University of Pennsylvania (805.018)

While the majority of the display was intended to be hung, drawings that predate Kahn's death also exist for display cabinets. Wall cabinets for vertical display of works on paper set behind canted glazing and associated with a "wood railing for note taking,"[57] were conceived for lining the perimeter of the third-floor gallery. Prown had admired such cases in the new gallery at Christchurch, Oxford, by Powell & Moya and had discussed them with Kahn as a potential approach. A freestanding cabinet on the same lines was also envisaged at one time for the Library Court.

The use of a consistent system of display throughout the building contributes significantly to the calmness of the galleries, despite the variations in their height and lighting.

Policy 53
To retain the use of the pogos. Their arrangement should follow the rules that can be deduced in Kahn's drawing for locating them. To respect in particular the following:
a. The consistency of the application of the same display method to all spaces
b. The relationship of the pogos and the display cases to the 20-foot structural bay
c. The constraints on the placing of the pogos
d. The relationship between the display areas on the walls and the pogos

Policy 54
To restore the design of the pogos with their original edge-trim details and linen covering to allow them to appear as floating screens rather than framed panels.

Policy 55
The periodic rearrangement of the pogos is welcomed, as it provides fresh opportunities for the display of the collection and the understanding of the building. However, the constraints imposed by the building should still be respected.

An example of this was the exhibition *Britannia and Muscovy* (2006), where the installation respected both the structure of the 20-foot bays and the progression through the galleries surrounding the Entrance Court. As a result, the works of art were enriched by the building and vice versa.

Museum fatigue and orientation
Museum fatigue was recognized by both client and architect as a serious problem to be considered in the design of the galleries.

It had first been intended that the Center would extend from High Street to York Street, "from river to river" as Kahn said. However, a simple application of the areas of the First Program showed that this would have resulted in only two floors of accommodation above the commercial base. Therefore Prown recommended to Kahn that the building should be reduced in length and that a more compact solution with an additional floor would be preferable. One of the main reasons behind this was that visitors to the gallery would be able to orientate themselves more easily, which would counter museum fatigue.[58]

Windows were also to play a key role in managing fatigue. As well as illumination, windows provided a view out, locating the building in the context of both the University

Top: In the exhibition *Sensation and Sensibility: Viewing Gainsborough's "Cottage Door"* (2005), the third floor was divided by a partition wall with a door cut within it rather than using two independent pogos disengaged from the sides of the gallery.
Center: *Art and Emancipation in Jamaica: Isaac Mendes Belisario and His Worlds* (2007) employed the pogos as Kahn intended.
Bottom: *Britannia and Muscovy: English Silver at the Court of the Czars* (2006) also respected the layout of the twenty-foot grid.

[57] Kahn office drawing, Third floor, February 18, 1972, Louis I. Kahn Collection, University of Pennsylvania and Pennsylvania Historical and Museum Commission.

[58] Prown, "Lux et Veritas," 51.

Facing page:
Views across the Entrance Court
provided visual relief from looking at works
of art in the second-floor galleries when the
openings were restored during the
Paul Mellon centennial exhibition in 2007.

and the city as well as providing relief from looking closely at works of art. Similarly, visitors enjoyed views within the building from the galleries by the creation of openings onto the Entrance and Library courts, the vistas from one gallery to another affording tempting and unexpected views of the paintings, the building, and beyond. To facilitate this, while meeting building codes, Kahn persuaded the authorities to accept fire shutters connected to the detection system at the top of each opening. However, they are not integrated into the paneling and, if revised codes allow, should be removed.

Even where conservation needs required low light levels, such visual relief was still seen as important to the enjoyment of the galleries. The third-floor gallery, designed without daylight for the display of light-sensitive works on paper, therefore, still had one window so that visitors could look out onto the street, and it was intended that the layout of displays would take this into account.

Kahn acknowledged that some form of shutters would also be necessary to control changing light from the windows. The "American" louvered shutters that slide into recesses in the wall were part of his original details but not installed until 1981–82 on account of cost-cutting. However, the "cloth shades" that had been intended to supplement the shutters were installed. The use of retractable shutters indicates that light was to be managed in response to immediate conditions rather than on a long-term basis. Over the years increased restrictions on lighting levels, primarily related to loan agreements, have meant that several windows on the second and third floors have now been blacked out and the American shutters are usually drawn in front of them.

Similarly, the adoption of part of the second-floor gallery as a temporary exhibition gallery has meant that some openings onto the Entrance Court have been blocked on a virtually permanent basis by partitions disguised to look like roller blinds when seen from the court. In each case the effect has been intrusive and reduced the quality of the visitor experience, especially as the legibility of the building has become confused by the denial of the openings.

The elimination of a primary axial view on the second floor from the elevator lobby across the Entrance Court to High Street has also eroded the relationship of the building to its setting. In 2007 the openings were reinstated for the Paul Mellon centennial exhibition. Not only was the building transformed by the relationship between galleries and with the vistas onto the city, but the actual paintings were enhanced by their setting.

Policy 56

The external windows and internal openings are significant elements related to Kahn's original organization of the internal galleries and the need for visual relief for museum visitors. The design and use of the galleries should work within this constraint.

Visitor experience and comfort

In addition to having views out of the galleries to provide relief from looking at detailed works of art, the Center was provided with relaxation areas for visitors and staff. The furnishing of the building included comfortable couches within the galleries, and the Library Court was envisaged with millwork benches on which visitors could sit and look at

Kahn's openings onto the Entrance Court are frequently blocked to reduce light levels in the second-floor galleries.
Top: Within the galleries, treated as a red damask background to an exhibition in 1999
Bottom: Within the court, made to appear as closed shades

Windows onto the surrounding streets are important in all the galleries to give a visual release from viewing works of art, as in the fourth floor (top) and the second floor (bottom). When necessary, sliding louvered shutters are used to reduce light levels.

Following spread:
Looking east across the Entrance Court to the galleries on the fourth and second floors, 2007. In order to control daylight, the third floor, intended for the display of works on paper, has no openings onto the court.

Garden Court at the Kimbell Art Museum.
Kahn planned similar courts within the galleries
of the First Program for the Center.

the paintings. In the First Program this feature extended to include external garden courts at roof level opening off both the galleries and libraries, very similar to those used at the Kimbell, but, sadly, these became subject to the cost reductions of the Second Program.

The importance of having space for relaxation within the building was emphasized by the concept of "The Room." This also characterized the link between the academic institution and the public gallery, forming a place for meetings, rest, thought, and contemplation. In the earliest designs it was symbolized by including a great hearth. In the Second Program this had been reduced to a meeting room at the northwest corner of the fourth floor, now the "Founder's Room" and largely used for formal meetings, particularly in connection with the Director's Office. On the third floor a room marked "Lounge" opened through double oak doors off the northeast corner of the gallery, allowing visitors to move from the display gallery to an area of relaxation with views to the University buildings beyond. By the time the Center was built, the Lounge had been connected by a door to the adjacent paper conservation studio and is now used for the paper conservation library, photography, etc. The colonization of these areas demonstrates a growing need for ancillary space as staff and activities have grown.

Policy 57
Relaxation areas connected with the galleries were an inherent part of the original concept and should be recognized as important to the gallery experience.

Organization of galleries within the building
The organization of the galleries arose from the two primary characteristics concerning the display of the works of art in daylight and within room-like volumes as described above. The most significant gallery space occupied the fourth floor in order to exploit the use of top lighting. This was supplemented by second-floor galleries that extended to the north side of the building to take advantage of generous areas of glazing onto Chapel Street, and were intended to be quite flexible, suitable for temporary exhibitions. The third floor was treated as a space for light-sensitive works on paper, with the galleries set inboard one bay from the north and south elevations. While the second- and third-floor galleries occupy only the east end of the building, clustering around the Entrance Court, the galleries on the fourth floor extend virtually over the whole plan.

So that as much of the collection as possible could be accessible to students and scholars, the whole of the south side of the fourth floor from the service core to the west corner was reserved for the Study Gallery. As the design progressed the two end bays of the space were developed by Kahn as offices that were glazed to allow supervision down the length of the gallery. However, the presence of these offices became less relevant once the introduction of pogos within the galleries made surveillance difficult, and even less so when the space was monitored by guards following its transfer to public display. It was renamed the Long Gallery in 1998. The physical separation of the area from the adjoining galleries made a great deal of sense when it was used for study storage, but it has no meaning now that the space is part of the overall hang of the fourth-floor galleries. The glazed doors at the entrance into the center of the gallery have done little to integrate it with the adjoining areas, and solid doors remain at the

Second-floor galleries with openings looking over the Entrance Court

Two photographs of the original Study Gallery before it was dismantled in 1998. The space now supplements the fourth-floor public display galleries and is referred to as the Long Gallery.

west end. The resulting isolation of the gallery makes it feel as if the material displayed is secondary, and this is compounded by each end appearing to be an area within the territory of the offices that overlook it. It is hard to understand that the structure of the two parallel galleries on the south side of the building is the same as that at the opposite corner of the fourth floor, where the display of works by Turner and Constable is celebrated in a space two bays deep.

The Library Court, always intended as a top-lit display area, rises through all three exhibition stories. Not only does it provide interconnections between the different areas of the collection, but it implies that all areas are available to the public, not only the display galleries but the libraries as well.

The clarity of the organization of the galleries has been diluted by the increasing use of the second and third floors as temporary exhibition space. Not only has this meant that the third floor is no longer specifically dedicated to the display of works on paper, a major element of the permanent collection, but the quality of space on the second floor, which was intended for changing exhibitions, has been eroded. The requirements to meet the conditions set out in loan agreements have meant the exclusion of daylight in the galleries and the blocking of external windows. Placing panels in the openings onto the Entrance Court to reduce light levels seriously affects the visitor experience. In contrast, the galleries on the fourth floor remain predominantly intact and make a positive contribution to the presentation of the collection.

Policy 58

To regain the original organization and configuration of the galleries with windows and internal openings treated as Kahn intended. This includes maintaining the galleries as daylit spaces and recovering the third floor as space dedicated to works on paper. In addition, exhibits should be arranged within the galleries so that they do not compromise the original design intentions for the building, while ensuring that no work of art is placed in unsuitable environmental conditions. To this end, the current stringent requirements for the display of loan items could mean that exhibits should be temporarily and locally screened within the galleries rather than impacting a whole gallery.

Policy 59

To site the temporary exhibition galleries in an appropriate location that is compatible with the intended organization of the building.

Policy 60

To respect the need for a dedicated, light-controlled space for the display of works on paper, rare books, and manuscripts.

Policy 61

To ensure that the subdivision of the galleries continues to be determined by their use and takes full advantage of the building's potential.

Offices on the fourth floor were constructed with glazed walls to allow monitoring of the adjoining Study Gallery.

The repetition of the twenty-foot, top-lit bays throughout the fourth floor implies flexibilty in the arrangement of the galleries. The open plan that this facilitates to the north of the Entrance Court (left) allows views through the buiding that enrich the visitor experience when looking at works of art. However, consideration could be given to opening up the galleries to the south of the Library Court in a similar fashion. They are still interrupted by the partition wall that originally defined the Study Gallery (right), despite the space being integrated into the public display area in 1998.

Given the pressures resulting from the growth of the collection, the requirement to house it on site, and the desire to make as much of it as possible available to visitors, it would be prudent to readdress the area originally occupied by the Study Gallery. This is particularly desirable since the adaptation of the space failed to integrate it satisfactorily into the public display areas when study storage was abandoned. Two options for the area are clear: the reinstatement of the Study Gallery with some form of dense, accessible storage that is available to scholars; or its conversion into a two-bay-deep gallery so that it acts as a seamless extension of the fourth-floor galleries with opportunities for the public display of paintings as rich as those in the northeast corner of the floor. Each option would be equally valid in terms of Kahn's view that the building should respond to the needs of the collection and the institution, but the decision has to rest on an in-depth study of requirements.

Library Court

The introduction of a three-story court in the western half of the building is a major innovation of the Second Program. Rising from the second-floor level, it unites the libraries with the galleries two stories above via the openings on the fourth floor. It was denoted as the "Exhibition Court" in drawings dated October 1971. The intention that it is a space to display paintings is confirmed in Kahn's sketches dated the same year that show various works by Stubbs displayed on the walls, as well as notes that describe the space as "Entrance Hall to Rare Books, Drawings and Photo Archives. Place for Exhibition of Photos, Paintings, Books related to studies and general interest."[59] The drawing also noted the importance of being lit from above.

The court is three bays long by two wide. The treatment of the main stair tower as a freestanding object straddling the east bays demarcates an entrance area outside both the Library and the Study Room, leaving a two-bay exhibition hall beyond, a space of the same dimensions and materials as the Entrance Court, which it recalls. The concrete of the elevator shafts form the walls on the east side, while the expressed concrete frame is infilled with oak paneling on the other three sides. As in the Entrance Court, the millwork linings indicate a relationship with the spaces that lie beyond. On the fourth floor openings reinforce the connection with the galleries; on the second floor, glazed openings provide the entrances to the Library and the Study Room at court level.

From the first, the Library Court was seen as an important location for the display of large pictures, and its presence extending up through the libraries confirmed that all the collections in the building were one, even if differentiated because of varying requirements for storage and conservation. In contrast to the galleries, pictures in the Library Court were not displayed on linen-faced wall panels or pogos. The display of paintings on the oak paneling is advocated in Kahn's sketches, as is the extension of the hang to the upper levels of paneling, achieved by suspending the paintings from a channel at the head of the paneling rather than bolting them to the wood.

Photographs of different installations show that the hanging of pictures is more successful when they respect the discipline of the paneling grid and certainly do not

. . . the British Art Center again opens to the roof in its most spectacular space, also paneled and hung with appropriately enormous English paintings, including two ferocious scenes of animal carnage by Stubbs. Kahn thought of it as the Great Hall of an English country house, but it embodies more of that primitive power that Kahn's work always seemed to have, especially as the enormous gray concrete cylinder of the stair tower stands out in it, not quite touching the roof. So the kind of Sublime that Kahn looked for in his ruins is not absent here, but most of all there is the Silence that he always loved, the Silence and the Light.

Vincent Scully et al., *Yale in New Haven*

[59] Interior perspective of library court, looking west, Louis I. Kahn Collection, 805.470, University of Pennsylvania and Pennsylvania Historical and Museum Commission.

Paintings by George Stubbs hang on the oak paneling in the Library Court.

trespass over the concrete framing. As elsewhere in the building, no works of art were to be placed on the concrete walls or the structural frame.

The space is vulnerable, as it is used as a main area for receptions, and there is a clear need for supporting service space. Having large numbers of people in the court has resulted in the introduction of rope barriers, replaced by stainless-steel stanchions in the summer of 2008, to protect the paintings hung on the lowest tier of the paneling during concerts and receptions. In addition, the use of the building for receptions places the Center at risk from insects and pests. The best solution for this is prevention, by keeping food service away from collection areas.

Policy 62
To maintain the Library Court as the link between all sections of the institution and as the heart of the Center.

Policy 63
To maintain the Library Court foremost as a space that celebrates the display of important works of art but is also available for receptions.

For example, any barrier should only be in place when absolutely necessary during a reception. Proper servicing facilities are necessary to support receptions.

Reference Library
Rare Books and Manuscripts Department
Prints and Drawings Department

It is important to recognize that the whole of the building is one research institute in which all of the collections work together to provide both public pleasure and to be the objects of scholarship. However, the collections contain material (sculptures, paintings, works on paper, and rare books) that is stored and studied in different ways. The building, therefore, divides between the galleries and, what we term for convenience, the libraries. The Reference Library, the Rare Books and Manuscripts Department, and the Prints and Drawings Department are grouped around the Library Court, which unites them with the surrounding picture galleries.

The Reference Library and the Prints and Drawings Department balance each other at the entrance to the court, and the Rare Books and Manuscripts Department links the two discreetly beyond the west wall. The group of rooms works as an entity, expressing the relationship between the materials held in the three sections, while each part is a distinct department symbolized by its own double-height reading room.

The entrances to the Reference Library and the Study Room denote the areas available to the public. Beyond these spaces, access is limited to staff, and rare books, manuscripts, and works on paper are consulted by scholars and the public in the Study Room.

The three departments can be considered as one in terms of the conservation plan: two stories of accommodation wrapping around three sides of the Library Court and articulated by three double-height spaces that act as the focus to separate yet related uses.

The Reference Library and the mezzanine above

Facing page:
The Study Room serves the departments of Prints and Drawings and Rare Books and Manuscripts

This photograph of the Reference Library was taken ca. 1977 while the building was being completed and the pendant lamps had not yet been delivered.

The introduction of computers has made the card catalog in the Reference Library largely redundant.

Additional storage cabinets in the Prints and Drawings Department have been integrated with those originally supplied.

The double-height volumes act as the reading rooms for each department and are exceptionally significant. Each is a distinguished architectural space in its own right, and each is a variation on the theme of a double-height, galleried space, generously side-lit along one of its long walls. Subordinate accommodation is provided in two levels of single-story space that extend inboard, the upper closed except in the library. Access galleries with bookshelves run across the external walls. The staircases to the mezzanine are minor architectural masterpieces. The flush millwork of the staircase, paneling, cases, and furniture provides a unity throughout and, in every instance, is a clear insertion to the built fabric. The characteristic that the internal arrangement of the space determines the external elevation is particularly strong in this section of the building: the double-height volumes of the reading rooms are acknowledged externally by the concrete frame, and the positioning of the desks and bookshelves determines the fenestration. The upper windows in the Reference Library are also important to the views from the mezzanine across the double-height volume. However, most of the shades were faulty and required replacement in 2010. Generally all on this level are permanently lowered, blocking views. This is unfortunate as it is only necessary when glare occurs at certain times to impact people working in the mezzanine and with personal computers.

The reading rooms are principally intact, but additional furniture has been introduced. An extra trestle table in the Reference Library has made its reading room less spacious, and the lack of a pendant light over the table confirms that it is an introduction. The replacement of fixed shelving with compact shelving in the Reference Library, in both the single-story extension of the reading room and mezzanine above, has made an impact on the quality of the main volume, as the ends of the compacted stacks now form walls to space that previously extended in depth at both levels. The facing of the stacks on the main floor with millwork, rather than standard, painted steel fronts as on the mezzanine, was unacceptable in its attempt to be polite and did not follow Kahn's approach of accepting things for what they are; this detail was greatly improved following the replacement with metal end panels in 2007.

Additional storage has been accommodated in the Prints and Drawings Department with the introduction of further cabinets housing solander boxes in the single-story area. While this has increased the number of cabinets, their low profile has not significantly eroded the quality of the space. More storage, however, is required for the growing collection of works on paper.

New computer workstations in the Reference Library are rendering the original card catalogs redundant. They need to be accommodated in a way that acknowledges that the library is up-to-date. If the card catalogs were removed, consideration would have to be given to the division of the space that the cabinets currently provide.

The requirement for additional office space has meant visiting research fellows have been displaced from the offices designed for them on the third floor and are now housed on the mezzanine of the Reference Library, colonizing an area that was previously for open use.

Policy 64
The reading rooms are of the highest significance, and there is a presumption that no change should occur. The reclaiming of the space now occupied by the compact

A carrel in the Reference Library

The Rare Books and Manuscripts Department Reading Room

shelving in the Reference Library as a more transparent area is desirable in the long term.

Policy 65
To maintain views out from the space. Shades in the upper level should not be permanently lowered but managed in order to resolve issues of glare at particular times of day and season.

The ancillary work spaces are significant because of their functional relationship with the reading rooms and because each space was carefully designed and outfitted in response to the brief. The unity among the spaces and the reading rooms is achieved with the consistency and quality of their treatment. However, the present subdivision of the plan arises from the original brief, which generated a number of internal rooms. They are not significant, and modification would be acceptable.

The mezzanine stacks were of some significance with their open racking and cluster lights using PAR38 lightbulbs. The refitting with compact shelving and the introduction of fluorescent lights is a noticeable change and has resulted, to a certain extent, in the loss of the sense of a sparkling treasure trove. The space is now no longer transparent and the material consequently not visible on its shelving. It is important to bear in mind that, if such spaces are modified, they should maintain the consistency that Kahn achieved throughout the Center.

Policy 66
To accommodate minor changes of the ancillary space to support changes in the brief, as long as quality is not compromised and the nature of the relationship not lost.

Offices and supporting facilities

The integration of the curatorial and academic offices with the galleries was an important part of the program as it was seen that, especially for a museum within a university, curators should be working among the objects in their care. It follows the pattern used at the Fogg Museum at Harvard, developed from the building type established in early nineteenth-century museums in Europe. The dispersal of the offices for both staff and visiting fellows throughout the building was one of the fundamental principles underlying both the First and Second programs.

Fourth-floor paintings storage, photographed in 2008

Fourth floor
The fourth-floor offices and storage areas all occupy space generated by the standard top-lit bay that extends throughout the whole floor except for the air shafts and fire stairs. Indeed, the skylights were appropriate not only for use in the public galleries but where art might be viewed in storage or in offices.

Founder's Room
The Founder's Room has its origins in the concept of "The Room," opening off the painting galleries as a place for casual encounters, that appears in all of Kahn's First

Top: The mezzanine bookstacks as designed by Kahn in the Rare Books and Manuscripts Department, photographed in 2002
Bottom: The same space refitted with compact shelving and new lighting, photographed in 2003

The interior and built-in cabinets in the Founder's Room were designed by Bruce Budd in 1998.

Facing page:
The Founder's Room

Program proposals. The earliest proposals usually focused on a working hearth at the heart of the fourth-floor galleries and adjacent to an upper lecture room.

In the Second Program it is replaced by a Meeting Room related to both the public galleries and the Director's Office. However, in the final building the axial double doors from the office are replaced with a single door set in one corner; not only did this reduce the strength of connection to the Director's Office but doubtless allowed that room to be planned more conveniently.

The space was converted into the Founder's Room in 1998 by Bruce Budd, Mrs. Mellon's interior designer. It is believed that the concept came from Paul Mellon in conversation with Duncan Robinson, the Director from 1981 to 1995, and follows the presence of a Founder's Room at the National Gallery in Washington, built by Mr. Mellon's father. The furnishings are introductions of that time, ranging from antique pieces from the Mellons' home to new, purpose-built, painted-wood display cabinets and bookcases in a style closer to the Regency. It also provided a permanent home for memorabilia of the benefactor's life, such as his Cambridge rowing oars that he particularly wanted to be housed at Yale. The redecoration included rosewood graining of the oak doors and gray-wool walling. Since its conversion, the room has been used as a formal meeting room, primarily in conjunction with the Director's Office, and its contents place a restriction on general use. The double doors that implied a relationship with the public galleries are always closed unless there is an event in the room to which visitors are invited. The treatment of the Founder's Room has placed it apart from the rest of the building, outside the consistency that characterizes all other spaces, and has reduced the architectural significance of the room. However, cultural significance can be enhanced by association with important figures, and it is this that gives the room meaning in its present state.

Policy 67
The concept of a Founder's Room at the Center is of importance, as it represents the wishes of the donor.

Director's Office
The Director's suite of offices and the two-bay Founder's Room are particularly distinguished, as they are based on complete bays. Their quality is enhanced by the immediacy of the views of the Yale University Art Gallery from the generous windows that occupy one half of the external wall. The adjacent office, originally designated for the Deputy Director, was given over to the Business Office and suffered from overcrowding. Its occupation by up to half a dozen staff contradicted the feeling of generosity of space that was intended. In early 2009 it was returned to use by a single staff member, the Center's Head of Research.

Offices adjacent to the Study/Long Gallery
The Study Gallery was originally intended to run the full length of the south side of the building, from the fire stair to the west wall. However, during the design process, a bay at each end was separated by glazed partitions to create offices that could also monitor the gallery. Renamed the Long Gallery in 1998, the space is now part of the general

The Director's Office

The office at the east end of the Long Gallery

public display, monitored by guards. Control from the offices is no longer necessary and the glazing of the partition wall is redundant. Although basically of the same form as the Director's Office, these two offices are not as satisfactory. The glazed screen means that the offices lack privacy, and the adjacent end bays of the Long Gallery are perceived as being off limits by visitors. The rooms are not as well outfitted as those overlooking Chapel Street: storage cabinets are not as generous, and the centrally placed window does not work as well as the offset window in the offices on the north side. In their present form and use, these two offices are not significant.

Paintings and Sculpture Department

The bays occupied by the curatorial offices at the west end of the building were partitioned when the building was constructed and demonstrate how difficult it is to divide the 20-foot grid, particularly when it is below the dominant skylights. Further alterations followed the increase in staff numbers, with extra subdivision to provide privacy in 1992. The work was carried out under the Architecture Studio. The art storage area located between the Paintings Department and the Registrar's Office, first indicated in Kahn's drawings at the east end of the Director's offices, was shown in this location by 1973. The spaces have only minor significance.

Third-floor offices

The third-floor offices on the south side of the building were originally the fellows' "study offices." Following the requirement that offices and teaching spaces should be integrated into the collection, the fellows' offices were not only approached through the third-floor galleries, but the corridor connecting them was treated as a display space to which the public also had access. The corridor led to the room allocated for the Chairman of Studies and to an internal seminar room, both of which connected to the mezzanine story of the Reference Library.

One of the principal changes in the Center is that the building is now very much more densely occupied than when it opened. Today the fellows have moved from their private half-bay offices to a continuous desk space along the balcony in the open-plan mezzanine in the Reference Library, and four postdoctoral research associates have workstations in the room that serves the Rare Books Reading Room. The original fellows' offices are now allocated to administrative staff. Several of the offices are occupied by two members of staff in place of one fellow; the original room intended for the Chairman of Studies and the seminar room now house the Education Department.

The reuse of the area is reflected in minor alterations carried out under the direction of Jared Edwards of Smith Edwards Architects in Hartford, CT, in 2005. This has included the replacement of a partition wall with a glazed screen to provide borrowed light into the internal seminar room now that it is used as a permanent workspace. The alterations followed a precedent in the Reference Library on the second floor designed by Kahn.

Policy 68

To maintain the requirement of the original program that offices should be dispersed within the building so that curators and academics are in regular contact with the

Offices in the Paintings and Sculpture Department, showing partitioning across the grid

Top: The third-floor office corridor was intended to provide additional display space supplementary to that in the adjacent galleries for works on paper, photographed in 2004.
Bottom: The low wall cabinets were introduced in 2005 to give additional storage for the fellows' offices once they were adopted as offices and accommodated larger numbers of staff.

An office on the third floor

works of art. The administrative staff and service departments, however, do not necessarily have to be housed within the Kahn building.

Policy 69

To accept change to the offices arising from pressures within (modifications to accommodate extra staff) or without (the need to increase public display areas).

Policy 70

To recover the generosity of space shown in the Center when it opened. The policy of recovering the spatial generosity is not only concerned with the density of occupation but with maintaining the quality of the environment within the rooms. Any change of density must be considered in relation to the effect on building services.

Policy 71

To maintain the Director's Office and the Founder's Room in their present locations because of their quality and status within the building.

Paper Conservation Laboratory

The Paper Conservation Laboratory is identified as such on Kahn's plans of the third floor, and it is supported by the matting and framing room that occupies the adjacent west bays. The room opening off the lab to the east has a story-high window and oak-paneled double doors to the galleries that confirm its association with the public display area. Originally intended as a lounge, it has since been taken over as a paper conservation library and is also used for teaching.

The space occupied by the Paper Conservation Department relates to the Prints and Drawings Department and the Rare Books and Manuscripts Department, as well as being convenient for the gallery intended specifically for works on paper. The generous window facing north that extends across two complete bays is the widest in the building. Not only does this provide illumination for detailed conservation work, in strong contrast to the conditions in which works on paper are kept, but it takes full advantage of the view of the Yale University Art Gallery. In 1998 the laboratory was partially refitted, but in essence it remains intact. It is one of the most uplifting spaces in the building and must be one of the most enjoyable within which to work.

The Paper Conservation Laboratory

Policy 72

To retain the Paper Conservation Laboratory in its present location because of the quality of the space and its functional relationship to the adjoining areas concerned with works on paper.

Policy 73

To recognize the conservation library as an adjunct of both the adjacent gallery and the Paper Conservation Department as originally intended.

Staff lounge and seminar room

The Staff Lounge

Although they remain as originally designed, these two rooms on the second floor are disappointing. In contrast with the rooms above on the third floor where three bays are subdivided to form six offices, here three bays form two rooms of one-and-a-half bays each with their doors coupled in the middle of the central bay. As with the third floor, these two spaces demonstrate the difficulties of subdivision of the very strong grid. The Seminar Room is convenient for use in conjunction with the galleries. However, the location of the Staff Lounge seems incompatible with the galleries as it results in food being brought into proximity with works of art, potentially encouraging the presence of insects and pests, as well as requiring a modicum of cooking facilities. The location of the room, therefore, has an inappropriate context.

Policy 74

To consider relocating the Staff Lounge, as the relationship to the galleries is not significant and its use is incompatible with public display.

Policy 75

To consider the use of the Seminar Room for other functions. A seminar room is appropriate for teaching near the galleries, but general meetings could be elsewhere. The Seminar Room and Staff Lounge could be relocated, and consideration could be given to their conversion to form an extension of the second-floor galleries.

Back-of-house

The back-of-house areas on the first floor and in the basement were treated by Kahn as utilitarian – a world of concrete, cinder block, and painted steelwork. However, the design was still carefully considered and executed to a high standard: joinery and doorsets are coordinated with cinder-block walls, and concrete details, sanitary fittings, lights, hardware, and signage remain of the same family and order as those used on the upper floors, thus ensuring a consistency and a hierarchy throughout the whole building. The complexity and precision of the installation of the building systems and equipment achieve a strong visual character in the mechanical rooms, which is supported by meticulous maintenance.

Basement service corridor

The white-oak millwork screens that form the security offices have been modified with the introduction of a louvered wooden screen.

The early Second Program plans show a much simpler layout of the service entrance area. The loading dock was initially planned to provide direct access into the building, through a clear sequence of spaces suitable for art handling; in turn, this allowed the security offices and guards' lounge to be placed along the south front. However, the planned location of the dock in relation to the movement of trucks proved unsatisfactory; the drawings were modified by October 1971, and the dock was moved one bay south to the corner of the building.

The route into the building thus turns inconveniently before the basement stair, and the guards' lounge occupies internal space previously destined as art transit storage and handling. As such, it provides a much lower standard of environment than that

The former wood shop was converted into the Paintings Conservation Studio in 2008.

originally envisaged. The "cage" enclosure was part of the fitting-out that followed the completion and is a detail found in several Yale buildings. An increase in staff has placed further pressure on the area, and caterers use the circulation space as a temporary set-up or staging area, hindering access, potentially affecting means of escape, and mixing entertainment support with an area also concerned with artworks.

The growth of the Center has resulted in the introduction of an additional conservation studio so that paintings, as well as works on paper, do not have to leave the building. To accommodate this, the wood shop was moved off-site, and its space was adapted for new use in 2008. Overall, the rear entrance area is the least satisfactorily resolved space in the building. It is clear that it is not ideal for shipping or receiving. When it is compared with that at the Kimbell, which is well considered in terms of security, receiving art, and the well-being of staff, this area of the Center falls far short.

The Control Room

Policy 76
To recognize that the back-of-house areas were carefully considered by Kahn and should be respected as such. However, the rear entrance and dock area are a prime area for improvement and can accept modification within the parameters set by Kahn.

Structure and building systems

Structure

Kahn described the structural system of the Center as "the bones of an elephant."[60] Architecture critic and author Carter Wiseman notes that, while Abba Tor, the structural engineer for the Center, recognized Kahn's own willingness to blur the line between "honest" expression of structure and theatrical effect, he admired the architect's fundamental desire to tell an architectural story in plain terms that laypeople could understand.[61] Working with Kahn and Tor, the firm of Van Zelm, Heywood & Shadford Inc. was responsible for the design of the mechanical and electrical systems and their integration with the building as required by the architect.

As Tor stated in his lecture at the Center in 2005:

This serene and modest looking building, with columns spaced on a 20-foot, or occasionally 40-foot grid, nothing to excite structurally, contains several well hidden structural innovations. Kahn had a unique talent to study, learn, and understand in depth the possibilities and constraints of the structural and mechanical systems, and integrate them in a most organic way with his architectural concepts. Like a great conductor, he could get the best results out of his orchestra.

Kahn, as in all his buildings, strove here to achieve full compatibility and maximum integration between the architectural requirements and the structural and mechanical systems, while avoiding any hung ceilings or other devices to hide air ducts, lighting systems, and other auxiliary elements.

This basic premise imposed several constraints on the structural and mechanical systems: e.g., the structural slabs had to be exposed and allow sufficient headroom as well as space for exposed ducts to be hung under the slab. This requirement eliminated the use of either a slab-and-beam system, or a waffle slab due to thickness limitations. A flat slab of minimum thickness had to be used.

60 Prown, *The Architecture of the Yale Center for British Art*, 19.
61 Wiseman, *Louis I. Kahn: Beyond Time and Style*, 246.

The fourth-floor galleries

Kahn felt that not only should the building reveal its making but also its history. With the building analogous to a living thing, the columns and beams are bones, the skeleton; electric wires are nerves; water pipes are blood circulation; the building breathes through air ducts that lead back to purifying lungs in the mechanical room where air is exchanged, humidified, and heated or cooled as needed. Kahn's convictions about structure, materials, history and the nature of a building at times led to small dilemmas. Once, when electricians had to run some wires from the basement to the first floor, the plans did not show the route so they snaked them through a convenient hollow rise where a column was subsequently poured. Convenient, but wrong. According to Kahn's principles, you do not run nerves through bones. On the other hand, the history of the building had to be revealed. What to do? A small but prominently located blank and functionless metal plate memorializes that history.

Prown, "Light and Truth"

The mechanical systems were to be concentrated in vertical "servant spaces," and fed off these spaces into ducts positioned under the structural slabs. The original solution called for two sets of air handling ducts, one for supply air and one for return air, to be placed directly under the structural flat slab. These were to be housed in two vertical shafts placed symmetrically north and south about the east-west centerline of the building. From these shafts the ducts would branch off horizontally at each level.

Early in the design a conflict developed between the required positioning of the return air ducts along the perimeter of the building and the architect's treatment of the fenestration. The ducts would be in the way, they couldn't be accommodated elsewhere, and therefore, they had to be eliminated. The structure itself, both horizontally and vertically, was the only system available to take over as a return air plenum!

The creation of the horizontal plenum was achieved at the second, third and fourth floors through the use of concrete "airfloor" flat slab, and at the roof through the use of large _/-shaped girders which performed three functions simultaneously. These precast girders supported the skylights and roof elements, housed the supply air ducts, and through the remaining voids acted as return air plenums; the inclination of the side slopes of these precast girders was chosen so as to bounce off most effectively the natural light to the paintings on the walls. The vertical return air plenums were created by using the free space between the walls of the shafts and the supply air ducts housed in these shafts.

The challenge of using structural floors as plenums required some unique design features. The airfloor used on the second, third and fourth floors had never been used as a structural load-bearing element before. Its primary use was as a slab on grade in assembly space, e.g. churches, where air circulation was required.

The construction sequence of the airfloor entailed three phases. A 4-inch-thick slab was poured first; this slab contained the major bottom reinforcement as well as the electrical conduits. Steel dowels were spaced on a 12-inch grid that projected about 8 inches above the slab. Four-inch-diameter light-gauge steel "cans" were placed over the dowels. 12 x 12-inch-square dome-shaped light-gauge steel forms were then placed and their ends "tucked" into the cans. These forms fit tightly and provide, together with the cans, a continuous surface.

Concrete was poured into the cans and over the dome-shaped forms, to a total thickness of 14 inches. The resulting flat slab contains a continuous air plenum, approximately seven inches high, interrupted only by the 4-inch-diameter stubs. The cost of producing this concrete plenum was higher than that of a conventional concrete slab, even if one considers the savings, i.e., cost of ducts and hung ceiling.

Not trusting the results of our calculations, which told us "not to worry," we made an unsuccessful attempt to load to destruction a 10ft x 10ft full-size airfloor section, supported by a column at its center. This floor sample carried the applied load, about 8ft high earth pile weighing about 900lbs per square foot, without any signs of distress.

The _/-shaped roof girders were precast in the plant, trucked to site and placed by crane on top of the 12 x 12 inch columns. Comparative studies showed that precasting would result in economy, as well as in greater accuracy and uniformity of finish. Four precast beams were placed on each interior column and were connected to each other by welding to embedded steel plates within adjacent beams, as well as by grouting a small pocket of concrete above the columns. These connections provided mutual lateral bracing for the beams and also allowed

Facing page:
The fourth floor under construction

The concrete frame of the building nearing completion in 1974, as seen from High Street

Policy 77
To respect the integration of the structural and mechanical systems in the building and their coordination by the architect.

Building systems

The mechanical room

The "Consultation Report and Conservation Environment Renovation Program," prepared in June 2002 by Garrison/Lull Inc., building systems engineers, found that the Center has shortcomings when considered in terms of providing the standard conservation environment anticipated in today's museum. These included: high levels of daylight arising from not only the skylights but also the windows and the openings from the galleries onto the courts; problems of glare associated with large windows in the galleries; and concerns that the concrete and cinder blocks were not sealed to control chemically active cement alkali particulates, that the use of fabric finishes to the walls and the carpet could hold particulates and be a major source of gaseous contamination, and that the oak millwork was too acidic. Several areas of the building that faced south were subject to solar gain that caused sudden humidity excursions and heat from the PAR38 lamps. Office equipment, such as photocopiers and laser printers that omit significant amounts of ozone, were in too close proximity to the collection, and food-stuffs posed a risk from vermin.

These problems were seen to indicate a collection environment that is inadequate to provide the most reasonable and practical protection and preservation of the collection. The firm recommended steps to protect the collection from building systems risks and to limit exposure to light in all collection areas. However, Garrison/Lull also recognized that an holistic approach had to be taken as other concerns affecting design decisions would need to be considered by the architect and structural engineer, and the building systems might need to be subordinated.

The Yale Center for British Art is a very special place, and it is not a standard museum. Elsewhere in this conservation plan is described how the works of art in the collection can be enhanced through their display within the setting that the building provides and how many of the environmental "issues" identified in the Garrison/Lull report contribute to their display in a positive way. Each of those concerns identified by the consultants has to be addressed, but a satisfactory response to many of the issues can be achieved through management or upgrading the services infrastructure within the mechanical room.

A real difficulty with the services is that, when they have to be replaced or modified, it is hard to find suitable cable and pipe routes that do not conflict with the significance of the building. Kahn had a very clear philosophy on their position and presence in the

[62] Tor, "The Structure of the Yale-Mellon Center for British Art and British Studies."

Second-floor galleries
showing air distribution ducts

building, and, as Kenneth J. Borst, Director of Buildings and Grounds when the Center was designed, noted: "Lou's buildings were very hard to build as there was no place to hide anything."[63]

HVAC installation

As he would not accept hung ceilings, Kahn had developed the idea in his design for the Yale University Art Gallery of incorporating the services distribution systems into the spaces of his tetrahedron vaults so that horizontal services could be linked to the core without intrusion into the galleries. Similarly at the Kimbell, he used "u"-shaped concrete channels between the vaults for horizontal distribution.

In both the First and Second programs for the Center, the clarity of the servicing of the building was also very important. In the First Program, utility services were distributed from risers that formed towers at each corner of the building, clearly marked by being clad in metal. In the Second, they are delivered through two rotated square ducts that rise through the building, again clad in metal, the material associated with the mechanical services in the Center. Like the structural columns that reduce in size as they rise through the building and loads decrease, the ducts decrease in size in response to the amount of services required.

Kahn and Tor struggled with the location of the utility conduits in relation to the structure. On the fourth floor air is distributed into the galleries by using the space between the sloping beams that carry the roof lights. On the lower stories, it enters through expressed stainless-steel ducts running through the spaces at a high level. On each floor the air returns through baseboard slots in the woodwork and filters back to the mechanical towers through the "air floor" slab. Through this, the mechanical systems became part of the aesthetic experience, and the mechanical installation was integrated with the architectural concept. Indeed, the exposed air ducts became pieces of sculpture in themselves; Prown recalls that when the exposed air-handling ducts were installed, workers had to wear white gloves to avoid fingerprints on the exposed stainless-steel surface.[64]

The HVAC systems are the main determinants for actively maintaining a proper conservation environment within the building. The collection should be protected from humidity extremes, high temperatures, high light levels, harmful contamination from particulates, and threats posed by fire and building systems. These issues also apply to use of the museum as a loan venue. The stated goal was 70°F and 50% RH. Garrison/Lull reported that the present fluctuations in environmental conditions, often arising from solar gain, need to be reduced.[65]

In addition, the changing pattern of use of the Center, with the growth in staffing levels, is placing pressure on the air-conditioning as spaces such as the original fellows' offices on the third floor can now be occupied by two or three members of staff rather than one. Services are thus perceived to be inadequate, but this is also primarily a question of outdated controls and balancing.

Garrison/Lull recommended that the pneumatic controls should be replaced with a modern direct-digital control system to provide a more timely response to the fluctuations in the environment,[66] and that the HVAC systems should be upgraded. In certain

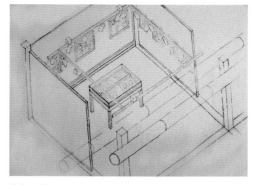

Kahn office drawing detailing the building systems in relation to the exhibition bay on the second or third floor, Louis I. Kahn Collection, University of Pennsylvania

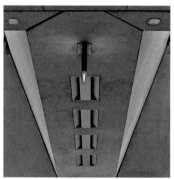

Top: Air distribution duct at the partition-wall penetration
Bottom: Air distribution through a skylight duct at the fourth-floor level

Air shaft at the fourth-floor level

[63] Wiseman, *Louis I. Kahn: Beyond Time and Style*, 260.

[64] Jules D. Prown, remark to Peter Inskip, late 2006.

[65] Garrison/Lull Inc., "Consultation Report and Conservation Environment Renovation Program for the Yale Center for British Art" (June 16, 2002), 29.

[66] Garrison/Lull Inc., "Consultation Report and Conservation Environment Renovation Program for the Yale Center for British Art" (June 16, 2002), 29.

areas the positioning of thermostats is poor, and this has resulted in makeshift arrangements such as in the Rare Books Reading Room, where lights have to be turned on in summer to generate heat in order to activate thermostats and bring in the cooling in the double-height volume. The work would include the replacement of the humidification systems, the removal of the remaining VAV boxes, and the installation of new room sensors. None of this equipment is significant in itself, and it can be replaced. However, the introduction of mounts behind sensors, the siting and choice of new fittings and cable routes, the replacement of cables and fittings, and the choice of equipment would all have to be done with the greatest care and following Kahn's philosophy if such changes are not to erode the significance of the building. In addition, the quality and neatness of the mechanical rooms and service spaces need to be maintained.

Policy 78
The air-distribution system is a significant part of the building.

Electrical Installation
Electrical socket outlets were carefully located in relation to the bays of the building. Alterations to incorporate additional power outlets required in connection with changing patterns of use or display have attempted laudably to conceal cables but have not been so rigorous in the location of outlets in relation to the building fabric.

The discreet introduction of audio cabling in the Lecture Hall, where any route is denied by the concrete box, has been attempted as carefully as possible, but the surface-mounted conduit clearly exemplifies the difficulties of working in the building.

Lighting
The lighting installation is largely that which was original to the building and devised with Richard Kelly, with whom Kahn had worked at the Kimbell and on other projects.

The installation throughout the building was primarily based on the use of a standard track suspended from the concrete ceilings. To this were fixed downlighter cans developed with Edison Price. All lamps were incandescent except in a few service areas.

The original display lighting is demonstrated in the second-floor galleries where Kahn and Kelly used diagonally cut radiused cans fitted with incandescent PAR38 lamps. These provided a wash of light over the walls that was intentionally not necessarily uniform and reduced towards the ceiling. The pictures appeared well lit against a background that had shadow and variation. This balanced the electric light with the large amount of daylight available in the galleries and supported the program to show the pictures in a small-scale domestic setting. Square-cut cans were used in circulation areas and would have been used if any specific picture was to be spot-lit. Many of the original cans survive. Kahn and Kelly were both interested in the shape of the light fittings. The form of the original fittings was, therefore, not generated just by the lamps and reflectors but by the desire for simplicity. They are now generally fitted with tungsten halogen lamps.

The original track is still recognized as very good and at the Center provides an excellent infrastructure. It is large in scale since it needed to span a considerable distance

The skylights over the Entrance Court (top) before the removal of downlighters in 2002 (bottom)

Top: Original fourth-floor lighting track set within the skylights
Bottom: Overscaled projectors suspended in the Library Court, photographed in 2007

The first-floor foyer articulated by the arrangement of downlighters

with a minimum of fixing points to the concrete. Transformers for the present cans are housed within the head of the fittings rather than on the track. Over the years spot-lighting of some pictures has been introduced, and other types of projectors have been added to highlight specific works or sculptures as the need arose. However, the predominance of one type of downlighter can has been always apparent, and some projectors, such as the supplementary lights added in the Library Court at a later date, appear discordant as their form is too complex. The size of the cans used in the galleries was quite large, but they provide an important transition to the scale of the air ducts in the lower galleries and act visually as an intermediary item between track and duct.[67]

In several areas these are used to decorative effect with clusters of cans marking the entrance to the museum foyer or carefully grouped beneath the skylights to emphasize the corners of the two courts. Elsewhere lighting is used decoratively, such as with the rows of downlighter cans set between the cross beams over the portico or the attached "festive lights" on the walls of the Entrance Court.[68] The latter, supplied by Edison Price, were chosen by Kelly in February 1974 but were not liked by Kahn.[69]

Today, changing requirements and the way that exhibitions combine different media mean that some flexibility is necessary, especially if the presentation of works on paper is to be balanced with adjacent paintings. At the Center works on paper have been generally lit with wall washers, while spot lighting has been introduced on oil paintings.

Policy 79

To ensure that electric lighting of the galleries serves to supplement daylight and incorporates a similar spectrum of light. The quality of illumination of the works of art should be to a high standard, at the same time accepting that illumination will vary depending on daylight conditions. A color temperature range of 2700–2800K should reflect the incandescent light that was seen by Kahn and Prown to complement daylight and be sympathetic to the materials in the Center.

Policy 80

To maintain a flexible lighting system appropriate to the variety of objects on view. Wall washers might be supplemented with small accent lights as long as standard cans remain dominant throughout the galleries. The track should remain clean and uncluttered.

Policy 81

The size, shape, scale, and detailing of the original track fittings used by Kahn make an important visual transition from the ceilings, skylights, and ducts to the display surfaces and should be respected. Original fixture forms should remain dominant as improved lighting technologies are integrated into the building.

Policy 82

Kahn's grouping of the fixtures is an important design element in emphasizing the relationship between spaces and should be maintained.

Lighting trials in 2007 experimented with replacing the original downlighters (left) with smaller fittings (right) using the same track. However, it was found that the smaller fittings no longer acted architecturally as a mediator between the track and the large-scale air ducts.

[67] Mellon Job Meeting, November 21, 1972:
    1. Dr. Prown thinks the library reading room is the main lighting problem and the exhibition court and library stack. Lou still likes the idea of lights hanging from long rods over tables.
    2. Lou likes the aluminum painted cans at Kimbell. Prown is not convinced though. Track lighting is OK for offices. Lights OK: galleries, elevator lobby, storage rooms, offices, stack lighting. Shadford doesn't need finishes for lights to go on.
    3. Prown says he cannot be assured on skylight design as it stands now. Needs verification from Kelly.
Louis I. Kahn Collection, University of Pennsylvania and Pennsylvania Historical and Museum Commission.

[68] Kahn, "Festive light strip added . . . ," February 28, 1974, Louis I. Kahn Collection, A22a, University of Pennsylvania and Pennsylvania Historical and Museum Commission.

[69] Prown recollection to Peter Inskip, 2005. Edison Price construction drawings MAC-1 and -2, Festive Lights Details, February 16, 1977. Louis I. Kahn Collection, University of Pennsylvania and Pennsylvania Historical and Museum Commission.

Policy 83

To strive for lighting systems that provide flexibility to respond to changing exhibition requirements with minimal lamp types, ease of handling and maintenance, and no ultraviolet light emissions.

Policy 84

To minimize the energy use and carbon footprint of the building's lighting systems by maximizing the use of daylight and selecting the most efficient electric light sources that maintain the quality of light provided by the original lighting system.

Stand pipe

Example of BKM office furniture in Tan Value 4 color

Stand pipes, etc.

Kahn resented the safety code requirements to include light switches, thermostats, and electrical outlets on his pristine walls. He derisively referred to the scattered hardware as "fraternity pins."[70] To meet the code, he artfully grouped them all on the vertical steel panels, where they would not interrupt the surfaces devoted to art but made a composition of their own.[71] Thus, stand pipes, fire extinguishers, alarm call boxes, and telephones were brought together into carefully considered assemblies throughout the building and relate to the vertical air shafts on which they are positioned. Minor modification of these over the years has resulted in additional equipment being placed adjacent, and their lack of integration is discordant.

Similarly, the fire shutters in the openings overlooking the Entrance and Library courts were Kahn's solution to avoid the installation of wired fire glazing required by the fire marshal. They are, however, simply mounted in a wooden shutter box at the top of each opening. Should management of the building allow the fire code to be met in a way that did not require the shutters, there would be no objection to removing them and recovering Kahn's original design intention.

Furniture and finishings

Kahn recommended Benjamin Baldwin to furnish the building, as the two had collaborated successfully on the Kimbell Art Museum and the library at Exeter. Although the furnishing of the building was not addressed until after Kahn's death, Meyers was confident that Baldwin was sympathetic to Kahn's vision. The use of upholstered two-seater couches supported the domestic appearance that Kahn had provided in response to the brief, and the Windsor chairs in the libraries and meeting rooms are to be found at Exeter and other buildings by the architect. Office furniture was selected from BKM and supplied in Tan Value 4 color. The restriction of the furniture to a few types that were applied consistently throughout the building was successful, as it was parallel to Kahn's approach to light fixtures, signage, restroom fittings, and other details.

The approach to furnishing the Entrance Court, however, suggests that the Center was made more comfortable under Pellechia and Meyers than might have been the case if Kahn had been alive. There the hard, sculptural benches, illustrated by Kahn in his sketches, were replaced in Baldwin's design by individual upholstered sofas arranged as a semicircle, set on either side of the lead statue of William III. It was a change that did

Top: Call boxes, alarms, and other such items were carefully located by Kahn on a stainless-steel panel set flush with the millwork. Later additions of a telephone and fire extinguisher have not respected the original logic and have been located on the return wall.
Bottom: A fire extinguisher is inappropriately fixed to the primary structure.

[70] Quoted by Marshall Meyers in Latour, *Louis I. Kahn, l'uomo, il maestro*, 83.

[71] Wiseman, *Louis I. Kahn: Beyond Time and Style*, 248.

The Oriental rug in the Library Court was purchased on Benjamin Baldwin's advice as part of the original furnishings in 1975.

Push bar

not respond so clearly to the architect's original vision of the Entrance Court as an external space open to the sky.

The large Oriental rug in the Library Court was also chosen by Baldwin from a firm in New York, and it forms part of the original furnishing of the building. Its presence contributes to the domestic effect and to the acoustics of the space for musical performances. It is thought to be from Sultanabad, as testified by the 1975 invoice. The conservation report of 2006 states that it is a Mahal carpet, possibly from the Arak area of Iran, dating from the twentieth century. As the rug is part of the first furnishing, it contributes to the significance of the Library Court. However, the handling of floor finishes and materials in the rest of the building was carefully used by Kahn to reinforce the way one moves through the building, and the choice of the rug seems discordant because its rectangular shape is at odds with the square plan of the space in which it sits. The choice of an Oriental carpet is also in contrast to the rigorous application of unpatterned natural materials in the rest of the building. The rug was temporarily removed, and a natural, cream colored carpet was laid for a while, but it was felt to be bland.

The majority of Baldwin's furnishings remains in place or survives as seating in staff areas (as was the case with the circular seating when it was removed from the Entrance Court). However, changing attitudes toward ergonomics have led to more suitable office seating, and wear and tear means that items such as the Lecture Hall seating are due for attention. Some visitors find the couches in the galleries too low for comfortable use.

Because the survival of Baldwin's scheme is significant, furniture should be refurbished when possible. Where new furniture is necessary, it should be supplementary rather than a replacement so that the ethos of Baldwin's design is retained. Any supplementary items should again be restricted to a limited range that can be applied consistently rather than as a matter of personal choice.

Hardware

The hardware was generally supplied by the Elmer T. Hebert Corporation of New Canaan, CT. Certain individual items, such as push-plates, however, appear to have been purpose-designed for the building by Pellechia and Meyers. As with the lighting, the hardware was applied consistently throughout the building, giving equal attention to the back-of-house areas.

Signage

The signage was developed under Pellechia and Meyers, advised by Alvin Eisenman, Chairman of Graphic Design at the Yale School of Art, who recommended Gill Sans Bold typeface as well as the choice of colors. The external lettering on the concrete screen walls are stainless-steel cut-outs, whereas the name of the institution within the portico and on the dedication wall just inside the entrance are both etched into the stainless-steel walls and reflect the quasi-extended nature of these spaces. To maintain a harmonious frontage, signage for the shops was restricted to inside each unit. For the interior of the Center, Pellechia and Meyers drew up the lettering following Eisenman's guidelines for typeface and color. Throughout the building signage is mounted directly on the doors. In front-of-house areas where the doors are in natural oak, it is silkscreened in rose lettering on metal

Facing page:
The steel-clad air shaft passing through the Prints and Drawings Department integrates both a sink for washing hands and alarm points.

Following the advice of Alvin Eisenman, the room signage developed by Pellechia and Meyers uses Gill Sans Bold as its typeface.

Steel lettering mounted on the screen wall
at the entrance to the parking lot

plates. In back-of-house areas where doors are painted metal, the signage is applied directly on the painted surface in white lettering. Glazed screens occur at the entrances to the Library and the Study Room, where the rose lettering (Martin Senour 22R127 Rose) is applied to the glass. In 1998 signage was extended to office doors.

Drawings show that the signage in the elevators dates from the original construction, with a stainless-steel panel engraved with directions for the fire department as well as indication of the floor levels and the activities on each floor. Additional signage in the elevators was introduced in 2001 and replaced in 2003.

Labeling of exhibits is currently on cards adjacent to the works of art. The typeface used for labeling within the fourth-floor galleries is Requiem, a serif typeface designed by Jonathan Hoefler in 1992. For the special exhibits, labels and fonts vary.

Treatment of intrusive items

A number of items have been identified as intrusive in the Assessment of Cultural Significance.

Policy 85
Items identified as intrusive in this Conservation Plan should be removed. Prioritization and a time-based program for the removal or modification of intrusive items should be established and incorporated into any program of work. However, some intrusive items are tolerable if only present for particular events or exhibitions.

General principles

The following principles of conservation should be observed when dealing with the maintenance, repair, or alteration of the Center:
1. Retention of much of the original fabric and its continuing repair is a principle of conservation/preservation.
2. To retain the original fabric in situ where possible.
3. To ensure that conservation is proactive rather than reactive and founded on the "little and often" principle to prolong the life of the material by repairing defects as they appear.
4. Replacement is the last resort, as there is much repair work that can be undertaken before replacement should be entertained. The repair should also be determined by an analysis campaign that leads to a program based upon significance, priority, health and safety, and extent of damage.
5. To ensure that all conservation work is safe, environmentally sound, and sustainable as far as practicable.

Repairs and maintenance
Intelligent and prompt cyclical maintenance and repair are the single most important actions of the conservation program. The Center should be cared for by a planned and detailed maintenance and repair program (Maintenance Plan) based upon a complete

Facing page:
Pages from the catalogs of
the furniture manufacturers
recommended by Baldwin

CB10

S2 2016 60"W

2042-N STRAIGHT LINE SOFA

WARD BENNETT DESIGNS FOR BRICKEL ASSOCIATES, INC., 515 MADISON AVENUE, NEW YORK 10022, 212 MU 9-0233.

CB12

designer:
Don Chadwick

Chadwick Modular Seating

herman miller

212 N

240 N

180-N

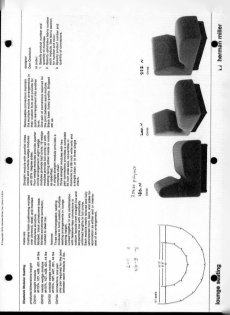

lounge seating

T4_T10_T16_T21_T24

1971 Phillips Oak living table
84x30x29½ H finish net buff

MAJESTIC FURNITURE CO.
19 Wareham St.

350.- N. 84x30 x 29½ H

STEELCASE TD

26" high typing returns.

Top sizes: 19½" d x 30", 37½" or 45" w.

15.

16.

17.

18.

19.

501.12 N

D   STEELCASE 5200 SERIES

Double pedestal desks.

Top sizes: 60" x 30" or 60" x 30"

1.

2.

3.

4.

336.25 N

S1 N

2234T ROLLED ARM TUFTED SOFA

W 84" D 33" H 25" SH 16"
Hand tufted; padded foam
and Dacron on coil springs.
Base: recessed round wood legs.
Upholstery: fabric 12½ yds.,
leather 225 sq. ft.

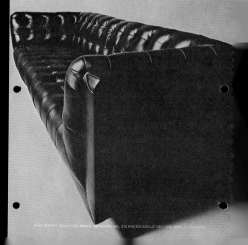

WARD BENNETT DESIGNS FOR BRICKEL ASSOCIATES, INC., 515 MADISON AVENUE, NEW YORK 10022, 212 MU 9-0233.

knowledge of the building and its materials and physical plant, regular inspection, and prompt preventative maintenance and repair. Any large establishment needs to guard against slippage in standards of housekeeping and maintenance. The existing management regime is to be complimented, as it is apparent that much of the knowledge and resources are in place. Additional pressure is exerted as the building itself is an international landmark for visiting architects, scholars, and tourists alike as well as for its famous collection. However, it is the aggregation of minor expediencies that detracts from the presentation of the place, and public areas are degraded as a result. A continuing vigilant regime of maintenance is vital.

Damage is occurring to the building, and thus a damage limitation strategy is necessary to respond to known threats, such as graffiti, chloride attack, and mechanical damage. Many of the original interior finishes are deteriorating or need repairing or refinishing. A strike of graffiti on the steel panels is more prominent and aesthetically disfiguring to the quality and presentation of the building compared to the slight, gradual, and collective damage that occurs to concrete, travertine, and oak that is less noticeable and less likely to be addressed.

Analysis of the forces acting on the building materials has led to the establishment of conservation-based trials, or "Trialing Protocols," prepared in collaboration with American conservator Michael Morris, from The Metropolitan Museum of Art, and leading British conservator Trevor Proudfoot of Cliveden Conservation Workshop, with the support of Center conservators Mark Aronson and Theresa Fairbanks-Harris. This is one of the first steps in the overall objective of developing safe cleaning methods for the various building materials and surfaces, together with "first-aid" treatments that are generally necessary as a result of defacement or deterioration. These methods and treatments will be compiled into the Maintenance Plan. Such an approach also entails appropriate maintenance operations, frequency, program, and costs.

Policy 86
To develop and adhere to a detailed and planned maintenance strategy or Maintenance Plan.

Policy 87
To develop and implement a comprehensive trial strategy, or "Trialing Protocol," of the decay mechanisms affecting the steel, concrete, travertine, oak, and glass surfaces in order to mitigate further damage and to inform the Maintenance Plan. The consequences of remedial treatments necessary to retard the degeneration of the steel, concrete, travertine, oak, and glass surfaces should be well understood and fully tested before use.

Policy 88
To carry out any remedial work on steel, concrete, travertine, oak, and glass surfaces in such a way that visual continuity with the original surface is retained; any joint between old and new work designed to achieve this should be executed with precision. As well as affording protection, treatments should match the color and texture of the original adjacent material.

Policy 89

To carry out photographic documentation of the external concrete and steel on an annual basis outlined in a Maintenance Plan for the first five years. In addition, areas known to be "at risk" should be documented before and after the winter de-icing regime to help determine the rate of decay. This would, in turn, inform any testing for remedial action (present and future) as outlined in Policy 87.

Advice

The Conservation Plan and a supporting Maintenance Plan are documents to guide the future care and development of the Center, but such documents will not be effective unless they are interpreted and implemented by persons with the relevant conservation-based expertise.

Where technical advice is needed and where work is required to be carried out, it is important to select consultants and contractors with proven expertise and experience in the relevant fields.

A low and apparently satisfactory bid often results in the degradation of the character and quality of the fabric and often proves expensive to rectify.

Continuity of relevant and experienced conservation advice should be provided to ensure that all work on the Center is compatible with its cultural significance.

Policy 90

To designate a senior administrator who will be responsible for overseeing the conservation program of the Center.

Policy 91

To make decisions and carry out any works or alterations in light of professional advice from architects experienced in the conservation of buildings and from experienced contractors.

Policy 92

To employ only persons qualified and experienced in treating the relevant material (concrete, stainless steel, glass, oak millwork, travertine, brickwork, etc.). Supervision should be consistent.

Policy 93

To formulate consistent cleaning, repair, and maintenance standards with the stakeholders (the Center, City of New Haven, University Properties, and business owners) and coordinate a parallel maintenance program with the stakeholders.

External steel curtain walling

The stainless-steel panels are of exceptional significance since they make a major contribution to the visual character and quality of the place. The Center's boundaries, spaces, and volumes are signified by the use of this type of steel curtain walling punctuated by flush steel "opaque windows." Its steel panels are flush with the fenestration and the front of the concrete frame, whereas the storefronts align with the back of the concrete columns, establishing a commercial zone distinct from the Center. Kahn's standard modular steel panel, 3 foot 5 inch x 9 foot, was designed around the 12-foot module of floor-to-floor height and the 20-foot-wide structural grid for the first, second, and third floors, which was determined by dividing the bay width by two and the floor height by three. Although the fourth floor is 14 feet high, the same panel size is used, and the residual vertical dimension forms another panel type. The typology is a direct result of the fenestration pattern determined by the design of the interior spaces. There are 379 standard panels out of a total of 882. There are 33 panel types ranging in size from 1 foot x 4 foot to 16 foot x 9 foot.

Allegheny Steel Corporation (now owned by Allegheny Ludlum) provided the raw stainless-steel-sheet material. Trio Industries of Ohio was one of the two competitive fabricators selected by Kahn to produce the panels. On October 12, 1972, Kahn selected sample #2.

In December he met Trio Industries and Allegheny Steel Corporation representatives who provided samples showing the diversity of finishes to the stainless steel. Kahn accepted the diversity of finish on the samples supplied to Macomber as the goal to match, and he later visited the factory in March 1973. Sample panels were placed as a mock-up, together with a window frame, and the cost for the mock-up was in the region of $5,400. Kahn chose a dark non-reflective, mill-finish, annealed, 12-gauge, grade 304 stainless steel, a basic chromium-nickel-iron austenitic stainless steel. Jules Prown recalls Kahn invariably referred to the material as "lead" or "pewter," and when a sample came from the manufacturer, he would reject it if any reflection showed.

The designed panel system for the exterior is a 2-inch double-pan construction infilled with non-combustible, rigid foam thermal insulation and reinforced with transverse stiffeners. The outer pan is the "pewter" steel; the inner pan is galvanized steel bonded to ¾-inch treated plywood. On the outer stainless-steel pan the rolling lines run horizontally, while on the inner 12-gauge galvanized-steel pan, the lines run vertically. The change from sheet material to a bent pan (with tight, rounded corners) results in a smooth margin to the panel edges, demonstrating the workmanship on the finished article. The inner pan is fixed to a marine-grade plywood base; the two pans are abutted and secured to the structural steel and concrete frames. Each bottom panel is formed with a drip, and each top panel is canted to discharge water down the face of the panel and away from the concrete frame. The outermost edges of the steel panels are kept away from the concrete frame, but flush, forming a shadow gap of 1½ inches to the concrete frame and the steel sill. Generally, all abutments between the steel panels, windows, and concrete are ⅜-inch wide and sealed with a sealant.

Facing page:
Steel panels cladding the lowest
story of the south elevation

Kahn's projecting sills or drip pans at each floor level were modified by Wiss, Janney, Elstner Associates, Inc. (WJE) in 1998 with the introduction of stainless-steel pins to hold back the ice and allow it to melt.[72]

Policy 94

To protect, conserve, and maintain Kahn's unique steel-and-glass curtain walling to best practice, avoiding replacement except in extraordinary circumstances.

Policy 95

To permit relocation of the curtain walling based upon Kahn's design philosophy that the glazing should respond to the internal use.

Stainless steel, the material

The stainless steel produced for the cladding appears to be unique to the Center. Former Associate Director David Mills discovered a small stainless-steel sample, which may well be an original approved sample. In November 2008, three large sheets measuring 12 feet by 3 feet were discovered by the Center's former Operations Manager George Conte in the basement tunnel and do match the originals on the building.

Stainless steel is defined by its chrome content, the minimum being 11 percent. Nickel is added for softening and malleability for the annealing process, and unique to Allegheny Ludlum is the substitution of manganese for nickel. The finishing mill attains a uniform thickness. The hot-rolling process gives the steel its apparent "black" color, although one suspects this is probably what Kahn described as pewter or lead, and is also characterized by the visible rolling lines that give the steel its texture. The pickling process produces a stable, protective chromium-nickel (manganese) film on the stainless steel for corrosion resistance.

Constance Clement, Deputy Director at the Center, has been instrumental in gathering relevant archives from the known two original companies and her work with Steve Wolff, metallurgist at Allegheny Ludlum, in late 2006 has resulted in an improved understanding of the probable manufacturing process. Wolff hypothesizes the following process:

1. Hot rolling of "slabs" to "hot bands" or "black bands"
2. Annealing and pickling of the hot-rolled band
3. Cold rolling to a thickness slightly heavier than the current panel thickness
4. Annealing and pickling of the cold-rolled coil
5. Leveling and cutting to length
6. Etching in an agitated acid bath to develop the surface roughness or an alternative method of placing hoses discharging the acid onto a horizontal sheet
7. Forming of the sheet into a panel
8. Low-temperature furnace exposure, probably with a reducing atmosphere to develop a tenacious oxide[73]

The manufacture of new matching replacement steel is a complex engineering issue. The steel appears to have been particular to the Center project, but current lack of knowledge of the original process of manufacture is serious since it means that the steel

Facing page:
Steel panels form Kahn's "opaque windows" on the Chapel Street elevation

[72] Wiss, Janney, Elstner Associates, Inc., "Sealant Replacement at Exterior Cladding," WJE #972866, April 6, 1998, Yale Center for British Art Archives, Yale Project No. 9709233-01.

[73] Steve Wolff, Notes, May 11, 2007, Yale Center for British Art Archives.

cannot be replicated. However, it has been suggested by Wolff that "reverse engineering" is a possibility, and this should recover the methodology. Any replacement panels would be very expensive, as the basic sheet material is dependent on factory-based processes which anticipate large-scale runs. With both maintenance and alterations proposed, it is certain that new panels will be required. It is likely that this would only be economically feasible if a reasonable quantity could be ordered at one time; that would mean a stock held for future use, in much the same way as the Belgian linen was procured in 1998 and stored in Beacon Falls, CT, for the interior walls and pogos.

The Center's stainless-steel panels have been damaged both chemically and mechanically. At street level on High Street and on the parking lot side, the steel panels are subject to graffiti attacks, as they are more easily accessible. The panels on all levels have been subjected to mechanical damage caused by humans and machines in maintenance and repair projects and by vehicle impact.

Chemical damage is caused by environmental processes interacting with the building materials themselves. The surface of the stainless steel is considered fragile by Wolff and other metallurgists. The steel is susceptible to mechanical and chloride abrasion because of the original manufacturing process and the marine environment of the City of New Haven in which it is sited. Damage has occurred, and there is reason to doubt that it can ever be fully prevented.

The opinion of the architects, conservators, and the metallurgist involved with the Center is that the chloride- and graffiti-damaged panels on the elevations can be retained, cleaned, and repaired to a good standard without causing damage to the original fabric.

The question of when and/or why to replace a stainless-steel panel is both a practical and philosophical issue and relates to maintenance and alteration:

a) **Maintenance**

Replacement panels will probably be needed in the future in the event of severe damage where:

1. Repair and retention is not a feasible option because the damage is so severe.
2. Management is of the opinion that it is visually intrusive.
3. Such damage allows significant water penetration into the building.
4. It compromises the security profile of the building.
5. It places the building and its contents at other risk.

b) **Alteration**

In Kahn's design philosophy the arrangement of glass-and-steel curtain walling is articulated by the functions within the Center. For example, if the use of a space changes from an office to a public gallery, the curtain wall on the outside of the building should also be modified to reflect the interior use.

Policy 96
To consider replacement of steel panels subject to proper research and development, testing and samples, and available human and financial resources. The feasibility of "reverse engineering" should be examined.

Facing page:
Concrete, shadow gap,
and steel panels

To ensure that any logistical or technical problems associated with the provision of new replacement steel panels for the elevations are resolved well in advance of requirement. Any order should include adequate stock for future replacement.

Cleaning

There is currently no maintenance or cleaning regime of the external steelwork. The panels have accumulated more than thirty-five years of urban dirt and grime, various human and machine marks, and abrasions that have resulted in the loss of "surface." When designing in stainless steel, it is often preferable to have the grain of unidirectional finish running vertically, since this improves self-cleaning and reduces dirt entrapment, particularly where coarser finishes are used. As previously described, however, the "grain" of the Center's stainless-steel panels was specifically chosen by Kahn to be horizontal. In addition, the effects of rainwater runoff into the horizontal surfaces between panels that may harbor dirt and water are potentially destructive. Grooves, recesses, and complex contours can hamper manual cleaning and lead to rust in concealed areas, which is, again, potentially destructive in the long term. Capillary action around these grooves, as well as at defective sealants and at other gaps, may permit such rust to continue unabated and undetected. In 2006 Wolff stated that cleaning of the steel is beneficial and is recommended as good practice by both the American Stainless Steel Association and its British counterpart. Cleaning should be an established precursor to repair and surface treatments and part of a regular maintenance regime.

If carried out, proposals to clean the steel panels in mid-2001 would have had disastrous results because the methods and coatings proposed were totally inappropriate, involving the use of acids. Fortunately, this was not carried out, but it does highlight the need for appropriate methods and contractors as well as peer review.

Policy 98
To give consideration to the cleaning of the external stainless-steel panels on a regular basis as part of the Maintenance Plan, subject to the trialing protocols.

Chemical damage

Chemical damage may have three causes. Except in the Lower Court, rust staining, also known as "orange bloom," is visible on the first-floor steel curtain walling. It may be due to the inherent inclusion of iron and carbon in the stainless steel or a result of chloride attack or both. In the winter de-icing salt (or chloride) mixed with sand is laid for the safety of pedestrians, which in turn produces a corrosive environment in which grade 304 stainless steel is known to corrode. Recollections by various staff indicate that the snowplow directs the spreading of the mixture onto the elevations rather than toward the parking lot or High Street. The stainless-steel doors to the commercial shops also exhibit similar patterns of rust staining, supporting evidence that it is chloride attack.

The simplest method for long-term protection is probably direct negotiation about snow removal with the contractor and University Properties. It would probably be best

Rusting stainless steel, photographed in 2006

Steel panels above the sidewalk
on the south elevation

to discuss this with the City of New Haven and contractor on an annual basis prior to the winter. The de-icing mixture needs to be kept away from the steelwork (and the concrete columns) to reduce and limit corrosion. It should not be sprayed toward or at the building. Snow should be removed from the sidewalk toward the road rather than at the building.

It is known that rust can be safely removed and that an application of a protective coating can retard future corrosion, subject to testing, and the coating may also act as a graffiti barrier. The application of a protective coating to steelwork should be tested as part of the trialing protocol described above.

Policy 99
To develop a maintenance strategy in order to limit damage to the steel panels by chlorides and rust.

Bimetallic corrosion
Bimetallic corrosion in the construction may be evident, as galvanized steel is also used in the construction of the stainless-steel panels. The parallel use of stainless steel and galvanized metal in the construction described above gave Wolff some concern, and this may be borne out by the rust staining visible on the concrete frame, particularly on the west elevation. David Mills reported that much rusting of the structural steel and bolts was found during the window replacement campaign in 1995–96, and all the newly exposed steelwork was wire brushed and treated with an epoxy-based paint system. Further investigations, first through the working drawings, historic photographs, and other documentation, are necessary, but these may eventually lead to some opening up from the interior to examine the extent of corrosion. The sills are stainless steel, but the anchors on the back are galvanized steel. The underside of the sills at street level and to the storefronts did not show deposits that cause concern.

Policy 100
To develop a "trial" study by opening up some internal walls to establish the extent of corrosion between steel types as well as sources of water penetration through the steel-and-glass curtain walling.

Mechanical damage
Mechanical damage from several causes has occurred to all elevations. The most significant is described below relating to the removal of graffiti. Above the first floor, marks visible on the panels of all elevations probably arose when hydraulic platforms were used to clean windows annually or during the Year of the Window in 1995–96. Joe Branco, a former member of the Center's operations staff, reported in June 2006 that the contractors dropped silicone caulking on the steel panels when installing the replacement windows and subsequently cleaned them abrasively. These abrasions are bluish in color and would have destroyed the film and surface. There are also scratches in the panels at higher levels. Mechanical impact damage has occurred to panels and sills on the first floor of the south elevation and is likely to have been caused by snowplows clearing the

Stainless steel suffering from chloride attack as a result of snow clearance on the High Street facade, photographed in 2007

pavement in winter. Such risks cannot be eliminated, because human error cannot be removed from the equation.

There are more bluish marks on the panels around the building, particularly above the second floor, and although their origins and natures vary, they are not considered problematic. All water-related runoff down the steel panels creates a bluish streak, including the panels below windows. A weathering pattern occurs along the base of the lowest panel above the sills, which is probably due to rainwater splashing back, also bluish in color. Below the exposed concrete beams similar bluish marks are visible. This is probably attributable to the presence of free-lime (calcium hydroxide, CaOH) in the concrete, which is caustic, as it combines with water and then runs down the face of the panels. Although access has not been possible to the face of the glazing, on balance the free-lime is probably not damaging the steel.

Along the top panels of the fourth floor is a white tide mark on all elevations that may be a runoff from the terne-coated stainless-steel mansard roof covering that was renewed in 1998. This needs to be checked with a metallurgist.[74]

There is significant damage on two panels on the east corner of the south elevation where there is now reflection. The edges of the adjacent panels were also adversely cleaned by inappropriate materials and contractors. This type of damage cannot be reversed because the original surface and oxide have been fully removed. Although a new oxide layer has probably reformed, it is much thinner, does not match the original, and is reflective. There is, however, a remedial and reversible aesthetic solution known as "re-patination" or "in-painting." The panel surface could be treated with a coating that is dull and matte and matches the adjacent original panels as closely as practicable, and the same protective treatment could be carried out on other steel panels.

Policy 101
To consider re-patinating the severely damaged exterior steel panels to regain their matte appearance.

Graffiti
Evidence of graffiti survives on High Street, the Entrance Portico, and the parking lot. Recent attacks have led to the establishment of trials based on conservation principles for the removal of graffiti. It is essential that graffiti be removed as quickly and safely as possible without causing damage to the original fabric. As the High Street elevation faces east and the parking lot south, solar gain in the panels probably increases the adhesion power of the graffiti medium and seems to embed it into the texture of the steel. The temperature of the panels significantly affects the urgency for its removal.

In 2006 Joe Branco reported to Constance Clement that a local contractor advised the use of a lacquer thinner in the mid-1990s to remove graffiti. At that time it was probably not known how such a treatment would affect the steel. It resulted, however, in the drastic loss of the original chromium-nickel film and surface (rolling lines) through mechanical abrasion, thus making the panel reflective, contrary to Kahn's design intentions. In time, it is possible that signs of corrosion will appear.

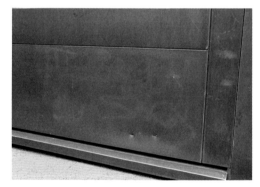

Graffiti and impact damage to steel panels above the sidewalk, photographed in 2006

[74] Policy 98 is also appropriate: To give consideration to the cleaning of the external stainless-steel panels on a regular basis as part of the Maintenance Plan, subject to the trialing protocols.

There is a residue of red paint on a concrete column on Chapel Street; paint was evidently reduced in appearance by using a lacquer thinner, probably in the mid-1990s. The concrete of the adjacent parapet also has a ghost of graffiti that may be contemporary with the paint on the column. Graffiti on steel and concrete can be removed safely, but it is a matter of testing for the correct products, techniques, skills, and timing.[75]

The Center is vulnerable to these attacks on High Street and the parking lot, and there has been limited security-camera surveillance until recently. The simplest, most effective method may be to establish such surveillance as a community initiative with the neighboring businesses. The light poles could double-up as camera locations. New cameras have been placed recently at the High Street end of the building, on the Yale Repertory Theatre, and at 149 York.

Policy 102
To develop a strategy for monitoring the vulnerable areas in association with the Center's neighbors, City of New Haven, and University Properties, with appropriate regard to character and significance.

Sealants to steel-and-glass curtain walling
Kahn carefully detailed the junctions between steel, concrete, and glass to be recessed and to create a shadow gap. The outermost edges of the steel panels are kept away from the concrete frame but set flush with them, forming an overall gap of 1½ inches to the concrete frame and the steel sill. Generally, all sealed abutments between the steel panels, windows, and concrete are ⅜-inch wide, which form the shadow gap between bent steel pans and the steel-framed windows. All jamb sealants are shown recessed between ½-inch and ¼-inch and generally about ³⁄₁₆-inch wide. The head detail to concrete shows a 1½-inch shadow gap with a ⅛-inch sealant width. The window-to-window jamb detail is 1½-inch wide sealant. The panel-to-window head or sill is ¼-inch wide sealant. Sealants and backer rods are used at the abutments of steel panels and windows with the concrete frame to maintain the weather tightness of the building.

The first recorded wholesale replacement of sealants occurred in 1998 under the direction of Wiss, Janney, Elstner Associates, Inc. and was carried out by Turner Construction Company. However, it appears that the importance of keeping the caulking to the minimum sealant measurements was not understood at the time, and it was incorrectly placed in a number of areas on the elevations. Some of the joints were made flush and others were over-caulked, resulting in the loss of the shadow gap. David Mills recollected that the sealants were replaced in 1996 when the windows were replaced. WJE's "as existing" drawings of 1998, therefore, record the 1996 work rather than Kahn's aesthetic of recessed pointing of joints as shown in Kahn's and Meyers's drawings. Alterations introduced in 1998 included over-filling of the shadow gaps in the concrete with mastic, which is a regrettable change of detailing.[76]

Sealants and probably backer rods will need to be replaced at regular intervals because of the inherent nature of their material. Repair is not an option. Defective sealants and backer rods can allow capillary action of water behind the steel panels and windows that leads to corrosion, which can continue unabated because it is concealed from view.

[75] The following policies are also appropriate:
Policy 87: To develop and implement a comprehensive trial strategy, or "Trialing Protocol," of the decay mechanisms affecting the steel, concrete, travertine, oak, and glass surfaces in order to mitigate further damage and to inform the Maintenance Plan.
Policy 88: To carry out any remedial work on steel, concrete, travertine, oak, and glass surfaces in such a way that visual continuity with the original surface is retained; any joint between old and new work designed to achieve this should be executed with precision.
Policy 91: To make decisions and carry out any works or alterations in light of professional advice from architects experienced in the conservation of buildings and from experienced contractors.

[76] Wiss, Janney, Elstner Associates, Inc., "Sealant Replacement at Exterior Cladding," WJE #972866, April 6, 1998, Yale Center for British Art Archives, Yale Project No. 9709233-01.

Water entrapment may lead to white precipitate staining on the concrete. Refer also to the section on External Concrete, page 156.

Policy 103

To replace sealants where visually detrimental, at the end of their warranty or life span, or earlier if failure occurs. It is important to follow Kahn's aesthetic of recessed pointing.

External steel doors

Kahn created a hierarchy in the use of steel (stainless, milled, and galvanized) for the door types and their finishes (pewter, brushed, galvanized, and painted).

The external fire escape doors – two in the east, one in the west, and one in the south elevation – are designed as part of the tartan-grid pewter-colored cladding. Similarly, the mechanical room doors and louvers on the first floor of the south elevation are integrated into the same design hierarchy. The single-leaf external door to the commercial loading dock is also pewter; however, the louvered panel above is galvanized steel.

The external doors are brushed stainless steel and glazed, and were made by Trio Industries in Ohio. The main entrance doors to the Center, contained within a 20-foot bay, are custom-height, 4-foot-wide double doors, with a steel-framed glazed fanlight, and flanked with full-height fixed glazing. The other pair of 4-foot-wide double doors with fixed glazing is in the Lower Court leading to the Lecture Hall lobby but contained within a 4-foot-wide bay under a deep beam reflecting the adjacent commercial space. All doors into the commercial shops fronting Chapel and High streets, including the restaurant in the Lower Court, are single-leaf, glazed doors, 3-foot-7¼-inch wide. Kahn specified finish No. 4 for the brushed stainless steel produced by Trio Industries, according to the 1973 specification. The steel was selected to withstand marring and finger-prints and be non-reflective. This was also approved on March 28, 1974, by Marshall Meyers, after Kahn's death. Lowest in the hierarchy of steelwork is galvanized steel described in the section below.

Damage to the various steel doors is arising from a range of circumstances, and all the results are disfiguring. There is evidence of excess lubricant leaking from door hinges, such as those to the Museum Shop on High Street. Chloride attack is visible on all exterior steel-door types. The changing of locks and handles and some attempts at forced entry have caused damage and subsequent rusting. The removal of pull handles without supplying replacements reveals the former fixing holes and allows some water penetration. Replacement of the straight pull handle to a curved handle results in similar damage, and this has occurred mainly on the commercial unit doors. The straight pull signals the Center, while the curved pull signifies a commercial property.

The glazing to the main public entrance doors to the Center, together with the commercial units and restaurant, is generally cared for. However, maintenance standards across the whole of the building are not consistent, and the first floor appears degraded in some areas. Maintenance of the doorsets and glazed walls is essential to the overall presentation of the place to the public on all four elevations. The glazed wall to the Lecture Hall lobby that was concealed by trellis work for a decade is particularly impaired, with its steel framing subject to corrosion. The accumulative effect of damage,

External steel doors in portico

poor repair, and lack of maintenance is a detrimental visual change and represents a loss of hierarchy in the elevations.

External galvanized steel doors

Galvanized sheet steel is used for the jamb and head surrounds for the motor-operated external roller shutters securing the two loading bays in the west elevation facing the Yale Rep. The pan-formed sheet metalwork has interlocking edges to permit concealed fastenings fixed to galvanized structural steelwork and serves to protect the structural elements from the weather. The external roller shutters consist of a curtain made of standard flat-face interlocking hot-dipped galvanized-sheet-metal slats. Galvanized sheet metal is the most utilitarian of the steels, and its external use is confined to the loading bays. Galvanized metal has weathered simultaneous with the curtain walling and appears in harmony.

Although the external roller shutters do not appear to be subject to the same degree of chloride attack as other steelwork, the bases of the jamb surrounds are heavily corroded due to the winter de-icing chloride mixture attacking such a thin sheet material. The metal at the bases is beyond repair, as the majority has disintegrated to a powdered oxide. The galvanized steel structure is also at risk, but not to the same extent because of its thicker galvanic coating. Dirt and grime have accumulated around the base of the steel structure, which, if not cleaned, will allow decay to progress unchecked beneath the build-up.[77]

Wholesale replacement of the galvanized-sheet-steel door surrounds is not recommended as a repair solution. Replacement would result in too sharp a contrast against the adjacent original steelwork, and periodic replacement of the surrounds (say every fifteen to twenty years) would have to be anticipated. Piecing in a new section at the base is feasible, but it would be visually at odds with the parent material and still equally vulnerable to chloride attack. What is of importance is the retention of much of the original parent material while, in parallel, the repair technique should address the vulnerable nature of the bases. The introduction of a robust stainless-steel baseboard would provide greater long-term protection because it could be considered sacrificial and replaceable. Such a repair represents a minimal visual change at the base and is not considered detrimental, but it also means the retention of much original fabric that can weather in harmony with the adjacent original fabric as far as practicable. Attention to such back-of-house items is important because of Kahn's consistent approach to design throughout the building.

Steel windows

The window frames are stainless steel in the same pewter color. The windows are insulated double-glazed units set within a sealed steel frame that has a dehydrated and hermetically sealed air space between. Two types were specified by Kahn in 1973. Type 1 comprised a 1-inch-thick unit of two lights of ¼-inch-thick clear plate or float glass with a ½-inch air space. Type 2 comprised a ⅝-inch-thick unit, also of two lights of ³⁄₁₆-inch-thick tempered polished plate and a ¼-inch air space between.

Problems with condensation meant that, by 1981, fourteen window units had to be replaced. In 1993 a one-year study of the condensation issues affecting the windows was

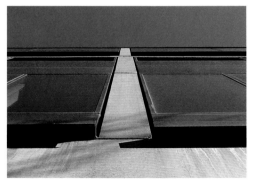

Recessed pointing separates the concrete frame from the steel surrounding the windows.

[77] Policy 98 is also appropriate: To give consideration to the cleaning of the external stainless-steel panels on a regular basis as part of the Maintenance Plan, subject to the trialing protocols.

undertaken by Ian Chin of WJE (Chicago). Following considerable debate, most glazing was replaced under a major campaign in 1995–96. The original steel frames were retained but were turned upside down for re-use, which facilitated a reengineering of the trough to the sill to include a weep system. The minor alteration to the sill is unobtrusive. All the external glazing on the upper floors has been replaced, and only the first floor and the Lower Court are original.

Water damage to the oak millwork abutting the windows throughout the Center suggests that the issues of water penetration and condensation have not been fully resolved.

Policy 104
To investigate the causes of continuing water damage to the internal fabric of the Center.

Fenestration pattern

Prown recalls that Kahn's philosophy dictated that the (asymmetrical) facade should express interior functions, and it is both the column-and-beam hierarchy and the window hierarchy that allow the external reading of the architecture of the Center. The windows are the key architectural expression of function. Variety is achieved through the arrangement of transparent windows and steel panels or opaque windows. The window height is always determined by the height of the cabinetry within to the underside of the primary exposed concrete beams, except in the absence of the beam between the second and third floors of the Library and Study Room. The variance in widths was determined by simple mathematical fractions; $\frac{1}{2}$, $\frac{1}{3}$, $\frac{1}{4}$ and $\frac{1}{16}$ of the 20-foot grid.

From this Kahn developed a clear hierarchy:

Entrance Court

The most important windows to the Center are the entrance door with its flanking side window lights occupying a single 20-foot bay and its double-bay counterpart to the Lecture Hall lobby off the Lower Court at basement level.

Public galleries and reading rooms

Next in the hierarchy are those windows to the public galleries on the east, north, and south elevations that extend over the three floors of gallery. They are a half-bay width, full height (floor to ceiling), subdivided by a transom equal to the height of one standard steel panel. The upper glazed section to the fourth floor windows is two feet higher than on the second and third floors. This window type always flanks a structural concrete column. However, there is an architectural conflict in one's reading of the third floor of the Chapel Street facade where the same window type is used in the Paper Conservation Department seminar room and the matting and framing room, but the latter has office cabinetry against the window. The Paper Conservation seminar room was once intended to be a public relaxation area. It is a change of use that initiates the conflict.

There are two window types for the reading rooms. Two quarter-bay-wide windows are used in one bay, and each flanks a structural column related to the furniture (desk and bookcase) arrangement. The desk height inside determined the sill, and the window

Facing page:
The fenestration on the second, third and fourth floors of the south elevation responds directly to the activities within the building.

The storefront of the Center's
Museum Shop on High Street

extends to the underside of the mezzanine gallery within the double-height space of the reading room. The other type forms the "clerestory" lighting to the mezzanines. Its sill height is also derived from the bookcases within. Together, they announce the function and volume of the three reading rooms on three elevations.

The vitrines to the entrance portico have curved sills matching the commercial units and are only half-bay-wide. They are an expression of the interior of the Center, as they contain linen walls for the display of graphic art and announce changing exhibitions.

Offices

Next down in the hierarchy are the several office types. The primary offices on the fourth floor have half-bay-wide windows. North-facing offices, including the Founder's Room, always flank a concrete column, while the south-facing are centered in the structural bay. The same was used for the Seminar Room and the Staff Lounge on the second floor. The office spaces west of the Study Room are based on a one-third module, two units being used and each unit abutting a concrete column.

Secondary office windows on the second and third floors facing west and south are one-quarter-bay wide and flank a column. The windows to the Department of Paintings and Sculpture and the adjacent art storage area were originally hinged as shown in the Kahn drawings and the 1977 published photographs. WJE recorded these in their record drawings. The hinges exist, but it is not known if they are operational.

The third-floor Paper Conservation Laboratory windows comprise two half-bay units set flush together to form a full-bay width to admit as much north light as possible.

Back-of-house

Windows to the third-floor book stacks are full-height, $1/16$-bay-width slot windows similar to the clerestory windows used elsewhere on the third floor.

There is an anomaly on the first-floor south elevation. Here the first-floor Public Education (now Docent) Room, the original wood shop (now the Paintings Conservation Studio), and the guards' lounge (now the Security Office) all share the same window type comprising two or four units derived from the 40-foot-wide structural bays representing the commercial zone set up for Chapel and High streets.

Storefronts

There are two types of storefront windows in the commercial spaces. The fenestration is determined by the central door and fanlight flanked by single, double-glazed units above curved stainless-steel sills. The other type exists at the western unit on Chapel, the only unit with two elevations, where the west storefront wall does not require a door.

Skylights and louvers

Set within the precast concrete V-beams of each 20-foot by 20-foot bay are four Rohm & Haas double domes covered externally by metal louvers to control sunlight entering the fourth floor. There are 224 skylights in total. All domes are constructed of acrylic Plexiglas. The primary outer dome rises 12 inches and is of ¼-inch-thick, clear and colorless acrylic type "Plex G," and the secondary inner dome rises 8 inches and is ³⁄₁₆-inch thick with an acrylic type UF-3 for ultraviolet filtering. Each dome has a 1-inch flange to facilitate fixing and sealing with a vinyl gasket. The first shop drawings were produced in August 1972, and following Kahn's approval on March 13, 1974, these were manufactured by Hillsdale Industries. The curb frames were all made from extruded aluminum by Fishman & Sons Inc. The louvers were fabricated in extruded aluminum that has an oven-baked finish (KYNAR), in a color that was to be selected by Kahn. Shop drawings commenced in December 1973 with approval by Kahn on March 7, 1974.

In January 1993 WJE performed a limited inspection of skylights and components of the roofing system. Selective opening in five areas facilitated observations of the existing conditions and recorded the as-built construction. Their report dated April 2, 1993, selected a location at the corner of the building to encompass the most typical conditions to which the roof and skylights were subjected. This enabled opening up an area of roof and partially dismantling a skylight that led to the development of drawings and technical specifications for a trial repair solution. A control sample of the proposed solution was monitored through a winter season, and a final evaluation of the efficacy of the trial was made. Turner Construction Company was appointed, and construction was carried out in 1998, now known as the Year of the Roof. In parallel with the re-roofing, both the original skylight assemblies and louvers underwent repair and modifications to combat the water penetration problems experienced in the past. The alterations have not had a detrimental effect on the significance of the building.

There are some visible signs of scratching damage to domes over the Entrance Court, which may have been caused when carrying out maintenance to the light fixtures or from the renovations in 1998. The damage is minor and should not be used as grounds for replacement of original historic fabric.

Atmospheric soiling on the domes may reduce the quantity and quality of light entering the space. This is probably more perceptible in the Entrance Court, where the skylights do not have the internal cassettes beneath them. An inspection of the skylights in 2008 revealed that defective sealants are causing condensation and promoting organic growth between the two layers.[78]

Plexiglas domes on the roof are shielded by louvers to reduce north light entering the galleries below, photographed in 2008

Policy 105
To give consideration to cleaning the domes, louvers, and diffusers on a regular planned basis.

Stainless-steel handrails
Kahn originally intended outer handrails for the public staircase to the Lower Court with no intermediate handrails. Pellechia and Meyers introduced the two additional rows in 1975 as a result of their widening of the staircase and adding an extra flight and landing. The form is much more complicated than Kahn originally intended, and similar to the way that Pellechia and Meyers altered the handrail and balustrade to the principal circular stair.

[78] Policy 103 is also appropriate: To replace sealants where visually detrimental, at the end of their warranty or life span, or earlier if failure occurs. It is important to follow Kahn's aesthetic of recessed pointing.

Kahn's painted-steel bollards at
the loading dock

Bollards

There are two types of bollards. Stainless-steel bollards at the top of the stairs leading to
the Lower Court were introduced in 1974 by Meyers, though the two western bollards
were added in 1987. Painted-steel bollards sited around the perimeter of the loading
dock to protect various walls from impact damage were designed by Kahn and engi-
neered by Pfisterer, Tor & Associates. The painted-steel bollards are constructed of reinforced concrete cores, structurally integrated with the beams forming the roof structure
of the restaurant/commercial space below. The core is encased in carbon-steel pipe,
12-inch internal diameter, to form the outer drum casing and set about three feet into the
concrete. The steel drum was sealed by welding a quarter-inch circular steel plate at
the top. Recent paint analysis of the metal bollards and the parking attendant's booth
has proven that the bollards were painted a rustic red-brick color (Benjamin Moore
#2091-20) and the booth a green color. Although bollards are utilitarian objects, they
were carefully integrated into the design.

The de-icing chloride mixture has led to severe corrosion along the base of all bollards.
The placement of the bollards adjacent to the walls forms a zone where snow can only
be cleared manually. If the snow is not cleared away, chloride-based decay continues
unabated under the snow. Rusting also occurs on the body and tops of the bollards. It is
likely that the snow plowing directs the chloride-contaminated snow at the body of the
bollards, which explains why the rust patches are randomly sited and the level of corrosion is so varied. The top steel plate has lifted in some cases, and one case is very severe.
Decay is also attributable to the lack of regular painting.

The corrosion is severe along the bases. Following trials it was decided that to repair the
bollards would not be economical, and the steel should be replaced.

Policy 106
To replace bollards when repair cannot be achieved economically.

External concrete

Treatment of the unpainted cast concrete
The elements of the primary structural fabric – floor slabs, posts, beams, and V-beams,
etc. – are of exceptional significance. Kahn took great pains through an extensive
process of samples to attain the quality and color of the architectural concrete. According
to Kahn's 1973 Specification, a Penn/Dixie Type II Buff cement mixed with the local red
sand would apparently produce the warm gray tone that would complement the stainless steel. New Haven Testing Lab reported (April 10, 1973) that the local red sand had
presented problems in maintaining consistency in gradation. It is not yet known what
sand was eventually selected by Kahn.

At first the quality of the concrete was erratic; Prown reported to Borst (June 13,
1973) that it was not up to the standard of the Salk Institute and far below the superb
quality at the Kimbell. He suspected inadequate Yale representation on site and felt that
the problem could be mitigated by on-site supervision to get first-rate detailing above
ground level. Kahn approved the sample for the V-beams on December 10, 1973.

Bollards protecting the top of the steps to the
Lower Court were introduced after completion
of the Center. Ad-hoc signage relating to the
restaurant colonized their caps,
photographed in 2008

Facing page:
External cast concrete with recessed
horizontal and raised V jointing with the
fixing holes left in place

Concrete parapet wall disengaged
from the west elevation

The columns are square-edged, with no chamfers or joints run within the column. Externally, at the column and slab intersections, the only joints allowed in columns at the slab intersections were kept as small as possible to prevent filling, and are recessed, not raised. Typical architectural-form details used 8-foot-by-16-foot sections. In the form work, absolutely smooth surfaces were achieved by using a polyurethane varnish on the ply-form to simulate Finn Ply, avoiding grain marks on the exterior and interior public spaces. Only in the basement story is the grain exposed, such as on the underside of the Lecture Hall raking floor and in the mechanical areas.

Policy 107

The architectural fair-faced concrete is of high quality and must be retained in good condition and unpainted. An analysis of the concrete should be carried out to determine the original mix so as to obtain a matching mix suitable for future remedial repairs.

Pollutants in the air can break up the more exposed surfaces or broken edges of concrete, which may lead to moisture penetration and consequent rusting of ferrous reinforcing bars. This, in turn, leads to spalling of concrete and an acceleration of the degenerative cycle, also known as "concrete cancer." There are several locations where this is apparent and has been addressed in the trialing protocols. For now, this does not present a risk due to the quality of the construction, but it should be borne in mind for the future.

"Free-lime" in the concrete mix is also able to leach out in the presence of water, and this is evidenced by the streaks of calcium-carbonate precipitate on the surface. Water entrapment behind the steel pans and between the inner wall linings might be a catalyst for the leaching precipitate. This is particularly visible on the concrete beams under the steel sills around the Center as a whole but appears more severe on the west elevation.

Exposure to chloride mixtures used for de-icing can lead to the decay of concrete, and the first signs of this are clearly visible on the column bases adjacent to the sidewalk on High Street.

Minor damage is occurring at the junction of beams and columns where there are minor losses that might be attributable to sealant and/or window replacement. Soiling tends to accumulate and darken these intersections.

The concrete has become soiled in areas and would benefit greatly from cleaning. Following the trialing protocols for the cleaning of concrete, the Center initiated its first cleaning cycle in April 2008, and this has been very successful in the Lower Court.

Bluestone coping in the cast-concrete parapets overlooking the Lower Court

Policy 108

To give consideration to the regular cleaning of the external concrete surfaces to remove dirt, grime, etc., as well as the lime precipitates.

Concrete boundary walls

The parapets and screen and boundary walls are of the same high quality and detailing as the Center.

The parapet walls to the Lower Court incorporate a flush, recessed New York State bluestone coping to half its depth, flush bluestone baseboard, and recessed flush lights

The concrete frame, screen wall, and steel panels above the Lower Court

to pedestrian routes. The tall screen wall of architectural fair-faced concrete between the loading bay and the Lower Court is carefully disengaged from the concrete frame of the Center. Before the renovations in 2010, the bluestone copings on the parapet had all become displaced, allowing organic growth to colonize some areas. Mosses and weeds had taken a foothold in some areas.

Two short walls flank the entrances to the parking lot on York and High streets. They are integral to the design of the Center and act as monumental freestanding screens guarding each entrance. However, they appear neglected. The two east walls on High Street are being displaced by the root system of the honey locust trees that are planted in close proximity. Upheaval of the sidewalk paving surfaces may present a risk to pedestrian traffic. The walls at both entrances suffer from ill-considered placement of later signs, emergency call points, and the like.

The southern boundary wall of the site is much smaller than those at High and York streets and is crowned by a wooden palisade fence to the height of the concrete walls, as shown in Kahn's drawings. The good-quality fence originally designed by Kahn is a double-sided picket fence; much of it remained, except that the rear pickets were removed in recent years. The fencing was restored in 2008.

Vehicles have caused impact and scraping damage to the south concrete wall. Wheel curbs were originally intended by Kahn to be fixed but were deleted from the construction phase as a cost-cutting exercise.

Cast concrete on the west side of the steps leading to the Lower Court

Policy 109
To consider the introduction of wheel stops based upon the original design.

Concrete pavement and curbs
The concrete sidewalk along the south elevation and the rounded curbs to the trees in the parking lot are shown on Kahn's 1973 drawings. The paving surface and curbs are in poured, reinforced concrete with large exposed aggregate finish. The design of the sidewalk follows standard details employed by the City of New Haven.

The tree beds were originally filled with fine gravel, but this has been partially replaced with white gravel and is being taken over by invasive weeds. The yellow dividing lines demarcating the parking bays were introduced in 2006, and the curved ends of the curbs have also been painted yellow to assist maneuvering by drivers. The paintwork is visually displeasing.

Policy 110
To repair the concrete sidewalk and curbs.

Policy 111
To strip yellow paint from the parking bays and tree curbs. White dividing lines are acceptable.

Policy 112
To clean out and return the tree beds to dark gravel.

External brickwork and masonry

Brick paving and bluestone paving

Portico

Prown recalls Kahn was opposed to the addition of pigments to achieve a color, which is confirmed by the architect's 1973 specification for the use of virgin clay for the manufacture of the bricks. The portico paving is a red-brown Stiles brick, laid in stretcher bond running east-west with a five-degree slope to shed water. The margins in 1-inch-thick New York State bluestone reinforce the structural grid and also express the threshold to the Center; similarly, the bluestone is used as the threshold to the commercial units opening onto High and Chapel streets. Exposed faces of the stonework were sand-rubbed. All brick and stone masonry was specified to be bedded in 1:3 (cement:sand) mortar. The same detailing is applied to the Lower Court and amphitheater west of the court adjacent to the Yale Repertory Theatre.

Sometime in the 1990s the paving bricks to the portico were sealed with various inappropriate sealers that have left a shine to the surface. In particular, at the north edge along Chapel Street, the sealer appears to be tar-based, and some minor repointing has been carried out; smoother and darker mortars than the original light-colored mortar testify to this.

Policy 113

To avoid the use of consolidants and sealers, as it is an irreversible process.

Policy 114

To analyze the pointing mortars so as to obtain an appropriate mix for future repairs.

Lower Court and staircase, terrace and amphitheater

The materials of the Lower Court, staircase, terrace, and amphitheater are the same as those in the portico that were used by Kahn to denote external space. The steps, landings, and bands forming margins and the division of the court paving are constructed of bluestone, while the paving itself is in Stiles bricks. As with the detailing at street level, the bluestone margins form a threshold between the Lower Court and the commercial units. However, because of the offset grid, they also form a threshold to the Lecture Hall lobby. The continuation of the brick paving into the Lecture Hall lobby associates the space closely with the Lower Court.

The tree bed within the brick paving is off-grid and implies the colonization of the ruined court by the single honey locust tree. Over the years earth has been built up to allow planting around the base of the tree, and this has resulted in the tree roots growing up into the deposited earth above the level of the paving; to reduce the soil would cause root damage, placing the tree at risk. When the tree has to be replaced, the ground should be restored to its original level, but, in the meantime, an interim solution should be adopted that indicates that the present arrangement is not original. The tree bed, therefore, was edged in steel in 2010 in contrast to the brick paving.

Facing page:
Brick paving with bluestone
margins in the portico

Structural movement in the bluestone steps and brick-paved landings, photographed in 2007

The staircase was in a poor structural state, as all the bluestone steps and brick-paved landings had displaced outwards by about 3 inches in the center. Dismantling of several steps revealed poor construction and detailing. The stone steps were not fixed to the concrete substrate, there were inadequate ties between steps, the concrete base was of very poor quality, and virtually all the cement pointing had been lost or reduced to sand.

The mortar mix to the stonework and brickwork to the Lower Court and the staircase had significantly degraded and failed, which suggested that a much weaker mix than specified had been used. This was also testified to by later pointing repairs using white caulking that had subsequently failed and led to biological colonization of the joints.

After a lengthy planning phase the Center embarked on the rehabilitation of its Lower Court early in 2010, in partnership with Yale's Office of Facilities, Knight Architecture LLC, Turner Construction Company, and Wiss, Janney, Elstner Associates, Inc. This was the first major project to be guided by this conservation plan. By November 2010 the bluestone and brick pavers throughout the courtyard, stairs, landings, were removed, repaired, and re-set by Capasso Masonry Preservation Group, Inc. of Middletown, CT; replicas of the original Edison Price step lights were installed by C. White Electric LLC. A final phase of this project will be undertaken in 2011–12, including the rehabilitation of the severely corroded double doors leading from the courtyard to the Lecture Hall lobby.

In the basement lobby off the Lower Court, salt efflorescence may be causing damage to the brickwork, though the source of moisture causing this is unknown at this stage.

Policy 115

To maintain the staircase and the parapets when necessary and repoint with appropriate mortars.

Facing page:
Bluestone grating to the central drain in the Lower Court, photographed in 2010

Bluestone margins in the Lower Court, offset from the main grid, form a threshold to the Lecture Hall lobby.

Internal steel panels

Steel panels, the same as those on the exterior, are employed in the interior to separate commercial uses from the Center and to clad the air shafts. The steel panels extend from the portico into the Entrance Court at first-floor level and wrap around the three sides where the court is surrounded by commercial units. Within the Center steel-clad risers recall the similarly clad service towers that stood at each corner in the First Program.

On the upper floors these mark the two primary air shafts, rendering them visible as they rise from the second to the fourth floor. Within the Reference Library and Study Room on the second floor, the shafts address the public as a two-story feature in the double-height reading rooms and back onto their respective staff offices and work areas. On the fourth floor they are reduced in size and altered in form to a square plan and are generally contained within the public galleries to form dominant visual features.

The insulated stainless-steel panels in the internal environment are less prone to the damage and risks that the exterior panels suffer. However, they are subject to the same human touch from museum attendants and visitors that leaves oils and greases. This is most pronounced in the Entrance Court. Pencil, pen, and eraser marks are also evident, most probably from school children. When the travertine floor in the Entrance Court is mopped clean, this results in a tidemark along the base of the steel panels. This tidemark may also be compounded by the annual mechanical cleaning regime to the floor.[79]

When environmental monitoring units have been replaced or upgraded at various times, new fixtures are often introduced, and the former holes in the steel are left exposed. It is visually unsatisfactory to notice such things in primary public spaces.

Policy 116
To re-use original fitting locations when upgrading units, whenever possible, rather than drilling new holes.

Internal steel: "pewter," brushed, galvanized, and painted

Doorsets

Kahn's hierarchy for the door types relates to the materials themselves. The public doors are brushed stainless steel compared to painted, solid, and semi-glazed steel for back-of-house doors. All doorsets are of high quality. The stainless-steel hardware is of good quality, universal and democratic in its use; the same lever handle types and locks were employed throughout, and pull handles and push plates signify public areas and commercial spaces.

The service doors in the exposed air shafts in the public galleries are pewter-colored stainless steel. All flush, steel-clad fire doors in the galleries, elevator lobbies, and the principal circular staircase and the two secondary fire escapes, elevator doors, and doors to the electrical rooms are brushed 2D stainless steel, probably 20-gauge. The basement double doors off the Lecture Hall and its associated lobby off the Lower Court are of the same material and hierarchy. Brushed stainless steel was selected following concerns

Facing page:
Internal steel panels are used vertically on the building-systems air shaft in the Study Room. The matte "pewter" finish contrasts with the brushed stainless-steel sink.

[79] Policy 98 is also appropriate: To give consideration to the cleaning of the external stainless-steel panels on a regular basis as part of the Maintenance Plan, subject to the trialing protocols.

over long-term appearance expressed by Prown in February 1974.[80] All doors are thought to be of stainless-steel construction, type either 302 or 304, with channel frames stiffened internally with 18-gauge channels. Hollow metal doors have flush, seamless, 18- or 20-gauge cold-rolled-steel faces, welded and finished flush on the edges. These are used in the back-of-house spaces and are painted blue. The cores are probably rigid foam. Sound deadening specified by Kahn was to be either compressed asbestos or mineral wool. (It is not known what was carried out.) All door frames are hollow metal, 16-gauge stainless steel reinforced with ¼-inch-thick structural steel plate and were assembled with accurately fitted welded joints. Frames were anchored into the walls through the jambs and heads. The jambs were fitted with three door silencers on the strike jamb and two at the top.[81]

All non-public (solid), steel-clad fire doorsets in the back-of-house areas are designated by their blue paintwork. The only two painted doors seen by the public are in the circulation areas discreetly located to the west of the freight elevator in the basement and on the first floor leading to the primary passages behind.

The doors have never been repainted since the Center opened in 1977, and painting is due. The paint finishes have worn in areas susceptible to abrasion by human hands, such as around the handles and locks, or they have been damaged by impact. Microscopic paint analysis has confirmed the original Benjamin Moore Polo Blue color #2062-10 that is in accordance with both Kahn's specification and Meyers's revision of 1975. The Center holds the original color swatches that were selected by Kahn.

Policy 117
To repaint to the original color and finish and to devise a planned maintenance regime.

Other stainless steel
The balustrade to the circular stair is constructed of 12-gauge, pewter-colored stainless steel, and the tubular stainless-steel handrail is brushed stainless steel. Meyers significantly modified the design, as Kahn's sketches show an elliptical handrail and a less complicated arrangement with the steel balustrade.

Brushed stainless steel is used for the elegant kitchen sink units in the Study Room and in the Reference Library; for the countertop, backsplash, sink, and exhaust hood in the kitchenette off the Founder's Room; another hood in the Paper Conservation Laboratory; and the free-standing kitchen unit in the staff lounge.

Internal galvanized steelwork
Galvanized sheet steel is used on the rolling fire shutters in the openings facing onto the two internal courts. These were introduced as part of the measures requested by the Fire Marshal in early 1974. Meyers designed horizontal slatted louvers, but these were abandoned. A change order dated March 12, 1974, confirmed the additional cost of $33,516.

Galvanized mild steel was used for the construction of the exposed stringers and risers of the fire-escape staircases and pipe handrails, steel ladders to the roof and air shafts, and for the fire-escape stairs, which were painted lime green, semigloss (Benjamin Moore Moor-o-Matic 20-70).

Matte-steel balustrading with polished-steel handrail

[80] Minutes of meeting, February 6, 1974: "Prown expressed concern about the appearance of stainless steel after a period of use. Brushed stainless steel is to be used both on the inside of the cabs and on elevator doors." Louis I. Kahn Collection, University of Pennsylvania and Pennsylvania Historical and Museum Commission.
[81] Policy 98 is appropriate: To give consideration to the cleaning of the external stainless-steel panels on a regular basis as part of the Maintenance Plan, subject to the trialing protocols.

Within the back-of-house areas, galvanized pipe work is exposed and supported by hangers fixed to the concrete ceilings.

Although stainless-steel ductwork is employed in the Paper Conservation Laboratory and Photo Lab exhaust systems, exposed galvanized steel pipe work was used for the toilet exhaust system.

Miscellaneous metal

Aluminum

Three types of aluminum alloy are used in the Center (extrusions, castings, and pipe), and all have a clear anodized finish. The exposed 24-inch-diameter supply ductwork is constructed of aluminum Alcoa 3003-H14 manufactured by United Sheet Metal Division with an anodized finish R201-R5. Ductwork was supplied with slotted external brackets to accept the custom-made aluminum rod hanger bolts and supported by special hanger plates set into the concrete ceilings that allowed for expansion of ducts. Slots are cut in the ducts for the diffusers. The ductwork is either insulated or not, depending on its function. The construction quality is high, with all the ducts perfectly aligned with the building, and all bends, junctions, and terminations carefully designed.

The "can lights" are all spray-painted with Krylon spray paint #1403 "Dull Aluminum."

Internal glass and plastics

Glass-block skylight in the stairwell

The glass blocks were either manufactured by Circle Redmont Corporation in nearby Stamford, CT, or by Pittsburgh Corning. This skylight is comprised of a flat grid of 196 solid glass Vue-blocks, 12-inch square, with no internal screen or filter because this function was performed by the skylight diffusers above. The blocks were laid in a grid of pre-cast reinforced concrete.[82]

Glass blocks admit borrowed light into the stairwell.

Diffuser panels to skylights

Each of the 20-foot bays of the fourth floor is roofed by four skylights, and below each of these, four cassettes diffuse daylight entering the areas where works of art are or might be held. (There are none below the sixteen skylights over the Entrance Court.) Each cassette is 3-foot square and is formed of two layers of Holophane Controlens #6339 set about 2 inches apart with their "points in line." This was a standard product marketed by Holophane Company Inc. as their "Refractive Grid for fluorescent fixtures – A scientific breakthrough in prismatic light control and lens design." Intended for use as illuminated panels in suspended ceilings, the manufacturer claimed it reduced luminaire brightness by up to 70 percent while increasing useful light. It was originally intended that retractable shutters would be fixed in recesses below the cassettes.

The scheme for the cassette was devised by the building contractor Kenneth Froeberg of Macomber as an alternative to Kahn's more expensive proposal worked out in collaboration with lighting designer Richard Kelly and supported by Jules Prown. Both schemes had the same performance in terms of light diffusion, but Kahn's design was

[82] Pfisterer, Tor & Associates. Drawing, SK-S70, March 7, 1974; received Macomber, March 18, 1974.

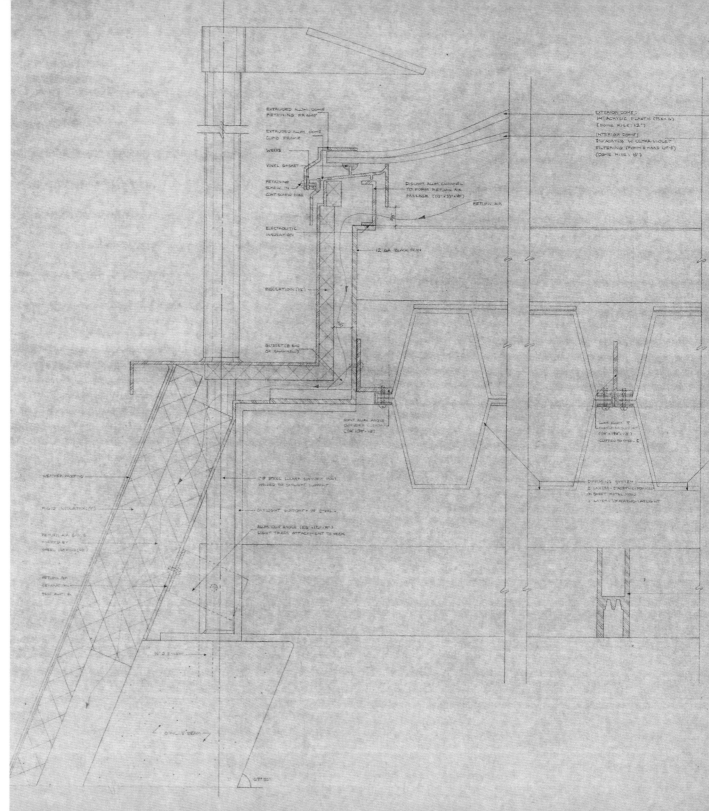

Kahn office drawings showing skylights with purpose-made diffusers designed by Kahn (right, March 1974) and the simplified diffuser cassettes proposed by Macomber (below, April 1974), Louis I. Kahn Collection, University of Pennsylvania (805.023)

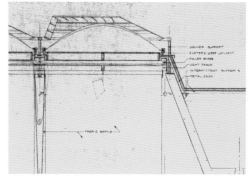

The top of the cast-concrete
stair tower below the precast
beam over the Library Court

more sculptural: two layers of acrylic sheet, specially formed on a metal mold to a 3-inch profile, were to be fixed to give a 6-inch-thick honeycomb cassette, the molded profile of which resulted in each cassette being modulated by a grid of twenty-five dentils.

Internal concrete

Architectural concrete

Kahn desired large cyclopean, monolithic surfaces for the primary walls: the shear walls of the elevator shafts, the circular staircase, ceilings, beams, and the V-shaped beams to the fourth-floor skylights. For the walls, the imprint of the forms in the concrete is an integral element of the architectural design and an expression of workmanship. Kahn and Macomber carefully developed the arrangement of the form work. The maximum panel size was 12 feet. Generally, for ceiling slabs, the joints are patterned by using column widths as a reference for edge joints. Joints intersect column corners, not within a face, and are placed to the longitudinal building axis. Panel sizes within the field do vary but only at perimeter panels. Corner details were expressed as a joint running vertically on the face about two inches from the edge. This was cited as most desirable, and Kahn reiterated that the use of a 2-inch vertical strip between plywood panels was only to facilitate the stripping of the formwork and not to achieve any contrived design.[83]

As water and sands tend to bleed at formwork joints, the edges of the form panels were slightly beveled to provide the place for bleeding, so "fins" were formed, about ¼-inch wide and projecting about ⅛ inch, for all walls and ceilings. Prown recalls that Kahn was not offended by the chips and breaks caused by the pouring or the removal of formwork, as this exhibited the intrinsic nature of the material and workmanship. Tie holes were left unfilled—small, precise, and clean with a maximum ½-inch-diameter for the desired unplugged effect. Larger holes were plugged with lead, hammered smooth, and recessed slightly. Floor slabs were monolithically finished to provide a smooth, even surface where they were exposed, or to be covered with a variety of flooring. The concrete stairs were finished with a soft-bristled broom after the finish troweling.

The fire alarm sounder illustrates how the building's systems are carefully accommodated within the cast concrete.

Policy 118

To leave unpainted interior and exterior concrete surfaces, including those in commercial units, so that their character and details remain visible.

The painting of the concrete is the antithesis of Kahn's approach to materials, but its use has been introduced over the years in limited areas of the building, both within the Center and within the commercial units.

In their report on environmental conditions within the Center, Garrison/Lull advocated the sealing of the concrete to reduce dusting, which could place works of art or equipment at risk. The treatment of the basement rooms has been necessary in connection with the use of spaces for storage. In the undercroft beneath the Lecture Hall, the change of use resulted in the concrete floor and raking ceiling slab being sealed to prevent dust adversely affecting sensitive computer equipment. While the reasoning is sound, such sealing processes are irreversible, the long-term effects unknown, and the

[83] Meeting February 22, 1973, attended by Louis Kahn; K. Borst (Yale); E. Cairns (Trio Industries); K. Froeberg, T. Burghart, F. Wales (G.B.H. Macomber Company), Yale Center for British Art Archives.

Facing page:
Internal concrete

visual change noticeable. Because of this, sealing the concrete on the upper floors would be unacceptable, and other steps should be taken to meet Garrison/Lull's recommendations. This might be achieved by management with the environment being monitored and the collection rotated.

The painting of primary elements of the building that pass through the commercial units appears to have occurred solely on the basis of a choice of decoration. The concrete columns and the air shaft need to be read architecturally as continuing through the building, and painting or concealing them makes this illegible.

"Migration staining"

In the galleries staff occasionally lean against the concrete frame; this allows the transference of various human-based oils, greases, etc., to soak into the concrete and cause staining, which has been coined "migration staining." Children in groups tend to run their hands along large wall surfaces of concrete such as around the elevator walls, particularly at the corners. Although the staining is non-threatening, it does affect the visual quality of the primary concrete structure. The use of double-sided tape also causes similar staining. It is thought that gloves are impractical; the simplest, most effective remedy is to encourage staff to wash their hands prior to going on duty and to ensure that groups are managed more closely.

Policy 119

To discourage staff and visitors from leaning against or gaining support from the concrete frame and from using tapes or glues that cause staining of the surfaces.

Policy 120

To base any cleaning or poulticing of greasy, unpainted concrete upon designed conservation trials carried out under policy 87. The methods and their consequences should be well understood and fully tested so that no change to the character or the original surface occurs. If the outcome is unsuccessful, it should remain uncleaned.

Policy 121

To consider the use of sealants or types of inhibitors to prevent staining, based exclusively upon testing before use, provided that such a treatment does not result in changes to the texture, color, or tone of the concrete surface. Where the outcome is uncertain, the surface should remain unsealed.

Internal millwork

American white-oak millwork

Kahn chose American white oak for its warmth and color to complement the uniformity of the gray concrete. Wall paneling throughout the Center is of flush construction with the stiles and rails of solid oak lumber and the flush panels of quarter-sawn white-oak-veneer plywood.

"Migration staining" on a concrete frame in the Long Gallery

Facing page:
White-oak millwork panelling
in the Reference Library

A corner of the Library Court

Custom-made wood doors are of the same flush and solid stile-and-rail construction, with a solid core and white-oak-veneer-plywood panels. The millwork quality is high.

Although Kahn produced working drawings for wooden shutters, now at the University of Pennsylvania, cost-cutting procedures saw them abandoned. However, oak shutters following the architect's original design were installed in 1981–82.

Prown recalls that Kahn wanted a natural, transparent finish to the woodwork. Woodwork was originally specified in 1973 to be finished with one full coat of Sherwin-Williams Dead Flat Clear Lacquer followed by two coats of Trewax, a mineral solvent-based wax. Samples of oak with Albert "DS" Fire Retardant Coating were received on April 3, 1974, but this does not appear to have been accepted. In late 2006 Rick Johnson, the Center's Installation Manager, tracked down the original craftsman, Helmut Guenschel, who reportedly worked with Kahn to develop the final finish to the casework and is still using the same methodology. The Center's former cabinet-makers, Henry Bayer and Phil Corvi, also worked on the casework and the finishing. The process was reported as follows: "The grain is filled using a Sherwin-Williams's vinyl sealer reducing to 60% using a lacquer thinner which, most importantly, is hand rubbed in using a French polishing rag. After a light sanding, a second coat of sealer is rubbed in with French polishing rag followed by a Sherwin-Williams's C system top coat applied. A medium rub effect produces an oil simulated finish."[84]

Originally, fabricating and finishing of millwork was to be done by the general contractor. However, in order to keep the University's Physical Plant carpenters employed, a decision was taken to remove some of the millwork from the contract for Yale employees to complete. This appears to have been limited to 43 bookcases, 12 large pull-out drawer units, and 30 small units. These units were coated with Pratt and Lambert No. 38 Dull Varnish in accordance with Meyers's specification.[85]

Microscopic analysis of samples taken from the woodwork in the building confirms the lacquer or varnish layer and possibly a wax treatment. These samples were taken by conservator Michael Morris, and the analyses were undertaken by Pascale Patris (The Metropolitan Museum of Art, New York), but further analyses are recommended.

Throughout the Center oak millwork continues to be damaged by exposure to moisture (water damage), and the finishes also degrade as a result of UV-light exposure, use, and lack of maintenance. Water damage to the oak millwork is most probably due to condensation of air in contact with cold windows. Pools of water form in the condensate tray and overflowing water leaches into the woodwork. This wetness causes the cellulose fibers to swell and create a spongy wood matrix. Swelling initiates tension in the finish, causing it to commence failing. The doors appear to have a slightly raised surface that has resulted from moisture penetration through micro-fissures in failing coatings leading to the expansion of the wood fibers. Another example of damage is in the Rare Books Reading Room and offices in the Prints and Drawings Department, where original solid oak cabinetry below the windows was replaced in veneered construction in 1998. Staff still report that water ingress and ice build-up remain problematic in winter and are injurious to the surrounding millwork and carpet. Water penetration is exacerbating damage, as the veneers are lifting and the substrates are swelling, while darkening the wood or substrate at the same time. Such damage can be

[84] Richard F. Johnson, e-mail message to authors, fall 2006.

[85] Minutes from the meeting held with M. Meyers, P. Basserman, et al., September 24, 1975, Yale Center for British Art Archives.

seen in the Prints and Drawings Curator's Office. Excessive dampness may lead to colonization of (suspected) mold already noted in the Rare Books Reading Room. Water damage continues unabated once the deterioration process has begun.

The degenerative effects of UV light and solar heat gain through the double glazing throughout the building on the oak sills, desktops, shutters, millwork, and cabinetry are becoming increasingly noticeable. Ultraviolet light causes a chemical breakdown of the lacquer by weakening its cohesive properties and loosening its adhesion to the oak surface. Scorching heat is damaging the fibers, leading to exfoliation and blanching of the hardwood and veneers around the windows. In the Entrance Court, which is lit by unshielded natural daylight, sills in the second-floor openings are particularly affected, and patchiness of the finishes is visible on the oak paneling, together with some abrasive marks where attempts have been made to rectify some damage that had occurred on the west wall. These effects are less pronounced in the Library Court, where UV-light diffusers are used to protect artwork.

From the exterior of the building, the shutters appear bleached and dried out, while on the inside the blades can be seen as warping. The pattern of deterioration of finishes and fading of the panels could possibly be mapped visually by an experienced contractor or conservator.

All oak millwork, free standing cabinetry, and furniture exhibit failure of their protective finish, together with numerous scratches, scuff marks, patchiness, and peeling throughout the whole of the building. For example, in Rare Books and Manuscripts and in Prints and Drawings, the finishes on the cabinets housing the solander boxes, trestle tables, and Windsor chairs, handrails, and oak steps are deteriorating. The finish on the oak doors throughout the building has aged, is soiled and greasy, and is exfoliating as a result of various cleaning products and greases and oils from contact with human hands. Cleaning trials indicate that the soiling can easily be removed with distilled water and cotton wool as part of a maintenance regime. After thirty years it is reasonable to assume that this original protective finish is degrading and has far exceeded its life expectancy. The rate of deterioration of the finishes can only be seen as accelerating; the time for renewal of finishes is long overdue. The finishes throughout the Center need reviving. In addition, the millwork is dusty and dirty on close inspection and requires general cleaning.

Condensation damage to millwork window sills and desktops, photographed in 2006

Policy 122

To remove original protective finishes to the oak millwork, doors, and furniture at the end of their expected life performance and to replace them with new protective finishes following the original specification. The millwork finishes should be subject to a regular planned maintenance regime every 4–5 years. Subject to analysis and respect for the original finish, consideration should be given to improving the specification of the finish to combat known causes of decay.

Policy 123

To analyze the existing finishes scientifically to corroborate verbal and written evidence.

Policy 124

To investigate the causes of continuing water penetration and damage to the internal millwork and concealed fabric of the curtain walling, including damage to the oak millwork abutting the windows throughout the Center.

Baseboards throughout the Center are regularly dismantled to gain access to the electrical routes or air plenum space behind for maintenance, or are relocated as a result of changing exhibitions. Unfortunately, after refixing the baseboards with cabinetry screws through the face, the holes are filled with a wood filler that does not blend with the appearance of the original finished millwork.

Policy 125

To blend in fillers to match the oak millwork at all times.

Electrical accessories, such as wall sockets in the baseboards, are occasionally renewed, blanked off, or installed in new locations as a result of changing exhibitions and rehanging of the collection. Early photographs show Kahn's and Pellechia and Meyers's symmetrical disposition within the room-like volumes.

Policy 126

To give due consideration to the relocation of power outlets so that symmetry in placement is respected.

Pogos, walls, and partitions

Structure and appearance

Kahn's 1973 working detail drawings show the original design as freestanding partitions separated from the soffit of the concrete V-beam and the travertine floor with aluminum "polecats" with a natural anodized-aluminum finish. Neoprene pads separated the polecats from the concrete and travertine. The frame was specified to be constructed of clear, white pine studs sheeted with 3/8-inch-thick pine plywood. On the fourth floor the studs were 4¼-inch deep while those on the lower floors were 3¼-inch deep. The linen was stretched and wrapped around the outer edges and then clamped into the reveals with a removable piece of ¾-inch-thick rift-sawn white-oak trim.

In 1975–76 Pellechia and Meyers's detail drawings of the demountable partitions show how Meyers altered Kahn's ideas.[86] For example, a typical 3-foot-wide partition has a pair of studs (2 x 4-inch studs for the fourth floor) at each end routed to receive the polecat with an intermediate 1 x 4-inch stud. The upper polecat mechanisms were retained, but the bottom polecats were replaced with a 3³/8-inch-high x ½-inch-wide rift-sawn white-oak baseboard as a removable base to facilitate dismantling, relocation, and reconfiguration. Behind the baseboards were maple legs with neoprene pads to sit on the travertine margins. Plywood, 3/8-inch fire retardant "Duraply," was then glued to the stud frame. At the top and bottom were 3/8-inch x ¹/8-inch-thick removable wooden grounds attached to the linen to tauten and stretch it before being clamped by

86 Pellechia and Meyers drawing, Louis I. Kahn Collection, SKA 319, University of Pennsylvania and Pennsylvania Historical and Museum Commission.

the ¾-inch oak trim inset to the reveals. The construction method for a 6-foot pogo was similar except there were three intermediate studs and another maple leg in the center. Each module had a pair of polecats. Meyers's details also show how two pogos were coupled with a removable hardwood spline at the meeting of two panels. To construct a 9-foot pogo, a 6-foot and a 3-foot were simply positioned together, and one could read the two modules by the locations of the polecats at the abutment. Meyers's details show that the linen was then stretched across the two or three modules to appear as a single panel. Similarly, a 12-foot module was constructed of two 6-foot modules and a 15-foot comprised of two 6-foot and one 3-foot module, yet all appeared as a single panel. Published photographs show this to be the case, as do the pogos in the former fourth-floor Study Gallery that survive as intended by Kahn and Meyers. All the remaining pogos on the three floors probably date from a later period.

In 1998 architect Glen Gregg introduced the surface-mounted, white-oak trim to the reveals. The pogos now have an oak frame on three sides but not the top. Both Meyers's addition of the oak baseboard and Gregg's subsequent reveal alteration have lost Kahn's intention of these floating planes of fabric and the ability to read the whole of the travertine margin.

When constructing new pogos, MDO (marine density overlay) is used in lieu of plywood. Rick Johnson reports significant problems are encountered when a rehang of the fourth-floor galleries occurs every five to seven years. The weight of a pogo may entail its dismantling and virtual rebuilding. Its strength may have to be increased. Damage is also caused to the travertine during the process of the rehang.

Policy 127
To devise a new construction technique for the pogos that pays great respect to Kahn's design principles.

The pogos in the exhibition galleries and walls in the reading rooms and offices are covered with linen for the display of art. In 1973 Kahn specified a fire-retardant, 54-inch-wide linen that was supplied by B. F. Ruskin in the Bronx through Macomber Company. The original linen supplied was Belgian, 52 inches wide, described as "natural" with a number of HA 1167. Recent testing by DesignTex has revealed that the original linen had a light tint and was single weave in a 2 x 1 construction (two yarns in the warp and one in the weft).[87] Kiesling-Hess provided "Scotchgard" that was treated with a fire retardant "Flamefoe KH." The weave was aligned with the panel edges and placed so as to be smooth, taut, and wrinkle free. The pogos with their neutral linen are of considerable significance for the display of works of art.

The linen within the public galleries was replaced in 1998, whereas the cloth and the pogos in the former Study Gallery are original, as is the linen in the offices and reading rooms. When it came time to replace the linen in 1998, the Center endeavored to match the old linen as authentically as possible. New products that were available comprised a single weave with an acrylic or paper backing and were installed like wallpaper, as opposed to heavy linen that is stretched. The Center contacted Carolyn Sears-Michaud, a sales representative from Knoll Textiles in New York City, who found a mill with an old

[87] As reported by Kevin Klier of DesignTex to Constance Clement via email, March 30, 2011.

Pogos in the fourth-floor galleries, photographed in 2006

loom that could produce a heavy weave, 58 inches wide: Tapetex in Helmond, Holland. The new linen was slightly tinted in order to match the original. The linen is fire-treated with Flovan CGN. The linen was installed by Stretchwall Installations from Long Island City, New York, a division of the same company that provided the original window shades. The Center stocks 450 yards of original cloth at a storage facility in Beacon Falls, CT, together with 429 yards of the new cloth. When new linen is required, light tinting and fire-retardant treatments are acceptable. The linen is also stained in areas by people touching the fabric, similar to the migration staining on the concrete explained earlier.

Policy 128
To discourage staff and visitors from touching the fabric.

Wood-and-glass walls
Oak-framed and glazed walls with glazed double doors articulate public entrances within the building. Of primary importance are those that signal the three departments on the second floor: Prints and Drawings and the Reference Library, off the Library Court, and Rare Books and Manuscripts, entered from either the Study Room or the Reference Library. Signage on steel plates was introduced in 1998.

On the fourth floor the original Public Education Office and the Registrar's Office were glazed to aid surveillance over the Study Gallery. Surveillance is now performed by guards. One side of the glazed partitions has been reduced in width next to the door jamb to accommodate a vertical service route containing light switches and card readers, which has resulted in a loss of symmetry.

There is one secondary example where the glazed wall between two second-floor offices (the Librarian's office and the adjacent work room) was used to borrow light into an "inner" room. An alteration in 2005 followed this example on the third floor, directly above those offices, in order to admit natural light into an internal room that previously had very limited natural light from the mezzanine of the Library.

Policy 129
To leave unaltered the glazed entrance partitions from the Library Court to the Prints and Drawings and the Rare Books and Manuscripts departments. When the function of the partition (glazed or otherwise) becomes redundant, alteration is permissible, providing that it follows an original precedent and maintains the original character and construction logic.

Gypsum wallboard partitions
This standard wallboard was used throughout the building for wall linings fixed to the steel partition structural framing. The walls were either lined with the linen to designate where artwork could be hung or it was painted and textured. Painted walls could have oak cleats fixed to them for hanging bookshelves or the placing of millwork.

Meyers specified a number of finishes ranging from a spray texture, a fast-dry latex primer and several satin latexes, to flat and semigloss paint finishes. The color schedule dated April 11, 1975, specified Moor-O-Matic 16-1.

Panel covered in natural linen
and framed in white oak, concrete,
and white-painted gypsum wallboard

To reinstate the original color scheme subject to microscopy to corroborate evidence.

Cork wallboards

The boards are ¼-inch thick, un-sanded, natural-tan cork carpet with burlap backing glued to gypsum wallboard. Corkboard was sited above the Registrar's desk on the west wall, on the north walls of the offices of the Curator and Assistant Curator of Paintings, and on the south walls of the offices of the Director and Assistant Director. In the Education Office corkboards were hung on the north wall and the walls flanking the central window. Cork was not specified in any other offices, including those of the three curators on the second floor. However, the introduction of cork wallboards in additional offices is acceptable.

Restroom walls and partitions

Cubicle partitions have baked-enamel finish over galvanized, phosphatized sheet metal and metal framing. These were, and still are, standard products: flush wing, cantilevered, wall-hung type supplied by Flush-Metal Corporation. Kahn selected American Olean ceramic mosaic "Pepper White" tiles to cover the floors and cinder-block walls up to a certain height with exposed cinder block above to the ceiling. However, on the third and fourth floors, the walls above the tiles are sheeted with gypsum wallboard and painted, representing the hierarchy of the adjacent office spaces.

Black plastic sheets have been fitted over the enamel partitions, perhaps to hide graffiti. One cubicle in the men's restroom in the basement was altered to create handicapped access. In doing so, minor damage was done to the concrete wall.

Policy 131
To consider removal of the black plastic sheets in order to restore the original finishes.

Basement water fountain and fair-face cinder blocks

Treatment of cinder block

In terms of hierarchy, hollow concrete block walls form the lowest tier. Kahn selected light-white concrete cinder blocks made with solite light-white aggregate by Plasticrete Corp. The use of cinder-block walls was confined to back-of-house rooms and passages on the first and basement floors, restrooms on each floor, the kitchen off the Founder's Room, and the secondary fire escape stairwells. Precast reinforced concrete lintels with an 8-inch bearing at each end were carefully integrated into the openings in these walls. Both were laid in a standard 1:1:6 (Portland cement:lime:sand) mortar. The cinder blocks and lintels were unpainted.

Policy 132
To respect the module and bonding pattern of the cinder blocks and lintels and avoid straying beyond the primary structural grid lines when carrying out alterations to internal walls, such as creating new openings.

Facing page:
The travertine floor abuts the concrete frame and pewter-finish, stainless-steel wall in the Entrance Court.

Internal flooring

Travertine floors

Kahn specified AR Light Roman Classic travertine from Sergio Lippielli, Bagni di Tivoli in Italy, and recent correspondence confirms the same source was used for the Kimbell Museum and exhausted by the J. Paul Getty Museum in Los Angeles. The stone was set on a bed of mortar comprising one part Portland cement and 3–4 parts sand. According to Kahn's 1973 specification, the travertine was to be scrubbed with Hillyard RE-JUV-NAL, rinsed, and sealed with two thin coats of Hillyard ONEX-SEAL II. This was later voided by Meyers in a letter dated February 28, 1975.

Cleaning

The same cleaning procedure used at the Kimbell Art Museum employing soap and water was intended to be adopted.

In 2002 New England Stone Technology LLC recommended cleaning the travertine in the Entrance Court with "Hurricane" stone cleaner (a corrosive liquid containing potassium hydroxide) and machine surface scrubbing, followed by Stone Kleen Neutral Cleaner. George Conte reported that the daily cleaning and maintenance regime in place comprised a dry mopping up of the dust, vacuuming, then a chemical clean using Image Deodorizing Neutral Cleaner. The annual "deep" clean was also chemical-based, using the same Image neutral cleaner, then a buffing machine scrubs the floor, mopping with clean water. This was followed by another chemical solution using one part Hurricane Intensive Cleaner to 2–3 parts warm water, then scrubbing with a buffing machine. Mopping up with clean water could take several applications. The final rinse was done with clear water. Other cleaning methods have been trialed.

Policy 133
To consider adopting a less corrosive cleaning regime.

Repair

Travertine is a soft limestone. The travertine margins in the galleries are being damaged or crushed by the pogos installed in 1998, which are heavier than the originals. The edges are susceptible to damage at the abutment with carpet, as there is a transition from hard bedding to soft underlay. To prevent damage arising from condensation in the winter necessitates the daily use of a mobile lift around the fourth-floor galleries. The weight of the lift contributes to damage of the travertine. Condensation falling onto the stone would tend to soften it, making it more susceptible to damage. In addition, the legs of the Windsor chairs grind into the soft travertine. Previous measures of capping the feet in plastic have helped to alleviate the situation, but point-loading via chair legs will continue to cause damage.

Policy 134
To consider consolidating the travertine with a stone strengthener to retard further damage, subject to the trialing protocols.

Unsightly fillings where the travertine margins have been damaged by heels, as well as dirt, sand, and salt

Policy 135

To consider modifying the use of the lift by laying pieces of plywood over the stone margins to prevent further damage.

Prown noted in 1975 that the voids in the travertine in the Entrance Court picked up dirt if the voids were not filled. Meyers instructed that voids larger than a twenty-five-cent piece be filled within ¼ inch of the top surface with matching color cement, and he also reported very few voids were filled at the Kimbell. Examination of some existing fills indicates that they are primarily cement-based and gray in color and were carried out in the mid-1990s when there was concern that the voids could potentially catch shoe heels and cause injury. The voids examined in the Entrance Court are filled with dirt and debris, which could readily be removed with the appropriate equipment. Due to the nature of cement, minor damage will be caused by its removal, but the benefit of removal outweighs that of retention.

Policy 136

To consider the removal of cement-based and other fills that do not match the travertine. Reversible replacement fills should only be carried out if the voids present a risk of injury and should be matched as closely as possible to the stone.

Wood flooring

Splined continuous-strip flooring, laid on sleeper cushions made of resilient rubber pads, with 2-inch yellow corkboard expansion strips at the wall abutments, is used in the Library Court and the elevators. Kahn used the same strip flooring extensively at the Kimbell. The product specified was Robbins Ironbound, $^{25}/_{32}$-inch x 2¼-inch x 12-inch, tongue-and-grooved white oak and was laid with staggered joints. The oak was specially selected to be heart-oak, without sap. The ends of the boards were grooved for the splines. For finishing, Kahn specified the oak to be sealed with Poli-Seal from Huntington Laboratories, machine buffed, and then a Trewax liquid paste wax with a mineral-spirit base applied.

At present the floor is dusted daily followed by a damp-mop clean. In July 2005 the floor was refinished by sanding down and finishing with four coats of a water-based polyurethane, and the work was carried out by Neal's Wood Flooring in Branford, CT. The cork strips appear to be degrading and will require replacement sometime in the future.

Policy 137

To reinstate and maintain the original finishing treatment at periodic intervals. Cork expansion strips should be replaced when degraded.

Carpet

Based upon a Yale University memorandum dated January 3, 1973, contained in Kahn's specifications, the fitted carpet used throughout the Center was a Yale University standard carpet: a velvet weave of wool from Bigelow Gropoint #2097 (or equal) of 216

Travertine paving in the elevator lobby and stair landings looking through to the wood flooring in the Library Court

The wood-strip flooring in the Library Court is similar to that used by Kahn at the Kimbell Art Museum and the Yale University Art Gallery.

pitch, 8 rows per inch, 100 percent wool with cotton backing, 3 ply. It was installed either with a conventional 40-ounce hair pad underlay, or it was cemented directly to the floor with Bigelow Broadlak adhesive. The selected color complemented the use of natural materials. Worn areas of the original carpet survive, such as in the Study Room in the Prints and Drawings Department.

In 1998 the majority of the carpet was replaced due to wear and tear and "off-gassing." The Center's Chief Paper Conservator, Theresa Fairbanks-Harris, carried out research on issues relating to wool carpeting in 1997, on which the following is based. Wool contains sulfur. The atmosphere is a source of sulfurous compounds, such as carbonyl sulfide, sulfur dioxide, and hydrogen sulfide, which can form sulfuric acid with moisture in the air. Sulfuric acid is destructive to materials used in the manufacture of art objects. Metals, primarily lead and silver, react adversely, as do lead pigments, such as lead-based whites, reds, and yellows, which form disfiguring black lead sulfides.[88] Silver tarnishes to brown. Natural fibers also can attract and trap pollutants and a build-up over time may cause the carpet to become a secondary source of pollutants. Changes in relative humidity or temperature can trigger a release of harmful chemicals from the carpet. Wool is also a food source for insects. While toxic chemicals are commonly used to eliminate destructive webbing clothes moths, for example, residual toxins can be harmful to humans.

The carpets proposed in 1998 were sampled and analyzed by the Center's Paper Conservation Department and the conservation scientists at the Canadian Conservation Institute. The replacement chosen was a synthetic carpet with low volatile organic compound emissions.

In their report of 2002, Garrison/Lull expressed their concern over the use of wool carpet because of the presence of carpet beetles and the consequential damage to works of art. However, if wool carpet was to be reintroduced, housekeeping standards would have to be stepped up to assure the best collections conservation environment possible. Food must be actively excluded from all areas except designated eating spaces and in these spaces the frequency of vacuuming must be increased, together with custodial monitoring. Filters used for trapping gaseous contaminants in the HVAC must be regularly maintained. Airborne pollutants must be monitored on a regular basis. Objects that are deemed by the Center to be particularly vulnerable to sulfur degradation and not on display should be properly protected from pollution scavengers.

Carpet set between travertine bands on the fourth floor

Carpet with travertine margins

Policy 138

To consider returning to wool carpet when conditions are appropriate.

Policy 139

To institute a cleaning regime to ensure that infestation does not occur.

The Oriental rug in the Library Court requires minimal conservation such as the removal of surface dirt by vacuum, the securing of fragile and unraveling edges, and washing after the testing of the dyes and pigments to ensure none are fugitive. Worn areas should be re-woven. It is also important that the rug has a padded underlay.

[88] Theresa Fairbanks-Harris, "Summary of Research on Carpeting Materials" (unpublished paper, Paper Conservation Department, Yale Center for British Art, October 1997).

Conservation work was carried out by Tina Kane in the summer of 2007, and a new pad was added.

Policy 140
To conserve the Oriental rug regularly.

Resilient sheet-vinyl flooring
The sheet-vinyl flooring is Congoleum, plain gray (IR/UV/black-out), ⅛-inch thick, homogenous vinyl with an edge strip that was probably waxed and buffed upon completion. It was used in the Paper Conservation Laboratory.

In recent years vinyl flooring has been introduced under new art storage racks, the new compact shelving in the Reference Library and the third-floor book stacks, as well as in the Paintings Conservation Studio.

Policy 141
To replace sheet-vinyl flooring when appropriate. When new vinyl is required, ideally it should be matched to the original as closely as possible. Its use should be restricted to storage areas and laboratories.

Concrete floors
Exposed, smooth concrete floors are found throughout the basement and the first-floor back-of-house area. A more porous concrete was used for the loading bays and commercial entry areas.

In 2002 the concrete floors of the loading bay and commercial entry were cleaned by New England Stone Technology using the Hurricane Stone Cleaner and a "grease-out" that was probably Cyclone Intensive Ceramic Tile/Grout Cleaner (another corrosive liquid containing potassium hydroxide), which would have been followed by an acid etch and neutralization by copious amounts of clean water. As mentioned previously, acid-based cleaning systems should be avoided as much as possible. Other cleaning systems have been considered, and another is due to be trialed shortly, so that the most appropriate conservation-based cleaning system can be adopted and incorporated into the Maintenance Plan.

Policy 142
To clean internal and external concrete floor surfaces on a regular planned maintenance program, subject to the results of the trialing protocols.

Floor plans

The following are the final revisions to the office drawings from which the building was constructed. Kahn's plans were over-stamped by Pellechia and Meyers when they took on the responsiblity for completing the Center following Kahn's death in March 1974, and they continued to update them during construction. Louis I. Kahn Collection, University of Pennsylvania

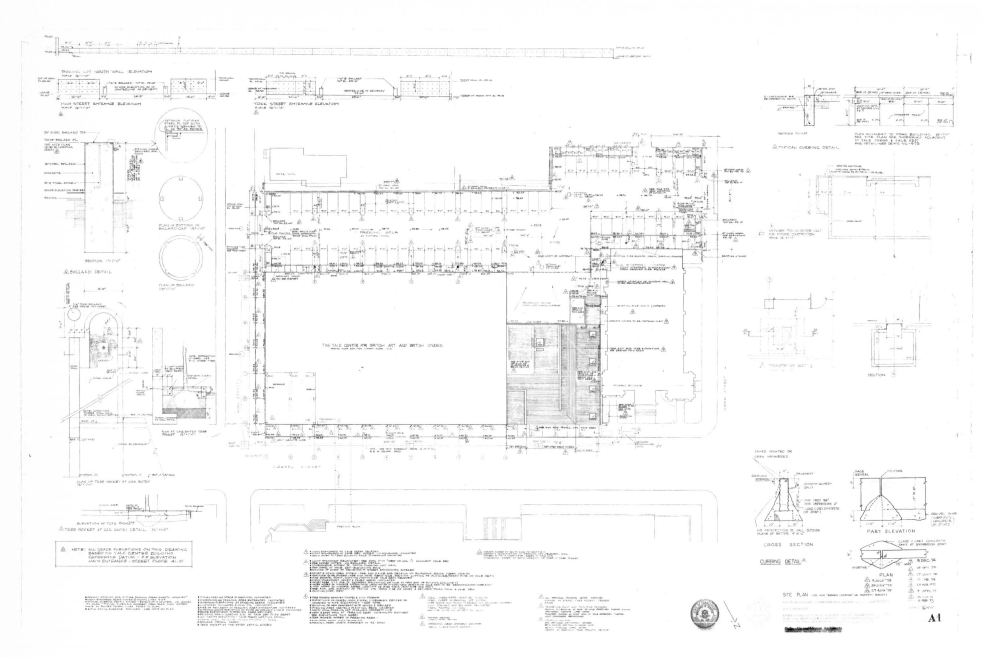

Site plan
A1 Rev 10, August 29, 1975

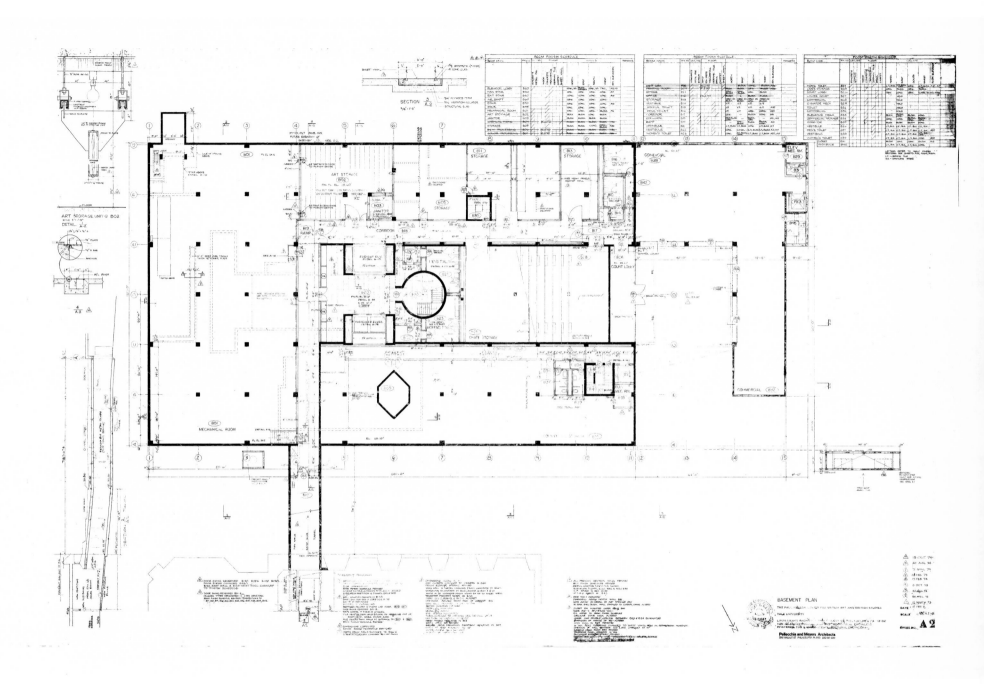

Basement
A2 Rev 9, October 15, 1974

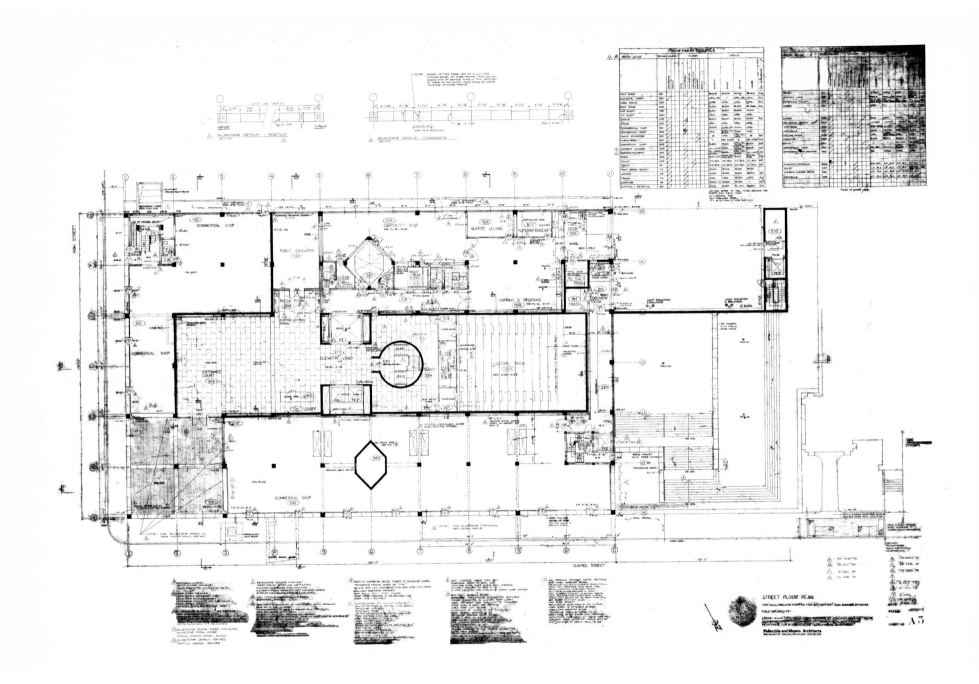

Street floor
A3 Rev 12, March 25, 1975

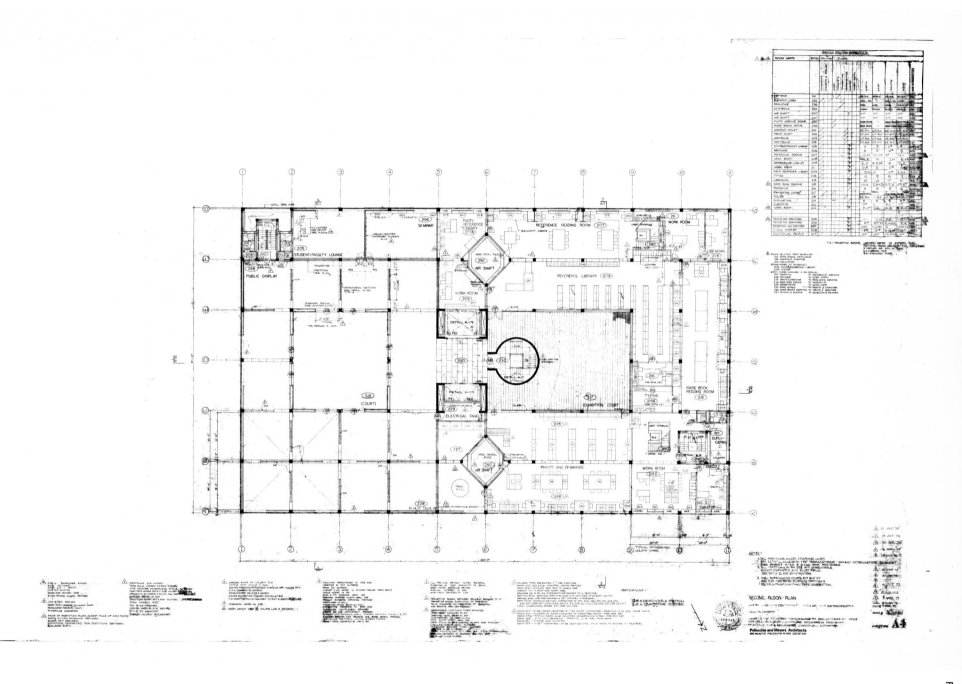

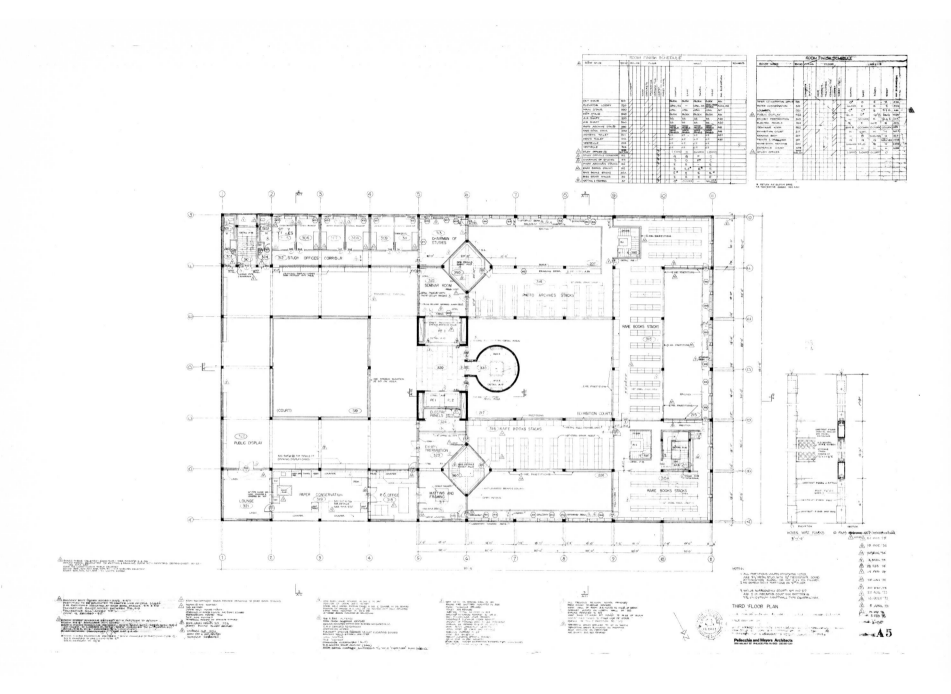

Third floor
A5 Rev 12, October 21, 1975

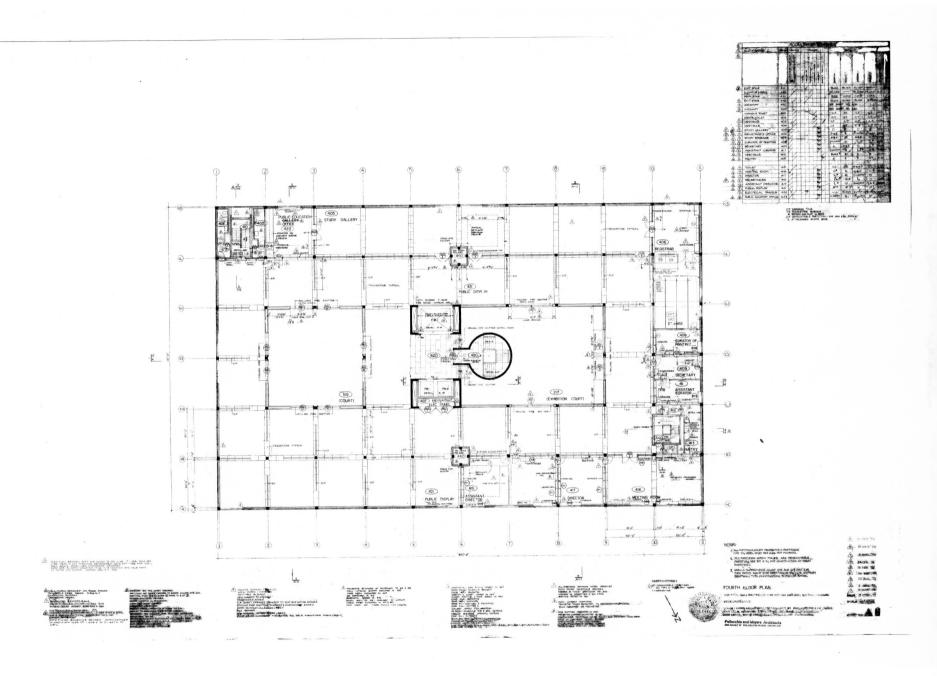

Fourth floor
A6 Rev 9, October 21, 1975

Roof
A7 Rev 5, April 3, 1974

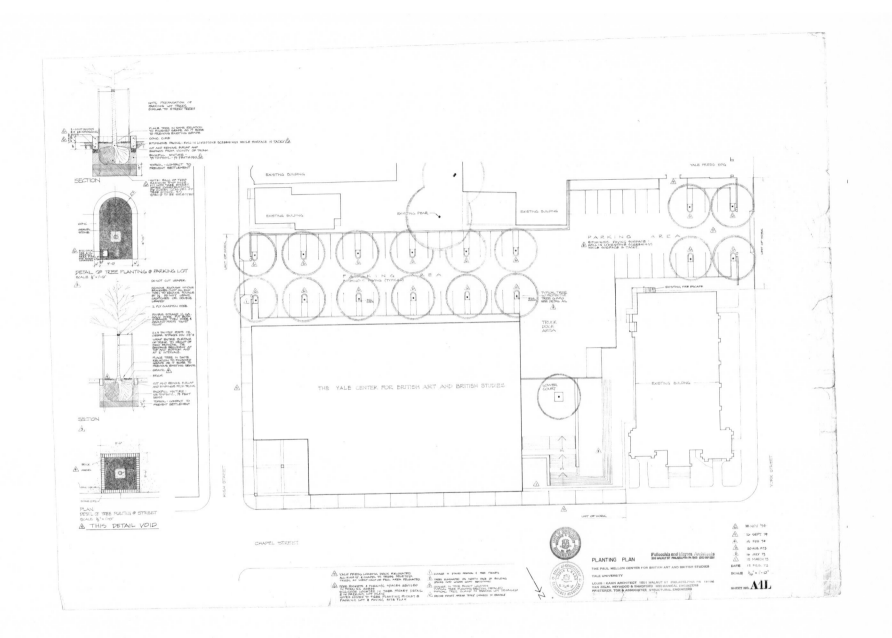

Planting plan
A1L Rev 6, November 18, 1974

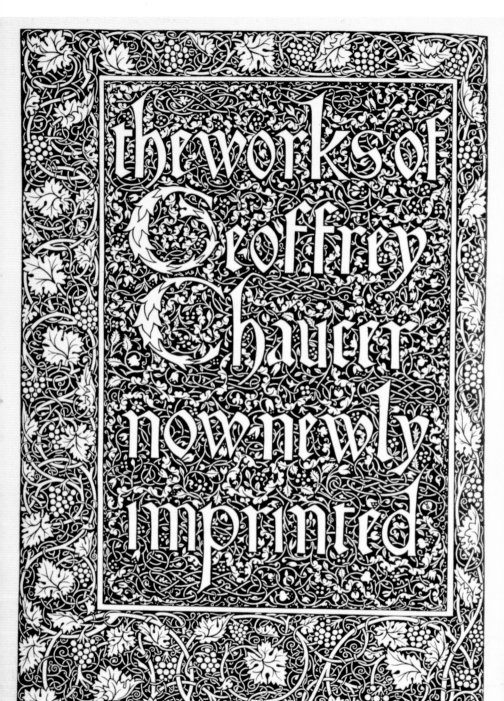

the works of Geoffrey Chaucer now newly imprinted

THAT Aprille with his shoures soote
The droghte of March hath perced to the roote,
And bathed every veyne in swich licour,
Of which vertu engendred is the flour;
Whan Zephirus eek with his swete breeth
Inspired hath in every holt and heeth

The tendre croppes, and the yonge sonne
Hath in the Ram his halfe cours yronne,
And smale foweles maken melodye,
That slepen al the nyght with open eye,
So priketh hem nature in hir corages;
Thanne longen folk to goon on pilgrimages,
And palmeres for to seken straunge strondes,
To ferne halwes, kowthe in sondry londes;
And specially, from every shires ende
Of Engelond, to Caunterbury they wende,
The hooly blisful martir for to seke,
That hem hath holpen whan that they were
seeke.

BIFIL that in that seson on a day,
In Southwerk at the Tabard as
I lay,
Redy to wenden on my pilgrymage
To Caunterbury with ful devout
corage,
At nyght were come into that hostelrye
Wel nyne and twenty in a compaignye,
Of sondry folk, by aventure yfalle
In felaweshipe, and pilgrimes were they alle,
That toward Caunterbury wolden ryde.

Selected further reading

Aloi, Roberto. *Musei: Architettura-Tenical.* Milan: Ultrico Hoepli, 1962.

The Australia ICOMOS Charter for the Conservation of Places of Cultural Significance (The Burra Charter). N.p.: 1979.

Banham, Reyner. *The New Brutalism: Ethic or Aesthetic?* London: Architectural Press, 1966.

Baskett, John, Jules David Prown, Duncan Robinson, Brian Allen, and William Reese. *Paul Mellon's Legacy, A Passion for British Art.* New Haven, CT, and London: Yale University Press, 2007.

Bellinelli, Luca, ed. *Louis I. Kahn, The Construction of the Kimbell Art Museum.* Milan: Skira, 1999.

Brawne, Michael. *The New Museum: Architecture and Display.* New York: Frederick A. Praeger, 1965.

Drury, Paul and Anna MacPherson. *Conservation Principles: Policies and Guidance for the Sustainable Management of the Historic Environment.* London: English Heritage, 2008.

Filler, Martin. "Opus Posthumous. Yale Center for British Art, Yale University, New Haven." *Progressive Architecture* 59 (May 1978): 76–81.

Glaeser, Ludwig. *Architecture of Museums.* New York: Museum of Modern Art, 1969.

Hargraves, Matthew. *Great British Watercolors from the Paul Mellon Collection at the Yale Center for British Art.* New Haven, CT, and London: Yale University Press, 2007.

Hitchcock, Henry-Russell. *Early Museum Architecture, 1770–1850.* Middletown, CT: Wesleyan University Press, 1934.

In Pursuit of Quality: The Kimbell Art Museum. An Illustrated History of the Art and Architecture. Fort Worth: Kimbell Art Museum, 1987.

Jordy, William. "Kahn at Yale, Art Center, Yale University." *Architectural Review* 162, no. 965 (July 1977): 38–43.

———— "The Span of Kahn." *Architectural Review* 155, no. 928 (June 1974): 318–42.

Kahn, Louis I. "Architecture Is the Thoughtful Making of Spaces." *Perspecta* 4 (1957): 2–3.

———— "Architecture: Silence and Light." In *On the Future of Art.* New York: Viking Press, 1970: 21–35.

———— "Louis Kahn." *Perspecta* 7 (1961): 9–28.

———— "Louis Kahn: Statements on Architecture." *Zodiac* 17 (January 1967): 54–57.

———— "Order in Architecture." *Perspecta* 4 (1957): 58–65.

———— "Order Is." *Perspecta* 3 (1955): 59.

———— "Order of Movement and Renewal of the City." *Perspecta* 4 (1957): 61–64.

———— "Space and the Inspirations." *L'Architecture d'Aujourd'hui* 40 (February–March 1969): 15–16.

———— "Structure and Form." *Voice of America Forum Architecture Series,* no. 6. Washington, DC: U.S. Government Printing Office, 1961.

"Kahn's Museum: Interview with Richard F. Brown." *Art in America* 50 (September–October 1972): 44–48.

Kerr, James Semple. *The Conservation Plan: A Guide to the Preparation of Conservation Plans for Places of European Cultural Significance.* 3rd ed. Sydney: National Trust, New South Wales, 1990.

Latour, Alessandra. *Louis I. Kahn, l'uomo, il maestro.* Rome: Kappa, 1986.

Letellier, Robin. *Recoding, Documentation, and Informed Management of the Conservation of Heritage Places: Guiding Principles.* Los Angeles: The Getty Conservation Institute, 2007.

Loud, Patricia Cummings. *The Art Museums of Louis I. Kahn.* Durham, NC, and London: Duke University Press, 1989.

"Louis I. Kahn." *Architecture and Urbanism* (special issues, 1971, 1973, 1975, 1983).

The Louis I. Kahn Archive: Personal Drawings. The Completely Illustrated Catalogue of the Drawings in the Louis I. Kahn Collection. 7 vols. New York and London: Garland, 1987.

Mellon, Paul and John Baskett. *Reflections in a Silver Spoon: A Memoir.* New York: William Morrow & Company, 1992.

Pevsner, Nikolaus. *A History of Building Types.* London: Thames and Hudson, 1976.

Prown, Jules David. "The Architecture of the Yale Center for British Art." *Apollo* 105, no. 182 (April 1977): 234–237.

———— "Lux et Veritas: Louis Kahn's Last Creation." *Apollo* 165, no. 542 (April 2007): 46–51.

———— "On Being a Client." *Journal of the Society of Architectural Historians* 42 (March 1983): 11–14.

———— *The Architecture of the Yale Center for British Art.* 3rd ed. New Haven, CT and London: Yale University Press, 2009.

Robinson, Duncan. *The Yale Center for British Art: A Tribute to the Genius of Louis I. Kahn.* New Haven, CT, and London: Yale University Press, 1997.

Ronner, Heinz, Alessandro Vasella, and Sharad Jhaveri. *Louis I. Kahn: Complete Works, 1935–1974.* 2nd ed. Basel and Boston: BirkhaOser, 1987.

Rykwert, Joseph. *Louis Kahn.* New York: Harry N. Abrams, 2001.

Scully, Vincent J. *Louis I. Kahn.* New York: George Braziller, 1962.

———— "Yale Center for British Art." *Architectural Record* 161 (June 1977): 95–104.

Scully, Vincent J., Catherine Lynn, Eric Vogt, and Paul Goldberger. *Yale in New Haven: Architecture and Urbanism.* New Haven, CT, and London: Yale University Press, 2004.

Smithson, Alison, and Peter Smithson. "Louis Kahn," *Architects' Yearbook* 9 (1960): 102–18.

Smithson, Peter. "Louis Kahn's Centre for British Art and British Studies at Yale University." *Royal Society of British Architects Journal* 83 (April 1976): 149–51.

The Travel Sketches of Louis I. Kahn. Philadelphia: Pennsylvania Academy of Fine Arts, 1978.

Wiseman, Carter. *Louis I. Kahn: Beyond Time and Style. A Life in Architecture.* New York and London: W.W. Norton, 2007.

Wurman, Richard Saul. *What Will Be Has Always Been: The Words of Louis I. Kahn.* New York: Access Press, 1986.

Wurman, Richard Saul, and Eugene Feldman, eds. *The Notebooks and Drawings of Louis I. Kahn.* Cambridge, MA: MIT Press, 1973.

"Yale Center for British Art: Kahn's Last Work." *Space Design* 155, no. 8 (1977): 5–24.

Facing page:
Geoffrey Chaucer (ca. 1343–1400)
Frontispiece and title page, with designs by Edward Burne-Jones (1833–1898) and William Morris (1834–1896), from *The Works of Geoffrey Chaucer,* Hammersmith, Kelmscott Press, 1896 Letterpress, with wood engraving Acquired by Paul Mellon in 1970

Note: Page numbers in *italics* refer to illustrations.

access, 95, 97
acoustics, 95
adaptation, defined, 65
alarms, *133, 171*
Allegheny Ludlum, 143
Allegheny Steel Corporation, 140
aluminum, 167
American Institute of Architects (AIA),
    54–55, 57
Architectural Studio/Gray Organschi, 76
Aronson, Mark, 138
Ashmoleum Museum, Oxford, 55
Atticus Bookstore, 76, *76*

Baldwin, Benjamin, 30, *30*, 54, 133–34
balustrading, 166, *166*
Barr, Alfred H., Jr., 53
baseboards, 176
basement, floor plan, *189*
basement lobby, 93–94, *94*
Bayer, Henry, 174
Beaux Arts tradition, 53
bimetallic corrosion, external, 147
Blake, William, *The Parable of the Wise
    and Foolish Virgins* (detail), 8, *10*
bluestone paving, 160, *161, 162, 162,
    163*
bollards, 156, *156*
Branco, Joe, 147, 148
Brewster, Kingman, 21, 22, 74
brick paving, 160, *161, 162, 162*
Brooklyn Museum, 105
Brown, Richard, 52
Bruce, Ailsa Mellon, 55
Brustein, Robert, 46
Budd, Bruce, 31, 121
Building Conservation Committee,
    7, 8, 31
buildings, drift from original forms, 7, 13
building systems, 128–33, *128, 129*
    call boxes and alarms, *133, 171*
    electrical, 131, 176
    HVAC, *129*, 130–31, *130*, 134, *135,
        164*, 165, 184
    lighting, 131–33, *131, 132*
    stand pipes, 133, *133*
Burne-Jones, Edward, design by, *196*, 197

Calvary Baptist Church, 26
    acquisition by Yale University, 46
    art library plans for, 46, *47*
    site of, 45, 70, 79
    as Yale Repertory Theatre, 27, 29, 45,
        46, *46*
Capasso Masonry Preservation Group,
    Inc., 162
carpeting, 31, 183–85, *184*
Chaucer, Geoffrey, frontispiece and
    title page, *196*, 197

Chin, Ian, 152
cinder block, 180, *180*
Circle Redmont Corporation, 167
cladding, 72–73, 74, 75
Clement, Constance, 143, 148
commercial premises, 75–76, *76, 77*
    doors of, 150
    storefront, *154*
    windows, 154, *154*
compatibility, defined, 65
concrete, *145*
    architectural, 171–72
    boundary walls, 158–59
    external, 144, *145*, 156, *156, 157,
        158–59, 158, 159*
    floors, 185
    internal, *170*, 171–72
    "migration staining," 172, *172*
    pavement and curbs, 159
    stair tower, *169*
conservation:
    defined, 65
    general principles, 136
conservation issues, 66
conservation plan, 8, 13, 32, 139, 162
conservation policies, 63–185
    exterior of the building, 68, 69–77
    external materials, 140–63
    external spaces, 79–85, *79*
    general policies, 66–67
    interior of the building, 87–139
    internal materials, *164*, 165–85
    method of approach, 65
consolidation, defined, 65
Constable, John, 113
    Stratford Mill, 56
Conte, George, 143
Coolidge, Shepley, Bulfinch & Abbott, 55
Cooper, Robertson & Partners, 8
cork wallboards, 180
Corvi, Phil, 174
cultural significance, 13
    as a building by Louis I. Kahn, 51–53
    concept and purpose of, 51
    defined, 65
    degree of survival and intactness,
        53–54
    and intrusive items, 136
    levels of, 60–61
    as a museum housing a specific
        collection, 55–56
    safeguarding via conservation
        policies, 65
    statement of, 59
    as urban fabric, 56–57
curbs and pavement, concrete, 159
C. White Electric LLC, 162

diffuser panels, 167, *168*, 175
Director's Office, 121, *121*
Docent Room, 93
doorsets, internal, 165–66
Duveen, Joseph, 21

Edison Price, 131, 132, 162
Edwards, Jared, 32, 122
Eisenman, Alvin, 134
electrical installation, 131, 176
elevator lobbies, 98, *98, 99*
elevator tower, 84
Entrance Court, 6, *13, 14,* 15, *86, 87,
    89,* 90–91, *91–92*
    Biolith (Hepworth), *6, 86, 89,* 91–92
    dedication panel, 17, *18*
    flooring, 180, *181*
    furnishings, 133–34
    Kahn's sketches for, 32, *33, 34,
        90–91, 91*
    and light, 71, 103, 113, *131, 132,*
        167, 175
    and portico, 74, *74,* 75
    steel panels, 165
    William III sculpture, 91–92, *98*
    windows, 152
entrance foyer, 92, *92*
exhibitions:
    *Art and Emancipation in Jamaica: Isaac
        Mendes Belisario and His Worlds*
        (2007), *107*
    *Britannia and Muscovy: English Silver at
        the Court of the Czars* (2006), *107*
    James Tissot: Victorian Life, Modern Love
        (1999), *106*
    Mellon Collection (2007), *109*
    *Sensation and Sensibility: Viewing
        Gainsborough's "Cottage Door"*
        (2005), *107*
exterior of the building, 68, 69–77
    cladding, 72–73
    commercial premises, 75–76, *76, 77*
    external form, 69–70
    frame, 71–72, *72*
    portico, 74–75, *74*
    roof, 70–71, *71*
external form, 69–70
external materials, 140–63
    bollards, 156, *156*
    brick paving and bluestone paving,
        160, *161, 162, 162, 163*
    concrete, 144, *145*, 156, *156, 157,
        158–59, 158, 159*
    fenestration pattern, 152, *153,* 154
    graffiti, 144, 148–49, *148*
    handrails, 155
    Lower Court and staircase, terrace
        and amphitheater, 160, 162
    mechanical damage, 144, 147–48
    sealants, 149–50
    skylights and louvers, 154–55, *155*
    stainless steel, 143–44, 146–48, *147*
    steel curtain walling, 140, 143
    steel doors, 150–51, *150*
    steel windows, 151–52, *151*
external spaces, 79–85, *79*

Fairbanks-Harris, Theresa, 138, 184
fenestration, *see* windows
fire escape doors, 150
first floor, floor plan, see street floor,
    floor plan
Fishman & Sons Inc., 155
Fitzwilliam Museum, University of
    Cambridge, 55
flooring, 180, *181,* 182–85, *183*
floor plans, 187–95
    basement, *189*
    first floor, see street floor
    fourth floor, *193*
    plantings, *195*
    roof, *194*
    second floor, *191*
    site plan, *188*
    street floor, *190*
    third floor, *192*
Flush-Metal Corporation, 180
Fogg, Elizabeth Perkins, 55
Fogg Museum of Art, Harvard
    University, 55
Founder's Room, 31, 112, 119, *120,*
    121, *121*
fourth floor, floor plan, *193*
frame, 71–72, *72*
Froeberg, Kenneth, 26, *31,* 103, 167
furniture and furnishings, *30,* 133–34,
    133, 136, *137*

galleries, 100–114
    display, 105–7
    fourth-floor, *12, 13, 50,* 51, *53, 58, 59,
        64,* 65, *88, 101, 103, 109,* 112, *113,
        114, 126, 178*
    lighting, 100–105, *101, 102, 103, 104*
    Long Gallery (originally Study
        Gallery), 31, 112–14, *113*
    organization of, 112–14
    and pogos, 105–6, *105, 106,* 112,
        176–78, *178*
    second-floor, 31, *89, 104, 108, 109,
        109,* 112, *112, 129*
    third-floor, *88, 109,* 112
    windows, 152, *153,* 154
Garrison/Lull Inc., 128, 130, 171, 184
Gee, Stephen, 7, 8
glass-block skylight, 167, *167*
graffiti, 144, 148–49, *148*
Gregg, Glen, 177
Guenschel, Helmut, 174

handrails, 155
hardware, interior, 134, *134*
Harrison, Laurence S., 101
Hepworth, Dame Barbara:
    Biolith, 6, 86, 89, 91–92
    Sphere with Inner Form, 93, 93, 98
Hillsdale Industries, 155
Hogarth, William, 21
Holophane Company Inc., 167

Howe, George, 51
HVAC, *129*, 130–31, *130*, 134, *135*,
 164, *165*, 184

Inskip, Peter, 7, 8, 31
interior of the building, 87–139
 back-of-house, 124–25, *124*
 basement lobby, 93–94, *94*
 building systems, 128–33, *128*, *129*,
  134, *135*
 Director's Office, 121, *121*
 Docent Room, 93
 elevator lobbies, 98, *98*, *99*
 Entrance Court, *90–91*, 91–92
 entrance foyer, 92, *92*
 Founder's Room, 112, 119, *120*,
  121, *121*
 furniture and furnishings, 133–34,
  133, 136, *137*
 hardware, 134, *134*
 Lecture Hall, 95, *95*, *96*, 97
 Lecture Hall lobby, 93
 Library Court, 114, *115*, 116
 offices and supporting facilities, 119,
  119, *120*, 121–23, *121*, *123*
 organization, 87, *88*, *89*, 91
 Paintings and Sculpture Department,
  122, *122*
 Paintings Conservation Studio,
  125, *125*
 Paper Conservation Laboratory,
  123, *123*
 Prints and Drawings Department,
  116, *117*, 118–19, *118*
 public display galleries, 100–114, *101*
 Rare Books and Manuscripts
  Department, 116, *117*, 118, *118*
 reception area, 92–93, *93*
 Reference Library, 116, *116*, 118–19
 repairs and maintenance, 136, 138–39
 restrooms, 94, *94*
 signage, 134, *134*, 136, *136*
 Staff Lounge and seminar room,
  124, *124*
 staircase, 98, *98*, 100
 structure, 125–28, *126*
internal materials, *164*, 165–85
 aluminum, 167
 balustrading, 166, *166*
 carpet, 183–85, *184*
 cinder block, 180, *180*
 concrete, *170*, 171–72
 cork wallboards, 180
 diffuser panels to skylights, 167,
  168, 171
 doorsets, 165–66
 flooring, 180, *181*, 182–85
 galvanized steelwork, 166–67
 glass-block skylight, 167, *167*
 gypsum wallboard partitions, 178,
  179, 180

millwork, 172, *173*, 174–76, *174*
 restroom walls and partitions, 180
 steel panels, *164*, 165
 wood-and-glass walls, 178
intrusive items, 136

Jarves Collection, 55
Johnson, Philip, 22, 54
Johnson, Rick, 174, 177
J. Paul Getty, Los Angeles, 182

Kahn, Louis I., 7, 8, *22*, *103*
 and architectural concrete, 171
 Art Museums of Louis I. Kahn
  (exhibition catalog), 23
 birth of, 51
 and brickwork, 160
 and building systems, 130, *130*
 death of, 30, 187
 design remaining intact, 32
 and door types, 165
 drawings completed by, 30
 and Entrance Court, 32, *33*, *34*,
  90–91, 91
 Erdman Hall, Bryn Mawr College, 53
 and First Program, 23, 69
 and gallery displays, 105–7, *107*
 Hurva Synagogue, Jerusalem
  (proposal), 54, *54*
 Kimbell, *see* Kimbell Art Museum
 on materiality, 51
 Medical Services Center, AFL-CIO, 54
 and museum fatigue and orientation,
  107, 109
 National Assembly, Dhaka, 53
 on natural light, 51–52, 103
 and the nature of public space, 51
 Phillips Exeter Academy Library, 30,
  30, 53
 and pointing, 149
 reputation of, 22, 51
 Richards Medical Research Building,
  University of Pennsylvania, 54
 Rochester Unitarian Church, 53
 Salk Institute, La Jolla, *22*, 54, 156
 and Second Program, 26, 32,
  33–40, 72
 and skylights, *168*
 and steel hierarchy, 150
 and steel panels, 140
 structural innovations by, 27
 Trenton Jewish Community Center,
  54, *54*
 and urban fabric, 75
 and windows, 73, 154
 Yale University Art Gallery, 22, *43*,
  45, 51, 52, *52*, 53, 72
Kelly, Richard, 71, 103, 131, 132, 167
Kerr, James Semple, 15, 51

Kimbell Art Museum, Fort Worth,
 22, 27, 30, 51, 52, *52*
 displays, 105, *106*
 external concrete, 156
 furnishings, 133
 Garden Court, 112, *112*
 internal flooring, 182, 183
 lighting, 53, 71, 100–101, *101*, 131
 restrooms, 94
Knight, George, 32
Knight Architecture LLC, 162

Labrouste, Henri, 69
Lanteri, Paul, 32
Lecture Hall, 95, *95*, *96*, 97
 double doors, 165
 glazed wall, 150–51
 lobby, 93
 Lower Court entrance, 79, *80*
Lee, Richard C., 21, 22
Library Court, 114, *115*, 116
 Kahn's sketches for, 32, *35*, *37*, 105
 lighting, 105, 113
 Oriental rug, 134, *134*, 184–85
 wood flooring, 183, *183*
light:
 diffuser panels, 167, *168*, 175
 electric, 101
 and Entrance Court, 71, 103, 113,
  131, 132, 167, 175
 natural, 51–52, 70, 100–101, 103, 175
 ultraviolet, 71, 175
lighting, 31, 51–53, *102*
 galleries, 100–105, *101*, *102*, *103*, *104*
 installation, 131–33, *131*, *132*
 objectives for, 101
loading dock, 84, *84*
 and bollards, 156, *156*
Loud, Patricia Cummings, 23, 52, 101
louvers, 154–55, *155*
 as "angry crabs" (Kahn), 71
Lower Court, 79–83, *79*, *80*, *81*, *83*
 bluestone paving, 162, *162*, *163*
 brickwork and masonry, 160, 162
 changes to, 54, 80
 Kahn's sketches for, 32, *40*, *78*, 79
 Lecture Hall entrance, 79, *80*
 as monumental ruin, 57
 salt damage, 162
 steel doors, 150
 steps, 32, *32*, 77, *83*, *156*, 162, *162*

Macomber Construction Company, 27,
 71, 103, 167, 168, 171, 177
maintenance:
 and damage, 144
 defined, 65
 and repairs, 30, 31, 136, 138–39
 of stainless steel, 144
Maintenance Plan, 138–39, 146

management principles, 67
Martz, Louis L., 21
McCaughey, Patrick, 31
mechanical damage, external, 144,
 147–48
Mellon, Andrew, 55, 121
Mellon, Mary Conover Brown, 55
Mellon, Paul, *20*, 21, *31*, *103*
 approvals from, 27, 31
 Brick House, Virginia, *23*, 55–56
 centennial exhibition (2007), 109
 collection of, 21, 22, 55–56, 105
 and Founder's Room, 121
 gifts of, 7, *18*, 21, 30, 55
 and Kahn, 22–23, 26
 site acquisitions on behalf of, 46
Mellon, Rachel (Bunny) Lambert Lloyd, 55
Mellon family, gifts to the nation from, 55
Metropolitan Museum of Art, New York,
 101
Meyers, Amy, 31
Meyers, Marshall, 30, 54, 95, 150, 156,
 166, 174, 176–77, 178; *see also*
 Pellecchia and Meyers
Mies van der Rohe, Ludwig, 69
"migration staining," 172, *172*
Mills, David, 143, 147, 149
millwork, internal, 172, *173*, 174–76, *174*
Morris, Michael, 138, 174
Morris, William, design by, 196, *197*
Munnings, Sir Alfred, 21
museum fatigue, 107, *108*, 109
Museum of Modern Art, New York, 53
Museum Shop, 76, 150, *154*

National Gallery, London, 101, 105
New Haven:
 and commercial premises, 75–76
 marine environment of, 144
 original plan of, 43
 and portico, 74
 sidewalk standards, 159
 and snow removal, 147
 taxable property for, 56
 and urban fabric, 56–57, 75
Nicholson, Ben, 21

Oriental rug, 134, *134*, 184–85

Paintings and Sculpture Department,
 122, *122*, 154
Paintings Conservation Studio, 125, *125*
Paper Conservation Laboratory, 31,
 123, *123*
 ductwork, 167
 sheet-vinyl flooring, 185
 windows, 154
parking lot, 84–85, *84*, *85*
 graffiti attacks, 148–49
 signage, *84*, 136

partitions, 176–78, 180
Patris, Pascale, 174
pavement and curbs, concrete, 159
Pei, I. M., 22
　East Wing, National Gallery of Art, 55, *55*
Pellecchia, Anthony, 30, 54
Pellecchia and Meyers:
　and display, 105
　and floor plans, 187
　and furnishings, 133
　and handrails, 155
　and hardware, 134
　Lower Court, 80, 83
　parking lot, 84–85
　partitions, 176
　portico, 74
　signage, 134
Pfisterer, Henry, 27
Pfisterer, Tor & Associates, 27, 156
Photo Archive, 31
Photo Lab exhaust system, 167
Pillsbury, Edmund, 30
Pittsburgh Corning, 167
plantings, plan, *195*
Plasticrete Corp., 180
pogos:
　in galleries, 105–6, *105, 106*, 112
　structure and appearance, 176–78, *178*
pollutants, air, 158, 185
Pope, John Russell, National Gallery of Art, Washington, DC, 55, *55*
portico, 74–75, *74*
　brick paving and bluestone paving, 160, *161*
Powell & Moya, 107
preservation, defined, 65
Prints and Drawings Department, 116, *117*, 118–19, *118*
　damage to millwork, 174–75
Proudfoot, Trevor, 138
Prown, Jules, 22, 30, *31*, 56, 71, 74
　and diffuser panels, 167
　and external concrete, 156
　and Kahn, 22–23, 26, 105, 171, 174
　"Light and Truth," 101, 103, 126
　and metalwork, 140
　"Preliminary Thoughts on Architecture," 22, 23, 100
public space, nature of, 51

Rare Books and Manuscripts Department, 31, 116, *117*, 118, *118, 119*
reading rooms, 32, *36*, 118, 131
　millwork damage in, 174, 175, *175*
　window types, 152, 154
reception area, 92–93, *93*
reconstruction, defined, 65
Reference Library, 31, 116, *116*, 118–19
　windows, 73, *73*, 118

repairs and maintenance, 30, 31, 136, 138–39, 144
restoration, defined, 65
restrooms, 94, *94*
restroom walls and partitions, 180
Reynolds, Sir Joshua, 106
Robinson, Duncan, 30, 31, 121
Rohm & Haas, 154
roof, 70–71, *71*
　floor plan, *194*
　Year of the Roof (1998), 155
roof system, 31
Rudolph, Paul, 43, 54
　Art and Architecture Building, 45, *45*
Ruskin, B. F., 177
Russell, Rufus G., Yale Repertory Theatre, 46, *46*

Saarinen, Eero, 54
Schinkel, Karl Friedrich, 69
Scully, Vincent, 72, 100
sealants to steel-and-glass curtain walling, 149–50
Sears-Michaud, Carolyn, 177
second floor, floor plan, *191*
security-camera surveillance, 149
sheet-vinyl flooring, 185
signage:
　interior, 134, *134, 136, 136*
　Lower Court steps, *156*
　parking lot, *84, 136*
site plan, *188*
Skidmore, Owings & Merrill, 54
skylights and louvers, 154–55, *155*
　diffuser panels, 167, *168, 171*
　glass blocks, 167, *167*
snow removal, 147, 156
Soane Museum, London, 105
Spiker, David, 79
Staff Lounge and seminar room, 124, *124*
　windows, 154
stainless steel, 72, 143–44, *145*
　alterations in, 144, 146
　balustrade, 166, *166*
　bimetallic corrosion, 147
　chemical damage, 144, 146–47, *148*
　cleaning, 146
　maintenance of, 144
　mechanical damage, 144, 147–48
staircase, interior, 98, *98*, 100
stair tower, *169*
stand pipes, 133, *133*
steel curtain walling, 140, *143*
steel doors, external, 150–51, *150*
steel panels, internal, *164*, 165
steelwork, galvanized, 166–67
Stevens, Stoddard, 22
Storonov, Oscar, 51
street floor, floor plan, *190*
structure, interior, 125–28, *126*

Stubbs, George, 21
　A Lion Attacking a Horse, 105, 114, *115*; (detail), 8, *11*
　Study Room, 114, 116, *117*
　　air shaft, *164*, 165
　　windows, 154
Swartwout, Egerton, Yale Gallery of Fine Arts, *43*, 55, 72

terrace, 79, *82*, 83–84, *83*, 160
Tetrault, Patricia, 46
third floor, floor plan, *192*
Tor, Abba, 27, 71, 125, 130
travertine floors, 180, *181*, 182–83, *183, 184*
Trio Industries, 140, 150
Turner, J. M. W., 21, 113
　Dort or Dordrecht: The Dort Packet-Boat from Rotterdam Becalmed, 56, *56*, 105
　Staffa, Fingal's Cave (detail), 8, *9*
Turner Construction Company, 32, 149, 155, 162

United Sheet Metal Division, 167
Utzon, Jorn, Sydney Opera House, *15*, 95

Van Zelm, Heywood & Shadford Inc., 125
Venturi, Robert, 22
visitor experience and comfort, 109, 112

walkway, 84, *84*
wallboards:
　cork, 180
　gypsum partitions, 178, *179*, 180
water fountain, *180*
William III sculpture, 91–92, 98, 133
Wilton, Joseph, portrait bust of Thomas, 1st Baron Dartrey, *20*, 21
windows, 73, *73*, 103, 118
　back-of-house, 154
　commercial storefronts, 154, *154*
　external pattern, 152, *153*, 154
　and museum fatigue, 107, *108*, 109, *109*
　offices, 154
　"opaque," 72–73, 140, *141, 142*, 143
　replacement of, 31
　steel, 151–52, *151*
　weep system of, 31
window sills, condensation damage to, *175*
Wiseman, Carter, 53, 125
Wiss, Janney, Elstner Associates, Inc. (WJE), 143, 149, 152, 154, 155, 162
Wolff, Steve, 143–44, 146
wood-and-glass walls, 178
wood flooring, 183, *183*
Wright of Derby, Joseph, 21

Yale Center for British Art, *2, 4, 48, 68*
　Building Design Program, Preliminary, 23
　Chapel Street facade (model), 23, *24–25*, 26
　commercial activities in, 56–57, *56, 57*
　conservation plan for, 8, 13, 32, 139, 162
　construction of, 27, 30, *30, 31*, 126, *127*
　costs of, 26, 30
　elevations, 56
　explicitness of space in, 52–53
　First Program, 23, *24–25*, 26, 27, 69
　High Street facade, 32, *38–39*
　lighting, 51–53
　maintenance and repair, 30, 31
　opening of, 30
　Second Program, 26–27, *26, 27, 28–29*, 70, 72
　site acquisition, 22, 45
　site and setting, 41–47, *42*
　in University context, 54
Yale College:
　development plans of, *44*, 45
　expansion of, 43
　original construction of, 43
　School of the Fine Arts, 43
　Trumbull Gallery, 55
Yale Repertory Theatre, 27, *29*, 45, 46, *46*
　security-camera surveillance, 149
　and terrace, 83–84
Yale University Art Gallery:
　building systems, 130
　commissioning of, 54
　connection to, 23, 79, *82*, 83
　displays, *105, 106, 106*
　internal flooring, 183
　Kahn's extension to, 22, *43*, 45, 51, 52, *52*, 53, 72